MORE PRAISE
for *Loyalty is Love*

"Beverly Koehn has assembled the best insights from her career into a book that introduces loving commitment into the building of people's homes. Thousands of personal observations, hundreds of site visits, scores of interviews, and years of listening are transformed into essential lessons covering integrity, loyalty, and craftsmanship."

— **Henry Cisneros**, *former mayor*, **City of San Antonio**, *former Secretary*, **U.S. Department of Housing and Urban Development**

"The quality and sustainability of any company rests on its ability to create loyal customers. Beverly Koehn offers a refreshing view about what goes to customer's hearts, and why it's important to understand *loyalty is love*. This book's excellent ideas and tools will help you recognize and embrace the intangibles that build — within every customer — positive emotion, trust, and respect. Beverly Koehn's work is inspiring for anyone who wants their company to resonate with *loyalty*."

— **Carroll Bogard**, *manager, trade segment marketing*, **Pella Corp.**

"In all my years in the corporate computer world and running my own businesses, Beverly Koehn made the best and most lasting first impression of any professional I've met. She's a real person who knows her business. This book is a *must* read."

— **Ralph Cataldo**, *president*, **Cataldo Custom Builders**, *former senior project engineer*, **Digital Equipment Corp.**

"Beverly has absolutely nailed all the key drivers behind the successful homebuilding company of tomorrow. As we move from a product economy, through service, to an experience economy — dominated by powerful consumers — passion, caring, and lasting customer relationships will be the difference between low profit margins and high ones. You've got to love that!"

— **Michael Dickens**, *CEO*, **BuildIQ**

"I've often said that a measure of career success is someone paying you to do something you love. Beverly Koehn takes 'love' to a new dimension. *Loyalty is Love* hits all the right buttons: customer loyalty, selling beyond price, communication, trust, and building sales. This book is a great read for anyone — new to the business, or with years of experience."

— **Omer "Butch" Gaudette**, *national director, trade relations*, **Whirlpool Corp.**

LOYALTY IS LOVE

HOW TO HOLD CLIENTS CLOSE FOR LIFE

BEVERLY A. KOEHN

with Joe Schuler, Jr.

For information contact:
Beverly Koehn & Associates Inc., 1000 East Basse Road, Suite 120, San Antonio, TX 78209-3252
210-824-3445
www.bkoehn.com

FIRST EDITION

Library of Congress Cataloging-in-Publication Data
Control Number: 2007903042

Koehn, Beverly A.; Schuler Jr., Joe
    LOYALTY IS LOVE: How To Hold Clients Close For Life/ Beverly A. Koehn, with
Joe Schuler Jr. — 1st ed.
        p. cm.
        Includes index.
        ISBN 9780975421291
        1. Client retention.   2. Company loyalty programs.   3. Employee training.
        4. Loyalty measurement and assessment.   5. Customer care and profitability.

DISCLAIMER
This publication is designed to provide accurate and authoritative information in regard to the
subject matter covered. It is sold with the understanding that the publisher is not engaged in
rendering legal, accounting, or other professional services. If legal advice or other expert assistance is
required, the services of a competent professional should be sought.

— From a Declaration of Principles jointly adopted by
a Committee of the American Bar Association, and
Committee of Publishers and Associations

To my father, James Anderson.

Dec. 28, 1930 — Jan. 15, 2000

To my uncles, Joe McMurtry and Tom Anderson.

And for three very special brothers, Barry, Bruce, and Ben Anderson.

Your love continues to inspire me.

ACKNOWLEDGEMENTS

I've been privileged to know many generous and loving souls throughout my life. This book made it to publication because of their encouragement and shared wisdom. To all of you who embraced my high concept and responded with stories, ideas, comments, and encouragement, I sincerely hope you're as proud of the results as I am, and feel your time was well invested.

Assisting me with the research were some of the best in the business: Carol Smith, Bob Mirman, Roxanne Musselman, Gust Nicholson Sr., Bruce Christensen, Michael Strong, Scott Sedam, and Martha Baumgarten. They were completely committed, and their expertise and influence are reflected throughout the book.

As a simple person from a very small town, I never dreamed it would be possible for me to write a book. Thanks to the encouragement of my friend Myers Barnes, it's a reality. I'm not sure what he saw in me the day he heard me speak in Orlando; I'm just glad he did.

Because of the support of my early mentors — Lee Evans, Bill Watson, and Becky Oliver — I've accomplished more than I could have imagined. And to my audiences, clients, and industry friends, thank you all for believing in me and allowing me to learn quite literally by the seat of my pants.

Through the creative charm and expertise of Christy Parrish, the cover and page designs came to life. As someone who can't even draw stick men well, I'm simply amazed. Thanks, too, to Dirk Aardsma, for his fine copy editing.

It's hard for me to put into words the thanks I have for Joe Schuler. Not only is he a gifted writer and "language architect," his uncanny ability to visualize and organize the entire project quite simply has been poetry in motion. His dedication, tenacity, and talent have been the fulcrum that made it all possible.

Finally, to the builders, remodelers, developers, and industry associates who continue to make America the best-housed nation in the world: **Thank you.** *I am proud to be a part of your team.*

FOREWORD

In January of 1989, I was hired from outside the industry to be vice president of quality and customer commitment for Pulte Homes. My job was to coach the company into the Twentieth Century, in both quality process and customer satisfaction. I'll never forget the first board meeting I attended that spring, where I was asked to give a brief presentation. As part of his introduction, Bill Pulte, founder and chairman of the board, told a favorite story that his plumbing contractor had shared with him when he was a young man, back in the 1950s:

" ... and then the plumber asked me, so now I'm asking you: *Do you know what the difference is between a satisfied customer and a delighted customer?*"

Bill was ready with his answer, which he knew the mostly Wall Street types on the board couldn't muster, but before he could get the answer out, the chairman of the finance committee and second largest shareholder blurted: "*Yeah! 200 bucks!*" After the chorus of laughter died down, a frustrated Bill explained how a satisfied customer *lives* with a home, while a delighted customer *tells others* about it — and why that makes all the difference. Yet the board member who answered "$200," depressing as it was, represented the mindset of a great majority of builders in North America at the time. You could run roughshod over a customer. Then, for the cost of a cheap microwave oven, you could win them back, presuming you cared enough to try.

My first years as a quality and customer evangelist were lonely ones. Only later did I discover there were others all across the country, pioneering the quality movement right along with me. One of the best was Beverly Koehn and although I'd heard her name many times, we finally met just a few years ago. When you meet Beverly, you've made a friend for life, for not only is she completely immersed in industry know-how, she's charming, gracious, and utterly genuine. So it came as no surprise to me that when she finally wrote this book, she called it *Loyalty is Love*, because that is exactly what she practices, and more importantly, how she lives.

Loyalty is Love appears at a remarkable time in the history of the homebuilding industry, now in the throes of the most severe downturn in 50 years. My first reaction when Bev told me about her book was, *"Oh no, bad timing."* After all, with virtually every builder operating at a loss, having laid off — in most cases — more than half their staff and cutting back on all things "customer service," who would buy the book? Yet after reading *Loyalty is Love*, I've changed my mind. I trust that you will, too. With a good dose of irony, it dawned on me that exactly *now*, exactly in this mess-of-a-market, builders, remodelers, suppliers, and trade contractors need to be reminded what it takes to romance the customer, to build a great relationship along with a great home and create a profitable outcome for all.

Bev writes with remarkable insight about getting to the heart of things, about who you are and what you believe. In our heart of hearts, my TrueNorth colleagues and I are more than anything else "operations guys" who spend our time helping builders create great production processes and systems. In our work with builders, we often have to insist that they include in the discussion their best salesperson, to represent the "voice of the customer," so they don't forget who they're working for. I now know that if everyone read *Loyalty is Love*, this wouldn't be necessary as the customer would always be on their minds. Use this book as your personal reminder of who *you* work for; use it as a trusted guide for how to do the right thing when it comes to your customers. Then share it with your organization.

During the downturn, take time to reconnect with your customers, or perhaps connect for the very first time. You will better weather today's storm, and prepare yourself to succeed at a much higher level when the tide finally turns.

It's time to rediscover that, indeed, *loyalty is love*.

— *Scott Sedam, president,*
TrueNorth Development,
Northville, Mich.

I've heard it said that in a book like this, love is a four-letter word. It's too feminine, it's too soft. *It's not business.* Well, let me tell you right off: I couldn't have written this book without using that word. In today's business world, for too long we've avoided using words that define certain experiences, emotions, actions, attitudes. For too long we've shrunk from a metaphor that defines long-term business relationships.

Look where it has gotten us in the past year. Housing hit an all-time low. Builders went bankrupt. The mortgage industry ran amuck. People were petrified to buy a home. People were petrified of their builders. Isn't it time we re-introduce a word that has been taboo for too long and make it a part of our everyday vocabulary in business?

I think so.

I think it's time to break old standards and start creating new ones. It's time to take words that have no meaning and start working with words that do. It's time to stop being tough and recognize that when everything is crumbling, it's time to hang on to something certain, something we know is true.

For most people, that's something that goes to the heart of what they think and feel for the business of building and renovating homes. They *love* this business. Despite its challenges, they love getting up in the morning and serving their customers. They sweat the challenges, but they *love* them. And they are learning that *love* is what it takes to keep their clients coming back again and again and referring friends.

Love, my friends, is what is winning business today.

So let's smash the taboo. You're going to see that four-letter word all over this book — *don't let it scare you*. Don't think you can never achieve the goal, even if you don't feel capable, or if it's too "soft," or if you don't feel that way for your customers today. Know that, with time, and care, it's possible. Not only possible, but the most probable route to business success.

Prepare to start smashing old ways of thinking and begin new ways of *doing*.

Yes, prepare to *love*.

CONTENTS

INTRODUCTION

LOVE'S A RUG & WE WALK RIGHT OVER IT

We abuse our customers so much, it's crazy.

We leave them waiting for weeks and don't call. We don't return messages on time. We don't acknowledge or recognize emergencies and diminish their importance. And when the situation draws TV cameras and newspaper reporters, we wonder why.

It starts with the little things. Our superintendent sees a switchplate missing and it's no big deal. The house is finished. But the customer's emotions are plugged in, and emotions run high. *You put in all this work, you gave me this beautiful space, and now you make me feel that I'm nitpicking for mentioning something that should have been done?* This buyer doesn't feel cared for — and rightly so. To you, it's nothing. To them it's 110 volts, through the heart. For want of a cover plate, or even the words, *don't worry, I'll throw one on*, you killed the love. *Good grief!*

Over the past 20 years, I've sold hundreds of homes. I've walked into thousands more. I've visited, spoken to, and consulted with builders, remodelers, and suppliers in the U.S., Canada, Europe, and Australia: companies as varied as BMC West, Brothers Strong, Centerline Homes, Centex Homes, D.R. Horton, Desert View Homes, GE Money, Hogan Homes, K. Hovnanian Homes, Kennecott Land Co., Newmark Homes, Pella Corp., Toll Brothers, Veridian Homes, Wellborn Cabinet, and WestView Builders.

I've been a featured speaker at the National Association of Home Builder's International Builders Show. I've received NAHB's highest honors, including Associate of the Year. I've been named a master instructor for the NAHB's University of Housing. All this experience has taught me:

The very trait that can make companies the best — their vision — often makes them the worst.

Welcome To Our Quality Home! Those are the words on the sign the builder sticks in front of the $500,000 model. And then, a filthy carpet remnant sits at the front door, a welcome mat … of sorts. *Step right in, we're all about quality!* The builder and the sales people constantly strut over this raggedy remnant. By being blind to this *nothing*, customers are lost.

Understanding customer care isn't intuitive.

GUTS TO LOVE

We *could* be, and *should* be, so much better if, just like in any relationship, we paid attention to little things. If we focused on what goes to the heart of buyers' emotions, we would know: Loyalty is love. Loyalty is a love clients return over and over — even when they suffer through total ignorance or blindness to their most basic needs.

When I write about love, I'm capturing my sense of seamless business practices and selfless service that create emotional connections. I'm not suggesting stuff that's too mushy for men, or women, to take seriously. I'm not saying "go out and hug your client," although at times, that's appropriate, or to have an affair (always inappropriate). What I'm trying to do is to get you to see that this thing you have with a client, it's a *relationship*, and relationships must be nurtured … or they die. Love is a metaphor, and in every understanding, it's a *commitment*.

I've met lots of crusty people in my life. But even if they've pushed their emotions down deep, they always have a soft spot. It's our responsibility to find those spots, within ourselves and our customers. Finding those spots will take the housing industry beyond where the best Japanese and American companies have taken quality, and more importantly, care, which matures into loyalty.

In business, as in life, we win people over with the most important thing and then focus on everything around it. But often, we forget what's important in the first place. In Texas, we turn to what we know and where we come from to understand a truth like that … *or we die trying*. This is how my understanding of the principles of enduring customer loyalty came about — believe it or not — from my childhood.

I was born in Temple, Texas, and I grew up in Troy, a town of 1,200 in the heart of the state, between Austin and Dallas. It was Mom, Dad, my three brothers, and me. We lived in a two-bedroom, one-bath house. When my grandmother got sick, she and my grandfather joined us — eight people living and breathing in 1,100 square feet.

Mom was a switchboard operator. Dad started as a policeman and became a die-caster. My grandparents raised livestock and farmed cotton, corn, and maize. In Texas, I learned that a person's soft side is buried deep, because in Texas, we've got guts. Guts rise to the top when things get tough.

I learned this from my mother and father's unpredictable discipline; many times set off by the slightest mishap. It took guts to face that anger. It took guts to love when love's shape twisted into fear, or cut love off from those we, as children, needed to love most. Although the love was always there, it was at times buried in layers. Inside, my appreciation grew for real love. What it is and what it means — at home, and later, in business.

AN OUNCE OF RESILIENCE

Because my parent's love was hidden, I was unsure of it. More apparent was the love that came from my cousins, aunts, uncles, and grandparents. My great Aunt Ollie was the kindest person you'd meet. Yet, she was one tough lady. Her husband died when their youngest of five children was only two. Everyone in Troy called her "Miss Ollie" out of respect, and she lived to nearly 100.

Aunt Ollie gutted out the Depression and cared every day for her five kids while living in a dirt-floor farmhouse. She suffered adversities most of us have only heard about. She had reasons to feel depressed or downtrodden, but never was. She saw the best in everything. She was the strongest, gentlest person I've known; she was always able to sense my basic needs.

When it comes to selling and servicing customers, you must understand their basic needs. Since my childhood, I've been keenly aware of my basic needs. Without question, they're the same needs as our customers. How you sense those needs is the tricky part. Often it means turning a want into a need. But deep down, we all need to feel loved. If I'm appreciated, I'll allow you to do almost anything to me — screw up my order, overcharge me, under-deliver, you name it. If you're constantly thanking me, I'm like putty in your hands. It flies in the face of good sense, but that's me.

I was grown before I realized how much I loved my father and how much he loved me in return. We simply weren't the Cleavers, the 1950s version of TV's *Leave it to Beaver*. Thankfully, dad and I took time to mend the flaws in our relationship before he died. I will forever be thankful for that.

We've all lost people special to us before we reconciled our differences. *This happens with customers every day.* We always think we'll have tomorrow. But tomorrow isn't guaranteed, not with friendships, not with loving relationships, not with customers.

Some customers will be lost. But customers are resilient if there's an ounce of love at the start. You need to trust that love. You need to build on it.

People think love is a weakness, but it's not. As Aunt Ollie proved, kindness and love require strength. It takes strength to care about our customers, and our employees. Kindness gets us in the door or out of a jam before strength can, anytime. Consider the incredible power of "I apologize." When did we last say that to a client? *Only the weak are cruel,* wrote Leo Buscaglia in *Love*, a 20-year bestseller. *Gentleness can only be expected from the strong.*

LOVING TOO LATE

Builders are strong people. Remodelers and suppliers are shaped by the same stuff. You've seen human beings at their worst and best, and if you've gotten this far, you've felt the top and the bottom of the roller coaster that is the building cycle. Think of the heroes still operating their businesses in Detroit, the worst housing market in the country, where, in early 2007, some homes were selling for less than a used car. Through the cycles, you've become tougher and resilient, like Aunt Ollie. And yet, you need to know it's OK to allow a certain gentleness to come through, in everything you do, no matter the cycle.

As I wrote this, markets continued to shift. Home prices were flat or declining in many regions of the country. Some economists feared a recession. Storied builder Levitt and Sons cited "unprecedented conditions" and filed bankruptcy. Other builders in the nation's top 100 also filed for Chapter 11 bankruptcy protection. Mortgage scams were uncovered and mortgage companies laid off workers or filed for bankruptcy. Federal lawmakers demanded that regulators and lenders provide answers about subprime mortgages, and many worried that rising mortgage defaults would hurt our banking system. The subprime crisis was blamed for stock market declines.

But, that wasn't all. Remodelers reported dips in business, and sales leads were the lowest in years. Nearly every homebuilding company announced workforce cuts, with some of the largest cutting their rosters by half — thousands of employees. Lennar Corp., the largest U.S. homebuilder, reported a 73 percent drop in first-quarter earnings when most orders failed to materialize. Then, it asked trade contractors in Southern California and other states to cut prices by as much as 20 percent and resubmit invoices — or be shut out of bidding for future projects. Every builder has had to find ways to cope.

At many homebuilding companies, it appeared the layoffs began to affect customer service by September, when customer satisfaction rating companies reported lower scores — perhaps the result of more attention paid to immediate gains and less attention on customers. The effect of this trend on the continuity of satisfaction and the evolution of loyalty will be critical, but as of this writing, the full impact is unknown.

I know that in the end, faced with fewer buyers, we must return to love — or whatever connection keeps our customer satisfied and referring us to others. Customers are our hidden, unpaid sales force. They promote our businesses in ways and places we can't. Referrals, the old word-of-mouth in the grocery store check-out line, are invaluable, because in slow markets especially, people turn to other people to avoid making bad decisions.

Where do we layer on the love? we ask our consultants. *The customer satisfaction rating companies are coming into my new community — what should we do?* As builders, remodelers, and suppliers, we try to set ourselves apart from our competition, examining our processes. We've discovered how sloppy we've been in boom times. Now we need to learn more about customer care; how care turns into loyalty; and how loyalty translates into longevity and takes business to the *next level*, whatever that means. We want to *enhance* loyalty. We want *customers for life.*

The good thing is, love doesn't have to add overhead. What's the price of a dead-on delivery process ... or a killer smile?

THE *YEE-HAW!* OF LOVE

First we must respect our client's home, even before it's a hole in the ground. The respect comes when the first bulldozer turns over this family's hallowed ground. Respect turns into trust and trust turns into loyalty — it's a never-ending cycle. One inconsistency can break the chain. It takes years to build loyalty ... and only a second to destroy it.

Until around 1996, 10 years after Carol Smith's ground-breaking work on customer service in home building, we built in the present, the here and now, focusing on tomorrow only when tomorrow got here. But as more builders went national, as more lawsuits drew attention to a lack of service or poor quality products, and as J.D. Power and Associates jumped into the market, customer care became the most important component for businesses of any size.

In that grocery store check-out line, it used to be that you'd tell your neighbor the headaches your contractor was causing you. Now, the Internet hosts consumer chat rooms where they share their pain. With a click, clients send their emotions to the world, adding pictures, which add power to those stories, and make them even more believable.

Through the influence of Carol Smith, an internationally recognized home-building customer service expert, friend, and contributor to this book, and through AVID Ratings Co., Eliant, GuildQuality, Customer Follow Up and others who rate consumer satisfaction, we've come to better understand the importance of measuring what matters to American consumers: How to live and grow as families in their homes. Indeed, some companies are basing everything they do on customer satisfaction scores, referral rates, and even the frequency at which clients provide referrals.

It only makes sense. Now we know, from companies rating homebuilders and remodelers, that loyalty returns bottom-line results. A preliminary study of John Laing Homes shows that an 8 percentage point increase in customer satisfaction with sales, construction, and customer service can yield 21 percent more referrals, and 28 percent more operating profits. In the remodeling world, we know that a 5 percent increase in customer satisfaction, from 92 to 97 percent, yields 11 percent more gross profit. If that's not a *Yee-Haw!*, what is?

LOVING IN MILLIONS OF PIECES

Homeowners have become our marketing departments because their homes connect to their hearts. These family refuges are places builders should always return to, because the emotional link is never lost. In their minds, customers never leave us. Their relationship with us began before the sale, at their first point of contact with a person in our community — Was it the mason on a jobsite? Was it the sales consultant? A laborer? — and it continues through the warranty process and beyond. Everyone, from supplier to Realtor to tradesman, is part of this life-long relationship.

More companies understand this and know how to keep clients close, but they've worked hard at it. The best see results. If the third largest builder in the nation by revenue can, in a year, cut warranty costs 14 percent — unheard of in homebuilding — why can't a company with 15 employees consistently satisfy customers before problems go to warranty? If Farnsworth Development in Mesa, Ariz. can build 250 homes and have *every single buyer* say they would recommend the company to a friend, shouldn't you be able to do the same?

You can, by doing what they did: Having the guts to make changes in how you look at employees and trade contractors, and yes, helping them love customers with the same care you provide. Look at the deep, ingrained systems that snake through the chain of service. I guarantee that you'll uncover habits going back to your company's "childhood."

In 1988, I started selling homes for Bill Watson's Denton Homes in San Antonio. Those were the "crash days" in Texas. Bill had a ton of product. But with Bill's help and commitment, and with my team, we sold those homes. How? By concentrating on each person who walked through the door. We never forgot what those men and women, moms and dads, even their children, wanted: *A home just for them.* Building, remodeling, and supplying thousands of parts to homes means you have to do a million things right, not in a *process* or for a *building*, but for *people*. It sounds simple, but how often do we *walk right over it?*

I'm not offering a magical, blow-you-away solution. I don't have a "Welcome Mat" system or theoretical lessons or recommendations. This book is like me. *Down to earth.* Real. *In your heart.* I offer perspective on how to go to the mat when it matters, where it means the most. I'll offer a look from ground level, not 40,000 feet. I'll remind you of what you know deep down, and what you need, in today's market, but may have forgotten through the boom cycles. My suggestions bloom from the experiences and recommendations of builders, remodelers, and all those connected with this business, true professionals who are — *here I go again* — loving their customers.

People say, "don't sweat the small stuff." I say it's *all* small stuff and you better sweat every bit. Lasting loyalty will take your business where you've dreamed. To make love last, you have to understand loyalty, respect, and trust. You have to know what's built into my idea of love. I see it not because I've loved more, but because I know, today, as a customer, what it means to be loved less.

It takes guts the size of Texas to love as we're meant to love. Let's find out how to share the love and see why customers won't let go. Let's rediscover why … loyalty *is* love.

Beverly Koehn, May 1, 2008

CHAPTER ONE

LOVE STORY
LOVE IS LOYALTY — LOYALTY IS LOVE

We're beginning to realize we're retail.

Those aren't my words, but the words of a savvy central California homebuilder — Karen McCaffrey of The McCaffrey Group.

In the next five years, McCaffrey's goal is to become like Nordstrom. Not that she'll sell shoes and killer clothes from the closets of the 250 homes her company builds each year, but her team will make *the customer matter in every interaction,* and building homes will be about the customer's *experience* from the moment they walk through the door.

When a customer arrives at The McCaffrey Group's Fresno headquarters, the team knows it must make the encounter meaningful. The gorgeous Mediterranean architecture sets the tone. Everyone in the office welcomes each visitor with a smile. They love their jobs and they're well-trained. Not only do they have several flavors of coffee brewing, but they'll offer freshly squeezed orange juice if that's your morning potion. Everything — coffee cups to silverware — is exquisite. Each item the customer touches has significance.

Are you focused on loyalty? Do you know why the orange juice is important? Why its smell, taste, and the feel of the cut crystal stemware matters? Do you understand why loyalty — the end result of an on-time, on-budget, professionally delivered construction project — a delightful experience — begins with the stemware? And retail?

HEART OF
THE MATTER

What to take to heart from this chapter:
- Loyalty is the new business driver.
- Building loyalty requires commitment, from everyone — leaders to laborers.
- Price doesn't matter; customer experience does.
- Care allows for forgiveness and feeds your business.
- Satisfaction is never an end; it's the route to loyalty.

Customers are loyal because of their relationship with you. It's that easy. Consultant, custom builder, and columnist Al Trellis reminds us that loyalty stems from satisfaction — even if the product is inferior. A great customer will apologize for our shortcomings! A great customer knows we're human, and we'll make mistakes. It's how we handle our mistakes and transform them into moments of love for our clients that makes the difference. Loyalty is given by customers we've hurt, but who will defend us, as we say in Texas, until the cows come home.

Retail understood this long before housing. It had to. Retail is highly competitive, and there are no guarantees that when a store opens its front door each morning that customers will come in. Perhaps you might understand more clearly in another language.

The McCaffrey Group, 35 people selling homes for up to $500,000, has up to a 40 percent repeat and referral rate in some communities. Even if McCaffrey approaches $1 billion in annual revenue, it won't make the list of industry giants, but think about it: *half a billion dollars* in business could come from friends of clients. OK, *now* think of the industry giants, with $15 billion in revenues. If 40 percent of their business comes from loyal customers, that's $6 billion that starts with  a single prospect and a single employee, smiling, taking time to squeeze the juice from an orange.

It doesn't get any sweeter than that.

We need clients for life.

But whoa, wait a minute, it's a long way from squeezing oranges to a well-delivered product and I don't know your superintendents, suppliers, or trades, do I? The economy's hard, and the cost of hiring and training competent building professionals is rising. There are labor shortages and environmental issues. Impact fees and regulations are stifling business. Unemployment is up and interest rates are unpredictable. How do I develop — and maintain — a system to keep customers not just satisfied, but loyal to the bone, given these conditions? *How can I possibly keep clients for life?*

LOYALTY DRIVES & PROVIDES

It's not only possible; it will soon be the only way to do business. If you're among the best, more than half of your future revenue in the next building cycle will come from this renewable client resource. How can you ignore it? How will you afford to chase after new business leads when your competitors rely on this powerful and longer-lasting source for their leads? Why not invest in it?

The best of the best have anticipated and built on these practices for years. It's a trend that will propel us beyond the uncertain world of "satisfaction" and into a more measurable and predictable world of loyalty. This movement has been prompted by many factors that have evolved over the years, among them the expectation that product-centric businesses like ours must deliver retail-rich experiences in ways that inspire lifelong loyalty.

Satisfaction doesn't drive referrals, says Bob Mirman, CEO of Eliant, a provider since 1984 of customer satisfaction monitoring services to about 300 homebuilders. "*Satisfied* is like getting a 'C' in school," he says. "It keeps people from complaining but a satisfied buyer is still a likely candidate for legal action. *Delighted* customers are loyal buyers, and much less likely to do that." The Irvine, Calif. company, whose clients include John Laing Homes and Ryland Homes, conducts more than 300,000 homebuyer surveys each year. These surveys show that unsatisfied people don't actively or eagerly initiate referrals. In fact, that's why Eliant began providing their builder clients with "customer experience management" services. Planned contacts, both ordinary and extraordinary, lead to delighted buyers and generate more referrals.

If you want to *drive* business, you need customers who are thrilled with the building experience and beyond, Mirman says. They need to be thrilled that you solved their problems. Delight doesn't come from just the product. The largest single referral driver for homeowners, defined as buyers after move-in, is the customer care *experience* — **about 47 percent of all referrals depend on this experience**. Eliant data also indicates that, for buyers, their *experience* selecting options and their *experiences* with your sales staff, construction reps, and customer care personnel combine to produce 42 percent of referrals. Who said anything about the new home?

Top 5 Referral Drivers: Buyers & Owners

Buyers			Owners		
1	Installation and Workmanship	29%	1	Customer Care Experience	47%
2	Options Experience	16%	2	Framing/ Wall Alignment	13%
3	Construction Rep Skills	10%	3	Plumbing	8%
4	Sales Experience	9%	4	Flooring	7%
5	Customer Care Experience	7%	5	Windows	7%

SOURCE: ELIANT, WWW.ELIANT.COM; TOP FIVE DRIVERS ONLY,
DOES NOT EQUAL 100%; REMAINING DRIVERS EACH HAVE AN IMPACT OF 5% OR LESS.

At least a third to nearly half of the referrals generated from customers, at any point in the process of buying and early ownership, are motivated by staying in touch and keeping clients up-to-date, by problem-solving, being on time for repairs, doing what you say you'll do, cleaning up, and all the niceties that touch the emotions. This is the honey that engenders trust and appreciation, whether it's a glass of orange juice, a quickly repaired drywall nick, ice cream for the kids in your new community, or a smooth, unhurried options selection process. Sense-driven emotions never stopped being a purchase motivator, so why overlook them when it comes to referrals?

Emotion-driven loyalty cuts costs. Just think how much less advertising you'd need if you, like one northwest builder that used a compelling emotion-driven branding message to grow its business exponentially in 2005-2006, had thousands of prospects and a 10-month waiting list.

Or if, like Destination Homes in Layton, Utah, you use well-honed systems and customer care to grow nearly tenfold, from 30 to 250 homes a year in just five years. Because of both population migration and immigration, Utah has been an anomaly in the national economy, not affected by economic dips until late 2007. But while Destination began to feel the pinch and had to lay off staff, it still knew that to continue to grow, whatever the economy, it had to invest — in its customers.

Destination Homes' sales team is on the front line for customer satis-faction, holding customers' hands from sales, through construction, to the walk through, managing expectations and helping clients better understand the roller coaster ride that we call home building. Each summer, Destination Homes rents ice cream trucks to delight kids in their communities and every spring they give packs of flowers to their new homeowners. In winter, they rent out the local movie theater to preview new movies. Destination Homes uses customer care to drive its entire business.

For these companies, even if their homes cost more, clients will pay the higher price because of the relationships they've developed. You know you have loyal customers when price becomes secondary. Price will never be a non-issue, it's a reality, but when you develop a relationship based on more than price, you'll have something that lasts. Price has no consistency, no life. It's a number.

The best builders and remodelers charge more because they sell *value*. There's value in relationships. Shouldn't you make price secondary?

LOYALTY — OUR FICKLE HISTORY

Don't forget our history or the history of industries that have yet to truly latch onto loyalty.

You can't deny history. But, before exploring how to arrive at loyalty, the best business driver, let's define what I'm talking about. In order to improve relationships, loyalty sometimes involves pain. But loyalty also encompasses trust, respect, and "keeping it real." Loyalty involves every facet of an organi-zation — employees, trades, suppliers, and customers.

Loyalty is the consequence of many actions and *builds* on satisfaction. For your client, purchasing a home or contracting a remodel doesn't hit them until, lying in bed, they're unable to sleep. And they're suddenly walking down a windy road at midnight, with doubts and fears about their decision besetting them. Loyalty is the assurance, the security that comes at that moment, putting to rest anxieties, fears, and confusion.

How do most of us achieve this loyalty? We tack on service at the end of the process. It doesn't work that way, yet that's exactly how it's been handled, for most, over time. Scott Sedam, president of TrueNorth Development, a well-known Michigan-based consulting firm, and a former columnist for *Professional Builder* magazine, says a good analogy of what builders want when it comes to loyalty is the fad diet. People don't eat right. They don't sleep right. They don't take care of themselves. They want a quick fix, but that fix has consequences and implications.

Builders resort to gimmicks — food baskets and coupons. If it's the right time on the right day of the week and it's a sunny day, the homeowner gets a pizza. Sedam says builders fail to look for the problems that are deeply rooted in their processes — seeking out what's critically wrong — what no one sees upfront.

He's right. Customer care can't ever be surface stuff — it must be deeply rooted. If you're not leading a well-run company, connecting customer care to your financials in every aspect of your business, forget it. A diet won't work. If your business is flabby and isn't running well, how healthy can it be on the inside?

Something caused your customer satisfaction scores to drop. You spot it like fat in the mirror: Wow, where did that come from? Do you ask: What's the cause? Do you change the system? Alter the process? If the surveys say plumbing or roofing leaks are recurring problems, you can't just keep fixing leaks. Was it design? Materials? The roofing contractor? Is it spread in layers throughout your process?

More important, is it rooted in training?

Sedam laments the utter lack of training for builders and even education for business owners. We don't spend enough on training for ourselves and our people. Mike Benshoof of SMA Consulting of Orlando, Fla., which serves 200

VERIDIAN HOMES Welcome To The Customer Experience

RECOMMEND TO A FRIEND	SURVEY OFIS/STRENGTHS	REGRESSION TARGET QUESTIONS
Survey: ⊙ 30 Day	Date Range (Survey Received)	View: ○ OFIs
○ 11 Month	⊙ Quarter Month : / ±	⊙ Strengths
○ Warranty Service	○ Year Year : / ±	
	View: YTD Q1 Q2 Q3 Q4	

30/45/60 Day Home Buyer Satisfaction
15 Strongest Survey Scores
Surveys Received between 10/01/2007 and 12-31-2007

Number	Question Number	Total Responses	Average Score
6c	Knowledge/Helpful/Courteous	45	99.62
6d	Dedicated To Building Quality	45	99.62
6e	* Pleasant to Work With	46	99.63
6f	* Overall Satisfaction	46	99.63
6a	Expl'd. Construction Process	43	98.42
6b	Responsive To Concerns	45	98.51
14	Time Till Closing	47	98.94
5c	* Knowledgeable/Helpful/Courteous	47	96.74
5a	Operations Clearly Explained	47	95.32
5d	Home Was Clean & Ready	47	95.70
15	Recommend to a Friend	47	95.68
1d	Available and Informative	47	94.23
5b	Warranty Policy Rev'd./Expl'd.	47	93.19
4b	Professional & Timely Approval	44	93.52
1e	Made Buying Pleasant	46	93.09

VERIDIAN HOMES' INTERNAL WEB SITE ALLOWS EMPLOYEES TO SEE ANNUAL, QUARTERLY, AND MONTHLY CUSTOMER SATISFACTION SCORES. THEY CAN CHANGE THE VIEW TO SEE BEST RESULTS OR AREAS THAT NEED ATTENTION. WITH A CLICK OF THEIR MOUSE, THEY CAN COMPLIMENT EACH OTHER.

---

clients building up to 800 homes a year, shares a similar perspective. SMA's benchmark for training is at least 5 percent of base salary, an amount which should increase to 10 percent as the employee is promoted and becomes a leader, teacher, and mentor. So much of customer care, and loyalty, ties directly back to training.

Based on the latest U.S. Census Bureau data, The Joint Center for Housing Studies of Harvard University estimates that 438,200 employers build new homes and remodel existing homes. I'd estimate that less than 5 percent, yes, less than 22,000, understand that for this best business driver to work, for loyalty to work, every person in the company must be trained in how to *engage* with each other and the customer.

No, I'm not talking *that* kind of love and I don't want to make our industry sound like Neanderthals. But some companies spend so much on studies and surveys and don't know how to interpret or act on the data they generate. They reprimand for bad scores and praise good scores. But too often — and I've seen it — that's the end of it. Think of the health care and auto industries. Before you think we have them beat, think again. We're no better. Like those business sectors, we ask our customers how we're doing, but we've yet to truly listen.

The scores are only the beginning.

It's astonishing to think that programs promoting customer care and loyalty are still in the early stages in housing. Loyalty is as new and revolutionary to our industry as warranty service was back in the 1980s, when nobody cared about warranties. Then, because of litigation, we saw an evolution. Things changed. Who would build anything now without a warranty service program?

LOYALTY — OUR FUTURE

When the housing market plummets, companies try to stop the bleeding. We cut back on training and customer care because we don't look at training and care *as the heart of the business.* It supplies our business with life. If you cut customer care in the recent economic cycle, did you first think how much business comes from treating customers as you would like to be treated — hear I go again — with *love?* Did you think that if they told six people about their experiences, those folks would walk in your door with new business?

How can you cut your marketing

driver, when you need it most? Some of these employees were the people who had the most impact on customer care in their companies. These executives made a difference, and accelerated the industry's understanding of customer loyalty. They are obsessed with care and are going places we've yet to see. I'll tell some of their stories. They're amazing. They are, and will continue to be, the best, the leaders. Why? They are *obsessed!*

John Maasch, vice president of sales, marketing and customer relations at Veridian Homes in Madison, Wisc., building about 400 homes and bringing in $90 million in revenues each year, has launched an internal Web site with a special field called "Customer Experience." Click on that tab and you'll see every question asked on customer satisfaction surveys, along with the results. Company results are compared to industry averages and to the benchmark set by *The AVID Award* winners, supplied by AVID Ratings. Maasch knows his people need to see these numbers *all the time.*

Mike Humphrey, vice president of operations at David Weekley Homes in Houston, one of the nation's 25 largest builders, uses phone surveys to obtain results in real time and allow the company to respond rapidly if needed. The surveys reach 85 to 95 percent of their customers. Everyone in the company can see where the company stands by looking at live survey data in Lotus Notes — tabulated

DOGGED LOYALTY: Keeping It Real

LOVE STORY

Chuck gimmicks. Add empathy. Fix the problem.

Peter Shands of Professional Home Improvements in Canberra, Australia says it's important to give exemplary customer service, with an attitude of respect, as if you lived in your client's shoes.

Shands has built or remodeled homes for 33 years, including three years with the home improvements division of A.V. Jennings Co. in Houston in the 1970s, and he now does about $5 million a year in sales. (See www.buildprofessional.com.au.)

Clients don't expect roses every Friday afternoon, or tickets to a football game. "But they want to be informed and looked after, and to feel secure," he says. "It's not about gimmicks." Builders and remodelers need to be alert for signs that clients need emotional support, especially when you have to tell them something difficult, and tell them straight: *As much as I want to help you, this is what I have to do, to get to the end of the job. What concerns do you have?*

Now suppose the clients have a pet dog buried under a rosebush and the excavator is about to dig it up for their home extension (Australian for "addition"). Do you ask: "How long did you have the dog? Can we put him in another place?" What if mother and daughter come home and the dog's gone? "We dug some bones up in by project, division, city, area, and total company.

But it's not so much seeing the data, but what they do to *act on the data*. But I'm getting ahead of myself. These tools are *driving* Veridian and Weekley as each business strives to keep its loyalty edge.

Consider, too, Gust Nicholson Sr., whose Team Blue got its name from the blue masking tape and language-is-no-barrier shorthand it used to communicate with its Spanish-speaking painting crews.

Nicholson, former director of customer relations at Engle Homes Orlando/Technical Olympic USA, spent more than 17 years developing and implementing quality assurance programs in Orlando at Pulte Homes including seven years with TrueNorth Development's Scott Sedam, who was, at the time, a corporate vice president of quality and customer commitment. Nicholson eats and breathes customer service. While he was director, his division had the best customer satisfaction plan in Florida, winning, in 2007, the Southeast Building Conference Excel Award. The same year, Engle Homes Orlando, up against many major builders, took the award for Best Customer Experience, 500+ Closings In The United States, presented by AVID Ratings and *Professional Builder*. Nicholson started working on this program in 2001.

Nicholson, now a customer relations consultant and trainer, refers to a customer's experience with their first

the back yard — 'oh, that was dad.' Sorry, he's gone."

Shands says we need to tell clients what's about to happen, what's happening, and then, what happened. "It's a part of being there and being engaged. It's like that little dog. The girl was devastated that mom and dad were putting the extension there because Patchy was buried there. Mom and dad figured it's not a big deal, we can live with it. On the other hand, they're attached to their daughter's emotion. The big deal for them wasn't the dog, it was their daughter. 'Oh, so there's a puppy buried there? We can handle it for you. We can arrange for something better so Patchy can be in a better place.'

"The daughter became right. The strain was lifted. It's called being responsive. And now, the client thinks, 'my daughter accepts the extension.' We 'exhumed' the dog and moved it to another place in the yard. The girl picked the spot. It's about empathizing."

Turn it around, he suggests: If someone was trying to make peace with you because you'd been wronged, you'd be outraged if they tried to do something extraordinary to make up for it — instead of just fixing the problem.

 Loyalty is just a stronger sense of 'keeping it real,' as Shands says. "The best answer isn't a box of chocolates and a bottle of wine. The best thing is to make sure you understand the problem, make sure you understand what you have to do to rectify the problem, make sure you fix it quickly, and then fix it the way they want it fixed."

home as a first kiss. He works from a principle-based foundation to put customers on a stable footing when they come in the door. While he believes referrals come from relationships, he knows that each customer arrives with his or her own baggage. If he sees promise in their DNA, he can build them up through faith, hope, and — he says it, not me — love. He's way beyond bricks and mortar here. "This might sound foolish," he says. "But we are dealing with human beings. Faith hits the body, hope hits the psyche, and love hits the soul. It's the human spirit that we're dealing with."

So he trained Engle salespeople to perform a "builder psychoanalysis" of sorts before starting with a client, asking questions to stimulate a response to questions such as: "Have you bought a home before? What was your experience?" These questions may bring out difficult emotions and even anger. He tries to spot "post-traumatic stress" from prior experiences with builders. Probing, he sees how badly the prospect's hopes were dashed. How was their faith attacked? How was their soul diminished by the last builder? What buyers' remorse did they have after that purchase? This isn't discussed with the prospect, but often simple questions can help determine whether buyers are "situationally depressed." Why? Nicholson believes we, as an industry, have psychologically damaged our buyers.

We have. And our buyers need critical care.

Sedam, who has called Nicholson "the most wonderfully fanatical customer service guy" he's ever known, suggests that his friend's approach can sound to many like "voodoo stuff." But he knows Nicholson, a master at back-end customer care systems, also appreciates good *process*, unlike a bankrupt builder he knows that wanted to pop champagne bottles for new home buyers while leaving 85 items outstanding on their completion list.

Sedam argues none of the voodoo stuff works without systems that begin as far back as the purchase of land. People were always probing for the great secret at Pulte Homes. But it wasn't that complicated, Sedam explains. Pulte has great systems and trains exceptionally well. Consequently, their field superintendents stay on top of their jobs and have more time to connect with customers. Sedam estimates that in the best Pulte operations, a superintendent can manage the job with 20 percent fewer hours than the typical builder. A customer shows up at the competitor's site, what are the chances the builder is able to look those folks in the eye, and listen to their concerns? Builders who are running and desperate won't be able to stop and connect. If you have a functioning management system, strong suppliers, and 20 competent trades on site, life's a dream. If you have only half that number of competent people, life's a struggle, just to get the homes closed. If that superintendent is lucky, he has a good customer service manager following him, who's able to repair some damage. At best, the customer will be OK, as will your scores. Little loyalty comes from that.

To many of us, Nicholson's approach might seem "out there," but when you understand the connection to their systems, you can't argue with its success. Following this formula allows Engle Homes Orlando to claim a referral rate ranging from 92 to 97 percent based on key questions in its AVID Ratings surveys, such as, "Would you recommend Engle Homes Orlando to a friend?" Or, "Would you work with Engle again?" (While the actual referral number isn't that high, it's significant, though proprietary.)

What isn't a secret is that Engle has a seven-year jump on the rest of the industry in understanding the key driver of business — the human psyche. Do you? I don't mean to be hard on you. For a nuts-and-bolts process-and-product industry, we've come a long way. We're used to building, moving on, building another one. We remodel, move on, remodel another one. Only in the last 10 to 15 years has the emotional, experiential side of the process been considered.

Times change. And our mindset must follow, or we'll die. When I train construction and administration staff, I see that they're building according to plans, ordering materials according to specifications, and stamping out homes like good workers. Don't tell them it's time to be a psychologist, nurse, mom, or communications specialist. Who wants that? I teach a class for the NAHB, for building superintendents. A large section of the class deals with body language. When I say to these superintendents — *look at you! Your expression says it all.* They counter, *what? What are you talking about?*

They're not the only ones who need to learn that a slouch or a surly look or the way they dress speaks volumes without a word being said. *If you're happy to see me, you need to tell your face about it!* They need to learn these hidden modes of communication. Training and communication are the only ways to tap the emotions that lead to referrals. Predictable and extraordinary customer service jazzes homeowners, and most referrals come from homeowners, not homebuyers. Referrals come down to expectations and customer experience and most of that experience is with your building superintendent or project manager, particularly if you remodel homes.

Do you know that if you promise to complete all the final items in a home in five days, and your competitor promises a more realistic 30 days, and you both complete the work in 20 days, only the builder who was true to his word is seen in a good light, and will generate the referral? Building expectations comes from tracking survey results and providing above-board inducements for better employee performance that meets or exceeds the client's expectations. A change by CEOs and management in the value placed on surveys and their use, says Mirman, can turn scores on a dime. If executives don't make satisfaction and loyalty a priority, they won't be. Scores inevitably drop for companies that stop the survey process. "When they stop holding people accountable, performance drops," he says.

And yet change, which Mirman tries to stir up within companies, is not impossible to achieve. Communication about construction progress is a good example. The Eliant CEO says if your salespeople turn in a log noting that they're calling buyers on their own initiative every two weeks to discuss construction progress, within 60 days you'll see an improvement in the scores on that question. When scores change, it drives loyalty and that drives referrals. A totally delighted customer will refer 6.1 buyers to your door, while a "C Buyer" will refer a third fewer prospects.

Sell 200 Homes a Year and Each Buyer Refers Six People?
That'll Be Enough Business For Six Years!

10 months after move-in: Average number of recommendations during first 10 months	
C Buyer	1.7
B Buyer	3.5
A Buyer	4.6
Evangelical Buyer	6.1

SOURCE: ELIANT, WWW.ELIANT.COM.

Evangelical Buyers — people who refer you over and over, forgiving your sins and spreading your gospel — are the clients you need to seek. They will provide more than three times as many referrals than C Buyers. It's all about a delightful 'ride.'

See why communication and the human spirit, as Nicholson calls it, are so important?

As builders, our processes and our company culture are getting better. We're more oriented toward service, or retail, as Karen McCaffrey puts it. But because of changes in the market, because of the influence of retail, expectations have changed dramatically. Buyers today have high expectations and they expect more from you than they do from FedEx or Southwest or Nordstrom because hey, the product you're building isn't a $14.75 next-day package, or a $99 plane ticket, or a $600 dress — this product, this new home, or this remodeled home, costs half a million bucks!

Eliant notes that in the 1980s, satisfaction scores for builders and remodelers were in the dismal 50 to 60 percent range. Some reached 90 percent, but most were much lower. Today, the range has narrowed, from the mid-70th percentile satisfaction level to the mid to high 90th percentile.

It has been a gradual transition from a focus on quality to one that includes experiences. Mirman pinpoints a turning point in 1994-1995 when the national

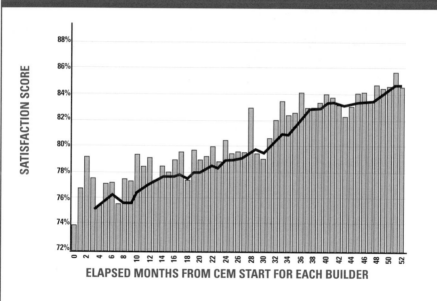

Experience, Not Quality, Improves Satisfaction
Impact Of Customer Experience Management Over First 4 Years

SATISFACTION SCORE

ELAPSED MONTHS FROM CEM START FOR EACH BUILDER

SOURCE: ELIANT, WWW.ELIANT.COM.

Customer Experience Management, or CEM as Eliant calls it, builds satisfaction scores. CEM designs loyalty points into each interaction. So quality isn't the only factor that drives referrals, says Bob Mirman, Eliant CEO. It's the sustained experience, and attention. This chart shows average improvement of 12% during this period for 200 Eliant clients. It begins at each builder's CEM start date (zero, at bottom), and the black line is the three-month running average. In the 1980s, quality was the driver of high scores; more than 20 years later, quality is now only the key that opens the door to high scores. The overriding factor is the experience. Without a great ride, quality will not carry referrals, Mirman says.

8 LOYALTY STANDARDS

Traits of Builders Rated Highest For Customer Satisfaction

- **Loyalty Is King.** A loyalty VP is in charge of customer experience/customer loyalty at corporate and division levels.
- **Experiences Matter.** A cross-departmental "E-team" handles "expectations management" and "touchpoint planning," disseminating data to employees and reviewing it with them.
- **Measurement Counts**. Companies measure customers' ratings of their homes and their ownership experience.
- **Expectations Are Exceeded.** The team exceeds buyer expectations through structured expectations management.
- ***Yee-Haws!* Happen.** Customers are wowed at each critical touchpoint through planned connections.
- **Teams Are Informed.** Department managers present customer satisfaction scores and trends on key issues quarterly, and share best practices across communities and divisions.
- **Teams Are Recognized.** A structured program recognizes individual and team performance.
- **Teams Are Rewarded.** Survey ratings determine a significant part of bonus compensation.

SOURCE: ELIANT, WWW.ELAINT.COM.

recession ended. Design centers came into being and people began to customize everything. Retail provided greater personalization. Blue jeans were available in over 27 varieties. In our design centers, we offered more options and 50-page catalogs weren't uncommon. (Now, the trend has been significantly modified: builders are trying to simplify the process, however, some still offer large option selections.)

What further accelerated this change in quality was when J.D. Power and Associates of Westlake Village, Calif., entered the market in the late 1990s. Now you had (at that time) a 30-year old global marketing information company conducting independent customer satisfaction surveys on product quality. To many, it was seen as the best — and worst — thing to happen to the industry.

Carol Smith of Home Address had rolled out the concept of satisfaction and loyalty before J.D. Power rolled in, and with others, including Eliant, who entered the market in the 1980s, they were the lone voices in the wilderness.

J.D. Power ratcheted up this view of a customer-centric model. It gave homebuyers a national voice in the ranking and rating of our companies. It helped set the bar across the U.S. and relied on public records so surveys were truly independent. Depending on your perspective, company rankings also established the thinking that the only way to survive was to be Number One in a market. That was an unfortunate development, and, depending on your perspective, it's still an (unnecessary) driver for many.

When we began tying employee compensation to customer satisfaction scores, that's when the focus on satisfaction grew exponentially. But that focus didn't come without costs. We've all watched with great interest developments in a federal investigation related to the gaming of surveys. Despite these cases, customer satisfaction rating companies have been a force for improvement in our industry. The old ways are dying hard. Companies are known to panic when J.D. Power announces it's coming to town to rate owners' satisfaction with their new homes. Last I heard, Alberta, Canada was expecting a visit from this consumer force.

Get ready to do better, Alberta, because we're all waking up to what matters most — the customer.

FASTENING ONTO LOYALTY

While focusing on products, we lost sight of the customer.

Sometimes we get so focused on numbers that we lose sight of the customer. We have enough sense to know we have to care, and there are enough people around us who do, says

Guts To Love

Setting A Care Standard
BY CAROL SMITH

Communication, documentation, and attention to the nitty-gritty are critical when providing care.

Nearly every company has employees whose service performance is stellar. Think of the top-selling salesperson, the "go-to" person in design, the superintendent who delivers homes that are complete and clean, or the warranty rep who "gets the job done" and in each case you'll find an employee with superior service attitudes and habits. These stars consistently and effectively manage the mundane everyday details of their jobs: returning phone calls, answering emails, and making suggestions at meetings. They are respected because they serve their customers well.

Builders often wish that they could replicate these attitudes and habits, yet they have no idea how to make that happen. Imagine the results if you identified and practiced the successful habits of these service stars in your organization. Imagine the clarity and confidence you would have when setting expectations with your customers.

The first step is to create Universal Service Guidelines. They're "universal" in that *every* employee practices these behaviors with *every* customer, *all* the time. Your company defines the guidelines. You develop them based on your company's values, practices, past failures, and current performance goals.

Marc Warren of Customer Follow Up, of Boalsburg, Pa., a market research consultant who specializes in customer satisfaction and loyalty surveys. But he says builders lose sight of a critical piece of the *Love* chain when they don't see the connections between what's viewed as just warm and fuzzy and the critical operations of the business. "If a builder uses a certain fastener and soon realizes they're going to be back in two years when the fastener isn't holding, they change something.

"The same goes for customer care. You need to give as much attention to it as you do the building process. A flaw in care can come back to haunt you if you don't take care of it right away." Take care of it, I might add, and your customer becomes your sales force. You can't afford for them to "come loose," as Warren might say. Every process should aim toward the goal of keeping close to your customer.

At the peaks, builders say they're too busy to put time into customer satisfaction and in the valleys, they don't have the resources. Everyone has excuses, but the good builders rarely have a problem. Top builders are totally committed and dedicate staff to quantitative measurements and provide incentives based on improved performance. For those unable to commit, well, their scores are flatter than Lubbock, Texas. And yet, it's been proven that if you're committed to changing how your company performs, your scores, and therefore, your referrals will go up.

You can define "customer" broadly to include homebuyers, trades, associates, and employees. In doing so, the opportunities to create across-the-board service expectations and consistent performance become readily apparent. Consider what would happen if everyone within your organization agreed to practice key behaviors designed to serve customers well. Not only could homeowner Jones expect a known level of service, so could the plumber, the design center, and the construction and purchasing departments — all the time.

With Universal Service Guidelines in place, every employee at every level looks forward to predictable company interactions. Management sets the tone in their interactions with employees that they want the employees to set with homebuyers. When trades and associates are treated well, their loyalty increases and their performance often improves. Companies are transparent to their paying customers and homebuyers will recognize the telltale signs of friction among functions, poor follow-through, and the lack of internal support. Committing to consistent and intentional Universal Service Guidelines helps manage the image customers see and instills customer confidence in your organization's ability to perform.

Service is one person doing something for another, whether they are a homebuyer, an associate, or another employee. The service provider might be the receptionist, a warranty technician, or the company owner. The service might be answering the phone or a question, providing a repair or conducting a

High-quality referral prospects are your most important target. Most salespeople don't realize how many of their sales come from referrals, says Paul Cardis, CEO of AVID Ratings, a customer loyalty management firm that provides research, organizational training, and consulting to more than 500 homebuilders in the U.S. and Canada. Yet most salespeople agree that sales generated from referrals are better than non-referral sales. AVID's proprietary system ranks referral prospects for its builders to help them concentrate not just on customers, but on the *right* customers, the most avidly referring customers.

Not many builders or remodelers have tracked or mined this data, even while, as AVID notes, some builders are generating up to 50 percent of their sales from their referral networks. Working with fewer customers, single-line remodelers often report a 100 percent referral base. Isn't it time to better understand who these customers are and why they are, or aren't, referring you to your friends?

I'm talking about thousands, millions, and for some, billions of dollars from die-hard loyalty. The enormous impact of this client base can no longer be ignored or taken for granted. It must be explored and understood. Why stick to systems that ignore people and training and ride the hard line on process and policy? If you can realize why loyalty is love, you'll need to weave love into everything you do.

meeting, filling out a form or even building a home.

Customer reactions to hundreds of such interactions compose your company's reputation for quality and service. You need to set clear service goals and develop a plan to achieve them. Part of that plan requires the identification and specification of nitty-gritty day-to-day behaviors that ultimately constitute "service" within your organization.

We find that few businesses make any effort to define the service that trades, associates, and company employees or even departments should expect from each other. These areas are usually left to manage themselves or are haphazardly planned. This means that the expectations of those groups are left to each individual's imagination. Performance, likewise, is left to the discretion of the responding employee or department.

The results will reflect the effort invested — some good, some bad. As a trade contractor observed about a company: *Their accounting department really has its act together; they always call back quickly when I have a question and they stay in touch until the issue is resolved. Sure can't say that about their purchasing department! I've called twice in three days with no response.*

There are a wide range of procedures you can use to manage phone calls, e-mails, faxes, and meetings. These everyday-everyone communication behaviors profoundly affect a company's service reputation. Why should an element of performance that is so significant to your company be left to chance?

We only have to turn to the numbers again to learn that for years, as an industry, we haven't gotten this message. Roxanne Musselman, Musselman & Associates, in Highland, Utah, has coordinated a homebuyer's survey since 1991, covering 25 major U.S. markets. Buyers are asked how competent, trustworthy, and helpful their Realtor, loan officer, and salesperson was when they purchased their new or existing home. The new home salesperson has perpetually ranked the lowest, with evaluations on all three points of service never greater than 60 to 65 percent. That's troubling to me.

Salespeople, Musselman says, defer providing the answers or help to loan officers and Realtors, and they don't communicate as frequently with their buyers. "I think you love someone because they serve you," Musselman says. "Service is huge in creating a love relationship. Why do people love their

Realtor? They believe their Realtor is serving them, chauffeuring them around, finding a loan officer … clients will seldom leave their Realtors."

On the flip side, we do know what builders and remodelers need to do to earn higher customer satisfaction ratings, the most direct route to loyalty. Mirman, of Eliant, using the best companies as models, developed eight traits of builders with the highest customer satisfaction ratings (**See 8 Loyalty Standards, Page 15**). Companies have bits and pieces of these traits, but rarely all of them. They may have a *corporate customer service concierge,* but no systems to review and share data; they may measure and gather data, but then put it all aside. Some say: *We know how customers feel, they tell us all the time.* They are "magic pill" believers, as Mirman calls them, believing that the satisfaction survey itself is the only thing they need to do to improve satisfaction. They're wrong.

It's not what you discover; *it's what you do with what you find.* How many builders or remodelers hire companies like Eliant, then get irritated by the results and ignore them? Mirman says from 10 to 15 percent of Eliant clients do little with their results, feeling pressured to get back to building homes. But in every company that does that, usually one or two managers take the results seriously, despite the company's indifference. "Our biggest challenge is to gain consistency, across divisions or departments," the Eliant CEO says.

How many companies have a consistent expectations management process that rides out the boom and bust cycles? How many companies have honest, straightforward recognition programs that are foolproof and can't be abused or gamed, in other words, deliberately manipulated to achieve desired results? Mirman says maybe two-thirds of companies have well-defined recognition programs, and only half of those are conducted with consistency. They might start with well-defined purpose, but 50 percent slip.

We have to continually fight the natural slide into mediocrity, in all that we do, to measure and reward our employees and our company performance.

Wherever you are in embracing loyalty for life, are you ready to better understand why you have no choice but to embrace its driver, *care,* in all you do? I will show you how you can feel comfortable seeing the words *love* and *business* in the same sentence and not get queasy. Yes, this is a business book, not a love story, I promise you. So sip a Pepto-Bismol in a heavy, cut-crystal glass and get ready to understand the only way to win loyalty is to give it, not necessarily giving more than you've given before, but knowing how to give well, when to give, and what to give.

Get ready to fall in love with a new way to do business. *Get ready to understand it's built on emotion and connections, not quality, and that loyalty is the new honey of love.*

Make Loving You Easy

The Commandments Of Customer Care

If you don't adhere to these basic principles, you might as well quit now. These commandments must be written in stone throughout your organization and must feed the heart of *Love*, if you are to achieve the loyalty I describe in this book.

✔ **Thou Shalt Never Forget The Customer**

The source and the summit of your focus is the customer. In everything you do, in any decision that affects your business, if it isn't good for you *and* your customer, you need to question why you're doing it. Even if the issue doesn't drive at your foundational principles, consider how it could affect all your customers, including the trades and people who do business with you.

✔ **Thou Shalt Remember Customers Need Us**

Customers come to us for one reason — they need us, they need help. They don't always say or know it, but they do. They might be afraid or concerned, and they've read nothing positive about home building or remodeling. CNN will never report how many happy families bought homes in your community. But they will report on the one client who didn't get into his home on time. Remember that for the next 30 years you will pay for decisions you make right now. So even if you've faced this situation 100 times before, know that for your customers, it's a life-changing experience.

✔ Thou Shalt Remember You Need Your Customers

After all, customers sell your business. If you don't have customers, you don't have a business. Without the customer, there's no reason to build homes. There's no reason to refine purchasing processes if you're not building for buyers. It doesn't do any good to train your superintendents to communicate better if you don't have any business. The customer is your best marketing source and more believable than any advertisement.

✔ Thou Shalt Forget The Numbers, Remember The Hearts

These are people. This isn't a lot and block, or a job number. This is a human being. Treat the customer better than you want to be treated. In some companies, customers turn into statistical algorithms on 10-point scales. But we have to remember names; we have to remember things about the family, and the issues of their life. What lifestyle are they searching for? Do you understand how you can deliver it to them?

✔ Thou Shalt Nurture Personal Connections

When you reach a loyalty factor with your customers, they won't let go. How often do customers get attached to your sales consultants? How many sales consultants or executives with key customer contacts leave companies to start their own firms, based on those connections? If your sales consultants changed their place of employment, would the customer go to the person they have the relationship with before coming back to your company? In any case, train employees to love your customers. Good companies train their trades, the Realtors who show their homes, their superintendents, even their purchasing managers. They don't normally see customers, but if they're taught to think about the customer, that purchasing manager will care about them, and let the *Love* filter through.

✔ Thou Shalt Love Interruptions

The customer isn't interrupting work; they're the *purpose* for the work. When they have needs or issues, or when they want to talk, that's part of doing business. We can't get so involved in our process or fail to build time into it that we forget customers are human. Human beings are different than products — they need care. When a car runs out of gas, it will sit until we fill it up. If a customer runs out of care, and we disconnect the life support system, they'll die. Past a certain point, you can't revive them.

✔ Thou Shalt Never Argue With Customers

If you get into a me-against-you or an either-or situation, you're done. It's like trying to match wits with a 16-year-old — you'll never win. Once you reach the adversarial position, you're opponents, not on the same team. Take this emotionally-charged event and turn it on its head. Make it a turning point — not a stopping point — in your relationship.

"Courtesy, up 25%. Effort, up 25%. Quality, up 25%. Customer retention, up 250%."

CHAPTER TWO

LOVE HONEY
LOVE IS PURE EMOTION

Do you drive a Ford Fiesta or a Kia Sephia?

I ask this question nearly everywhere I speak, and I've yet to see a hand raised. *How many of you drive a Ford F-350?* The hands fly up. *Do your trucks drive on different roads than Fiestas or Sephias?* No. *Do you ever haul anything?* Rarely. I can tell because I've seen the beds of your trucks — there are no scratches. Why not buy the cheapest pickup around? Did you buy an *F-350* because it smells and feels different? Was it the sound system? Do you feel the engine's vibration in the soles of your feet? If your Ford pickup travels the same roads as a Fiesta or a Sephia, what's the difference?

We know, in our hearts, that buying decisions are based on experiences. They grow from the emotions we feel when we see the truck, smell and touch its interior, hear its dual exhaust, and feel the thump of its subwoofers when we click on the radio. It's the same for homebuyers or remodeling customers when they buy building products. They employ all their senses — sight, smell, touch, taste, and hearing — from their first look, to the first click on your Web site, when they drive through the entryway of your new community, or when they meet your first smiling trade contractor. From our senses, we create emotions. The way we experience our cars isn't different from the way we experience our homes, remodeled spaces, or kitchen faucets.

Create this emotional *honey* within the buzz of the buying experience and you'll create a relationship of respect, trust, and *loyalty:* The most emotional connection of all.

YEE-HAW!

I write and talk a lot about satisfaction, but satisfaction is a temporary thing. As we see in research from AVID Ratings, Eliant, GuildQuality, and Customer Follow Up, satisfaction is a moving target. But if you have systems in place that manage the service you provide to your customers, you can drop the ball and pick it up again later in your process. *That's what makes customers loyal.* In home building, says Marc Warren of Customer Follow Up, people don't expect

perfection — yeah, they'd love to get it — but what they expect is *professionalism*. That means anticipating and correcting mistakes, bringing them to the client's attention, asking for forgiveness, and moving on. Not getting *stuck* in honey of another sort.

HEART OF THE MATTER

What to take to heart from this chapter:
- Good emotions feed loyalty.
- Senses feed emotions.
- Professionalism — not perfection — is the goal.
- The last 5 percent of the job causes the most problems, but offers the highest returns in customer loyalty points.
- Forgiveness is what makes loyalty stick.

If you examine the data from customer satisfaction rating companies, what takes builders over the top in customer satisfaction are "touchy-feely" things — things that connect them with the customer. **And in no study did the builder with the lowest price win the award.** Builders who score highest in customer satisfaction command higher prices and are more profitable. If that's not proof that *Love* works, what is?

How do we manage our customer's emotions as they make a lifestyle change within their home, or when they decide to move into a new neighborhood? It's not simply a decision to buy or remodel their home — they're choosing to alter something dear to them, something about how they live.

eliant

2007 Homebuyers' Choice

John Laing Homes

Builder of the Year
Overall Satisfaction

Multi-Division Builder

For many people, loyalty is only an intangible goal, but once you have a better understanding of how it is based on respect, trust, forgiveness, and yes, *Love*, you will understand it better. You will understand that by creating a unique and pleasurable experience, you'll drive higher profits, more referrals, and lower warranty costs (**See Love Mode, Page 53**). I'm not talking about sugar-coating business processes, but about following proven methods for best practices. While companies like Pulte Homes, David Weekley Homes and others understand this and take it to heart — right to the bottom line — you don't need to be big to have a real impact and create lasting relationships.

How do you create this honey of *Love?* It starts with how you look at what you do and how you convey that to customers. Do you convey a "process?" Or do you convey a series of sweet emotional associations that, in the client's mind, create an experience of *Love?*

Marc Warren says businesses get so organized that they forget how to treat customers with respect and care. Carol Smith of Home Address goes further. She calls it "customer abandonment." We love 'em, then we leave 'em. Warren says builders ask his company, a marketing research and consulting firm, to query customers about how the builders' processes are working. Warren asks them, how can processes matter when customers are complaining employees don't show up on time?

Warren's comment makes builders angry and they insist — *well, what about our new processes?* From the customer's perspective, process is passé. Focus on *experience.* You need to pour on the good stuff to feed that experience, to make it stick. And, you need to face the obvious: *Showing up on time goes right to the heart of respect and trust.* So why not start with the basics?

I'll walk through seven processes to show you how to avoid bad emotions, feed good feelings, and focus on positive experiences while you layer on *Love.* These seven processes — sales, design, selections, construction, change requests, closing, and warranty — put you into the most contact, and potential conflict, with your customers.

When customers live through a "process," their emotions light up. They can get excited and angry. Or they could get excited and exhilarated. If their bells are really ringing, they might yell, as we do in Texas when a customer experience blows our hinges off: *Yee-Haw!*

This is the honey of *Love*. It doesn't have a dollar sign written beside it, but it has tons of deeply held value. If your competitors aren't doing these things, they'll never match your level of client satisfaction. *Never.* What am I talking about?

Well, do you know that touch is one of the most deeply felt senses because it's the first to be formed? Babies feel their mother's touch even in the womb. Perhaps you've read about historical experiments with children who died from a lack of touch. How do you touch your customers and reach their deep, basic needs? Yes, let's go really *basic*. Have you ever thought about how you shake hands?

Every handshake — whether I let you in or clasp the pocket of your hand — tells you about my style and how I'll connect with you personally. I'm a hugger. A hug tells you something, too. Did I pull you in close, or keep you at arm's length and clap your back?

The proof that this need for touch lies deep within our psyches is that we still fly to conventions when we could learn 90 percent of the same information online or over the phone. Why? At trade shows for builders and remodelers, people walk the aisles. As many as 120,000 people turn out for some shows, and people still walk the aisles. Why? *To shake hands.* To connect. We look, *we touch* the products, we shake hands. We're *connecting*. We can't find the human touch online, but when someone is standing in front of us, looking at us, we can read body language, and we can touch them.

Homeowners have the same need. This connection doesn't always have to be physical, but it has to be heart-to-heart.

HITTING THE SPOT

So how do you cover the business basics while still connecting with basic needs?

Did you know that Bill Mischler of Genesis Construction, of Bluffton, S.C., begins his projects by dropping off the Port-O-Let and immediately erecting an architecturally pleasing lattice around it? The portable toilet door never swings toward the street, but always toward the interior of the site. Mischler, who builds $1.5 to $7

million custom homes around Hilton Head, paints the lattice green and erects it on three sides of the toilet, so, from the street, you don't see an eyesore, you see something that blends in with the site. Cost: about $250. The perception? This guy not only loves us, he loves the neighborhood. That's the best $250 Mischler ever spent. That's a *Yee-Haw!* And yet, such a "little thing." A basic thing. A *nothing.* And now, his competitors have begun doing the same thing. Who knows? Soon, they might add English ivy!

John Laing Homes posts a "construction speed limit" of 10 mph at the entryway and along the streets of many of its communities. It created its own speed zone for construction vehicles, 10 mph below the 20 mph speed limit. What does this tell the community? Even better, Laing enforces the 10 mph zone, back-charging trades or superintendents when they don't mind the limit. It's jobsite protocol. John Laing respects the community. The message is clear: Our builder loves us — and our children.

They care about us. That's all clients want — care. Touch them with care. After all, we affect their *lives. We affect their basic needs.*

As you can see from these examples, the way you carry out your *Love* has to be planned. The ways of *Love* have to be consistent. They must drive toward creating a connection. It takes time before you, as a company, become sensitive to these needs. Understand, that for clients, emotional attachments and the perception of caring only happen over time. So connect. Communicate. *Listen.* Build trust.

HERE ARE THREE WAYS TO LOVE:
Exceed expectations.
Make customers important.
Tailor every experience.

How do you exceed expectations in everything you do, make customers feel important, and tailor every experience, when you build two, or even 40,000 homes a year? How can you make the experience personal, and enduring, in an instantaneous culture where anyone can withdraw cash from an ATM in 20 seconds or less, but it takes three weeks to get a change request quote?

Let's discover how to make loving you easy.

PICTURE IT, HEAR IT, SMELL IT …

Because we live in a world where quotes take three weeks to prepare, product selections take weeks, and construction takes months — sometimes even years — we must build into our processes the words, pictures, smells, sounds, and tastes that will transform systems so people feel that their needs are always valued and that their experiences exceed their own expectations.

People buy emotionally, not logically. They'll justify their purchases logically after the decision, but it's their feelings that determine whether the sale takes place. Our processes must satisfy all their senses. About 83 percent of what we experience comes to us through sight. That's why so often "what you see is what you believe." Hearing makes up 11 percent of our experience. Smell, 3.5 percent. Touch, 1.5 percent. Even taste contributes an important 1 percent.

The impact of appealing to the visual senses can't be overestimated. Confucius said: I hear and I forget, *I see and I remember*, I do and I understand. Walk people through using their sight, and in the end, they will *understand*.

You must light up their senses and their emotions, to create a *Yee-Haw!* at nearly every interaction the customer has with you and your company. As Bob Mirman, CEO of Eliant, notes, customer satisfaction, and therefore referral drivers, are made up of different satisfiers at different points in the homebuyer's and then, homeowner's, life cycle. These referral drivers change over time.

> **ELIANT HAS DISCOVERED THAT IN THE BEGINNING OF THE RELATIONSHIP, THE MOST CRITICAL CUSTOMER CARE ISSUES ARE:**
> Getting it right the first time.
> Cleaning up before and after the work.
> Providing service quickly.

Yet when buyers move in, they pay attention to workmanship quality and installation, features, and products. Initial quality is the highest-rated referral driver after move-in — 29 percent. But once there's a problem with a floor squeak or paint, homeowners focus on the builder's problem resolution process. They've transitioned from homebuyer to homeowner, Eliant says. All the while, the builder must maintain the buyer's trust.

Mirman suggests that the buyer's experiences through these steps must be extraordinary. Why? Almost half (47 percent) of the homeowner's willingness to refer a friend to the builder is directly related to the experience with the builder's service process and personnel. Quality is important, but how a builder responds to warranty or service requests makes or breaks the relationship with the new homeowner.

To develop unconditional trust, steps to cement the perception of extraordinary service should occur particularly during the warranty period. Eliant says top builders have "engineered" ordinary and extraordinary touchpoints into every phase of the ownership experience, first defining the experiences and expectations they want buyers to have, and then designing processes around these goals — not vice versa.

By systematizing touchpoints, you create trust deposits, says Martha Baumgarten, Eliant's vice president of customer experience management and former Shea Homes customer experience executive. One builder, who has 12 touchpoints, ranked 31st in Eliant's system, but in six months moved to Number 1 by examining first what the buyer needed, and then fitting the builder's processes to those needs. Builders often identify too many touchpoints — Baumgarten recalls one who had 180 ... of which only 12 were required. Another builder discovered that the gifts it was giving customers, at $600 per home, had real costs, but analysis showed that they made no difference to the customer.

Wouldn't your buyers be surprised if you offered, unannounced, three-month, six-month, or 11-month inspections to see if anything needed repair or touchup? Typically in these visits, smoke alarm batteries could be changed and air filters replaced — insignificant costs. What if you provided a log for homeowners to note minor imperfections as they discovered them, giving them numbered adhesive dots to mark areas corresponding with the log entries? It's a lot of work? Maybe. But your next project could come from one of those brightly colored dots — after all, what company pays attention to details like yours?

What if, on one of your spring service visits, you brought a flat of flowers for the homeowners to add color to their landscaping? If your required touch-points are functioning well, and this extraordinary one cements them, maybe for you, that will work. Talk about lighting up the senses!

STOCKING THE SALES POOL

The connection begins during the sale. Actually, it starts in the words you use in your marketing materials. The message should capture a lifestyle choice, not just square footage and room count. Price and product don't do anything to connect your community or your company to an emotion. In your ads and promotional material, do you show families living and enjoying their

WITH VIVID PHOTOGRAPHY AND INVITING GRAPHICS, THE WEB SITE OF KENNECOTT LAND CO.'S *DAYBREAK* COMMUNITY CAPTURES A LIFESTYLE CHOICE AND CREATES STRONG EMOTIONS IN ANYONE WHO VISITS THE SITE.

community, or their new space? What do black-and-white floor plans and elevations really show? What if you showed people *using* the space — creating a memory, an experience, an emotion?

One of the most extraordinary examples of this is Kennecott Land Co.'s *Daybreak* community at the base of the Oquirrh Mountains south of Salt Lake City, Utah. Going to www.daybreakutah.com, it's easy for a buyer to envision himself or herself in the vibrant pictures — the bright hues of its homes are back-dropped by clear blue sky, snow-capped mountains, intense sunshine, canoeists plying colorful lake waters, smiling children, happy moms and dads — a true community.

If, like Kennecott and its builders, you've created a feeling in your marketing materials, then when a buyer approaches the sales center, every emotion they're expecting has to be accentuated. Everything they see in the home has to look like a real family lives there — this is merchandising, not decorating.

Every time they drive up, the streetscapes, the lighting, the signage has to be so inviting that they absolutely have to stop — they can't drive past. And whoever greets them must look and feel like they are part of the neighborhood. They should smell coffee or tea brewing inside the home. This is a place to spend time, not a place to rush through and pick up a brochure on the way out.

Kennecott's *Daybreak* not only builds these emotions into its inviting Web site, that emotion carries through to its contemporary entry monuments — unlike any people have seen. As visitors drive up the hill into the community, they spot a beautiful glass building, an information pavilion, not a sales center. It's staffed by warm, knowledgeable people, and is decorated with fresh, fragrant flowers. Walk through and they discover little surprises: a map provides context, then a bicycle is a point of conversation about the vast open space, and paddles from a canoe reveal a different world about sailing and water conservancy and the community's lake. Another display shows what a low-energy window does for a home, and there's a kid's zone so parents can talk while keeping an eye on their kids at play. Last, there's a diorama of the community, a scale model of its master plan. It shows residents walking in parks and paddling canoes. Its detail is second to none. Kids can push buttons to make sailboats spin, or get landmarks to light up.

Information pavilion hosts talk about the fish they're stocking in the lake, and everything works to create an emotion about a lifestyle. Kennecott Land's select builders have made *Daybreak* the hottest community in the Salt Lake City Valley — and it will be for years to come. Clearly, every sales professional and Daybreak representative conveys an appreciation for their work and for the people who come to the community. Prospects aren't "ups" or "traffic units" or "be-backs" — they're *people*. Just one encounter with Barbara Breen at the information pavilion, or with Shelli Bown at the Rainey Homes model, and you'll know you've arrived.

The sales consultant has more impact on referrals than any other employee, according to a preliminary study by Professor Kenneth A. Merchant, Ph.D., chair of the Leventhal School of Accounting at the University of Southern California. Examining more than 5,000 sales at John Laing Homes, one of the largest privately-held builders in the U.S., early study results showed that sales employees' satisfaction is closely associated with customer satisfaction. Sales, customer service, and construction personnel have the most direct contact with customers and employee-customer satisfaction relationships will be strongest in departments with the greatest customer interaction. This is why the sales relationship is so important at the beginning of what is one of the most emotional processes in a homebuyer's life.

A salesperson must quickly assess the clients' hot buttons — the reasons people do what they do — understanding that everyone has different buttons. But sales consultants must also connect with buyers and not simply view them as part of a scripted sales process. They need to gently drive to the underlying motivations, yet live by *the platinum rule* — doing unto others

A HOME THAT FEELS GOOD

LOVE STORY

Some builders understand that you can design emotion into homes, not just into people or processes. Jennifer Hurst at Kennecott Land Co. in Salt Lake City believes, like I do, that home design should carefully consider a woman's desires and needs. As Kennecott's marketing director, she has worked on a series of homes designed by women architects, based on focus groups with 30 women from different walks of life.

Hurst worked with designers and architects to dovetail the preferences of these women and their lifestyles into plans. Surprisingly, they have found that when they add in certain design features, men like them, too. She has completed pilot designs and plans to build models. If the models catch on, the designs may be worked into homes. Among the affected issues are space allocations, finishes, textures, overall design, and functionality. For instance, Hurst will as they would like others to do to them. We have to help our people understand how to be sensitive to emotions without being too "feminine" or sappy. This is about connecting emotionally. Even the most dominant left-brained thinker still has emotions.

Gust Nicholson Sr., when at Engle Homes Orlando/TOUSA, trained Engle personnel to be sensitive to the emotions and psychological baggage a client brings to a transaction.

Nicholson tapped concepts he learned through association with life coaches, psychologists, and spiritual mentors, and used as a counselor to couples and at-risk youth. Are you feeding prospects the antidote they need? Are you feeding them psychologically — giving them the experience they crave, to want to come back and to refer friends? "We want to make sure we get the customer's bad experience upfront, end it, re-cool it and get rid of the situational depression that causes it so we can deal with the psychological problem they had with 2-3 other builders," Nicholson says. "Once they have a good experience, their faith is built up. People think we're kooky, but if you don't value the well-being of a customer, forget it. All we care about is the customer and putting people in a home." You can't think that just because someone gave you $400,000 to build them a home, that you don't need any psychological or moral standards, or that this person has faith in the system even if you make them sick, or hassle

create a "drop zone," a place where a working mother, at day's end, can drop her cell phone, PDA, briefcase, and coat and yet still feel organized and balanced. This simple design tweak could make her feel that she has her act together as she juggles a job, kids, husband, and all their activities. Hurst knows her young, married clients value convenience.

That's cutting-edge stuff. It's being sensitive to buyers' needs when buyers don't know how to voice those needs. No one came to Kennecott and said, "I haven't been able to find a home that feels good to me." But Hurst thinks women live in homes differently than men. And her data shows 91 percent of new home purchases are influenced by women. So she's looking for ways to enhance the homebuyer's experience. These are subtle differences in the way homes are built and sold today.

The new designs won't always be readily apparent, but will contain as many as 10 different features from ordinary homes. Several focus on creative use of space, such as "bringing the outdoors in" through a pivoting fireplace that opens the family room to the deck, allowing the homeowners to take advantage of the sunny weather that bookends Salt Lake City's summers and frequents its temperate winters.

In another example, in most master bathroom designs, intense vanity lights cast shadows. In her focus groups, Hurst learned women want lights that point straight up off a mirror, so they don't start their mornings with artificial circles under their eyes. The vanity was designed like an old school desk: the mirror pops up, it is lit from underneath, and makeup trays are them every time they make a change. "I'm giving you money," says Nicholson. "You actually work for me, yet you are hassling me. The building industry has to wake up to that, and we did."

I don't want to stereotype anyone, but this is why women tend to be better at connecting, at least in the homebuilding, remodeling, and building products industries, primarily because women are more sensitive to emotion. Women are proud of the fact that they're better communicators and listeners. Men, too, often realize this, saying, "Gosh, she never shuts up." But women are naturally more sensitive to other people's needs, perhaps due to their nurturing instincts. Sensitivity training is a big plus in sales as it allows both men and women to become more closely attuned to clients' needs. When men walk through homes, many men look at functionality while women tend to think, *how does it feel? How does this room feel* versus *is it big enough or does it have enough closets?*

During the sales process, salesmen tend to want to take the interstate. Saleswomen like to take, as we call them in Texas, the farm-to-market roads, the back roads and byways en route to their destination. In other words, if there are six steps to a sale, women also have six sub-steps. They stop in each room and help the buyer create a sense of how they would live in that room. Man or woman, if you're not sensitive to the emotional needs attached to a home, you have to learn how to sense them. It's no secret

hidden from view so that women feel organized. Her designers also added a pocket door in the master bath to allow a "family bathroom." By opening the door, parents can keep an eye on their kids as everyone uses their respective bathrooms.

Off the kitchen, the designs better reflect how women appreciate a place to celebrate their children's artwork while not cluttering the refrigerator door for everyone to see when the family entertains guests. If there's a large master closet, Kennecott's builder models will lay out storage differently for men and women, recognizing that they put their clothes away differently.

These designs, while only subtly different, may not be inexpensive to execute, and Kennecott understands that it will need to actively seek the right partners to bring the designs to life.

When most women walk into these homes, they will *feel* the subtleties and intricacies within the rooms that make them special. They'll *sense* something *is* different. Each subtle feature will be carefully emphasized by the sales specialist, who will create a story around them, most likely before the cost of the home is shared on paper. Hurst says that just as a new car dealer suggests that you "go drive it" before sharing the sticker price, so prospects will be asked to walk through the home before they're faced with the cost.

Just like when you stepped into your new *Ford F-350*, these homebuyers will feel comfortable. They'll feel great. They'll feel at home. Jennifer Hurst and Kennecott Land Co. are driving to the heart of emotion and what makes people buy … their very basic needs.

that women make most of the home buying and home remodeling decisions. During the sale, men may dominate the talking and negotiations, but if you want to get to the heart of the final decision, you have to connect with the lady.

Guys think, women feel, says Myers Barnes of Myers Barnes Associates of Kitty Hawk, N.C. Barnes also notes that 38 percent of all first-time home buyers are women, and more than 60 percent of households include a working woman. So in sales, eye contact is important. His rule of thumb is if you're a salesman, give 49 percent of your eye contact to the woman; 51 percent to the man; *vice versa* if you are a saleswoman. The biggest mistake is spending all your time answering every logical question of the man — and forgetting the woman is there.

TURNING WANTS INTO NEEDS

In America today, there are few desires that truly qualify as needs. The desires are nearly all wants. So in sales, we must help create emotions that turn these wants into needs.

Pete Halter, a partner in V.R. Halter & Associates in Atlanta, once told me that if someone wants something badly enough, in their mind it becomes a need. It's no longer a want. Getting to need from want is a rocky road. After all, the only person who really *needs* a home is homeless.

Throughout the sales process, you need to create levels of discontent so that the buyer takes action. Until the emotion is there, nothing will happen. Everyone's threshold for discontent is different. I have a low threshold. I would rather seek forgiveness than ask for permission. If I make a mistake, I'll fix it. But there aren't a lot of people like me.

Many builders, remodelers and sales consultants know how to connect emotionally with people. They know that showing five floor plans and three elevations in a range of prices is about as emotional as surgery. When you buy that *F-350*, even if you are 100 percent logical and left-brained, you still want to test-drive it. You might ask about performance, crash results, and safety, but you still have feelings attached to the purchase. Great sales consultants know how to connect on all levels.

What do you say to single buyers who insist they need 3,000 square feet, with 4 bedrooms and 3½ baths? Do you ask about overnight guests? Do you wonder aloud if they switch rooms each night when the linens get dirty? Clearly this is not a need — it's a want, a status symbol. They might have some lifestyle plans for the rooms — a hobby or exercise, perhaps. But until you determine what's important, you'll disconnect, thinking, that's *stupid, why do you need four bedrooms? And what about your budget?* You have to get into the way they live, the things they've experienced in the past, and the things that are missing in their current home. If you write down criteria and specifications and don't understand why clients have a need, you'll never be able to deliver a *Yee-Haw!* experience. You'll have a stock plan with no emotional connection.

On many customer care issues, you can connect at a variety of levels through basic needs. Can you spell the buyer's first and last name? Do you remember their name when they come back? Can you pronounce the name correctly? That alone touches a lot of people. Do you eliminate bias, and are you sensitive to multi-cultural buyers and how they pronounce their names?

The more notes you take and "memory points" you develop for yourself, the easier it is to connect. Over time, you'll have to follow up with many people. You won't remember who had two kids and who had five, or who liked the open kitchen and who liked the compartmentalized kitchen. Being meticulous in your note-taking allows you to develop touchpoints for that person. Everything, *and I mean everything,* has to be personalized — this is not mass production, even if behind the scenes it is. Michael Strong of Brothers Strong in Houston makes each presentation packet unique and personal, and connects with people, not as prospects — he already treats them like customers. He walks into each presentation with the feeling that he's there to help them make the right decision, not to get the job, even though that's his objective. Just look into Michael's eyes and you know he's completely in the moment, at each and every presentation. Clients become friends; they keep coming back.

Emily's New Classroom

Emily's New Friends

Emily's New Teacher

When I was selling homes, I met a couple who was moving from St. Louis to San Antonio with their 8-year-old daughter, Emily. With permission from the school, I took pictures of teachers in the classroom, of kids on the playground, and of the front of the school. On each picture, I put a note: *This is Ms. Smith, Emily's new teacher.* Or on another, with an arrow pointing to a child: *This might be Emily's new best friend.* We made some mistakes in the process of delivering their home, as builders usually do, but this family allowed those things to pass because they felt there was a connection. I added a human touch to the process.

One of the most confusing things for buyers is the process they must go through to build a home. If you're attuned to the help they need, you can develop visual cues for them, similar to what author and former custom home builder Al Trellis did for Westbridge Homes (**See The Westbridge Process, Page 41**). Instead of verbally talking people through the process, he visually walks them through it. Trellis developed a multi-colored, 27-step roadmap for buyers, with the last step being, *Enjoy many years of happiness in your new Westbridge Home.* Trellis uses different colors for each step, indicating milestones, customer decision points, meetings, and construction timelines. Does that make doing business with you easy, agreeable, and visually apparent? *You bet.*

ALIGNING LOVE & DNA

The greatest potential challenge is in the disconnect between customer expectations and your reality. For instance, it's seemingly impossible to create a set of plans that is 100 percent complete. Even DNA matching is only 99 percent accurate. A forensic pathologist will say there's a one in a billion chance that the test is fallible. Fallibility is built into every step during construction, so you've got to anticipate it and head off disconnects before they happen, or as soon as they happen.

When the lot is staked, before you've poured the foundation, does your salesperson walk the footprint of the home with the buyers and paint a picture of the home so the homeowner can understand and visualize changes on the raw ground? Do you ask them, *please, stand right here. This is your daughter's bedroom. This is her view. How does it* **feel**? *Oh,* they say, *we thought she had a view over here.* If that's their perception, think: Well, the way this plan is staked out, this is the view, so we need to address this issue now because once the foundation is poured, you can't change it. You can't implode it and start over. Few people can take plans and visualize views and layouts. They have to stand on the site and *see it for themselves.* When you add this step to your process, it provides a tremendous connection — you're anticipating *needs.* The standard process is to give homeowners the plans and expect them to

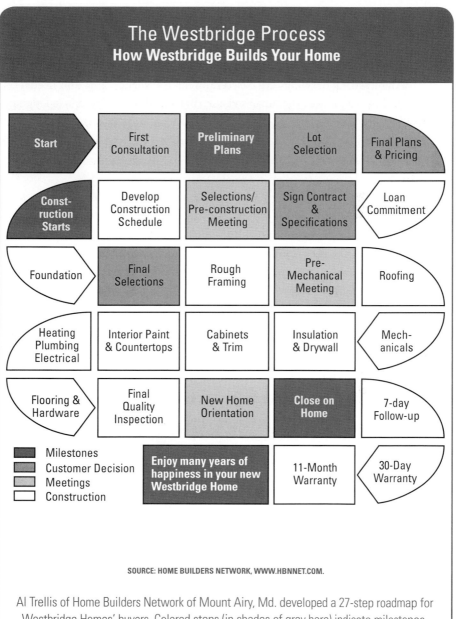

The Westbridge Process
How Westbridge Builds Your Home

Start	First Consultation	Preliminary Plans	Lot Selection	Final Plans & Pricing
Construction Starts	Develop Construction Schedule	Selections/ Pre-construction Meeting	Sign Contract & Specifications	Loan Commitment
Foundation	Final Selections	Rough Framing	Pre-Mechanical Meeting	Roofing
Heating Plumbing Electrical	Interior Paint & Countertops	Cabinets & Trim	Insulation & Drywall	Mech-anicals
Flooring & Hardware	Final Quality Inspection	New Home Orientation	Close on Home	7-day Follow-up
	Enjoy many years of happiness in your new Westbridge Home	11-Month Warranty	30-Day Warranty	

Legend:
- Milestones
- Customer Decision
- Meetings
- Construction

SOURCE: HOME BUILDERS NETWORK, WWW.HBNNET.COM.

Al Trellis of Home Builders Network of Mount Airy, Md. developed a 27-step roadmap for Westbridge Homes' buyers. Colored steps (in shades of gray here) indicate milestones, customer decisions, and other waypoints in the process. A straightforward, no-nonsense visual like this makes it easy for customers to understand how you do business.

visualize the home and on their own feel how it all fits on their home site. But this visual check isn't just helpful — it's a huge touchpoint. It's a connection with real value. It allows you to create emotion and allows you to turn up the volume on the experience.

Architectural drawings are based on what the client wants and needs. But there's always a piece of the buyer's vision that can't be translated into language. So the more time you spend discovering things about that person, the easier it is for you to interpret their vision. Then, it's up to you to translate that into the product you are delivering.

THREE PLACES TO SEED LOYALTY

Design is closely connected with selections. Selections and change requests can be two of the most cumbersome processes to work through with clients. Paperwork is always stressful. Clients have a million and one decisions to make. So the easier you can make it for the customer to make decisions and ease the stress, the better the experience and the higher the loyalty. Sometimes offering fewer options works best.

BY ALLOWING CLIENTS TO EASILY SELECT WINDOW STYLES, COLOR, AND OTHER OPTIONS, PELLA CORP.'S INTERACTIVE ONLINE TOOL CREATES AN EMOTIONAL CONNECTION WITH BUYERS AND BUILDING PROFESSIONALS, AND INFLUENCES BUYING DECISIONS. THIS TOOL AND OTHERS HAVE SIGNIFICANTLY INCREASED PELLA'S WEB SITE TRAFFIC.

If, for instance, the K164-NF9 model number in the paperwork isn't associated with a picture, selections can be a disjointed process. If you expect me to know PB is polished brass and NF is nickel finish, as a client, I just can't remember that.

Online tracking systems help with this process, at least for the first pass through the selection process. At K. Hovnanian Homes, they offer a design center orientation so clients can see what's ahead, before the actual appointment. It's an extra step, but it reduces stress. Who can make all their selections — brick, exteriors, flooring, countertops, fixtures, hardware, wallpaper, paint, textures, and so on, in two hours? *Good grief!* The more choices I have, the harder it is for me to make a decision and stick with it. The more places you send me to make selections, the harder it is. Going to different suppliers to look at a splotch of this or a swatch of that or one-inch samples of countertop, well that's just crazy. And by the way, does my lighting allowance include the cost of bulbs? There's no form to coordinate this, there's different paperwork at each step, and I'm supposed to remember how much money I spent in the process? What would be the value of a personal assistant to our clients?

Too often we waste opportunities in sales, selection, and design — three of the best places to make emotional connections of the magnitude needed to create long-term loyalty.

Guts To Love

Cookies & Balloons?

BY CAROL SMITH

Before adding touchpoints, learn the basics of client respect.

A builder called and asked for my suggestions on adding touchpoints to his processes. As I listened to details about procedures, alarms went off in my head. His problem was not with how many times to contact buyers, but the nature of the contacts. His company's focus was on rules, cut-offs, disclaimers, disclosures, prohibitions, and boundaries. He rambled on about all these limits and the efficiency with which his company wrenched selections from customers. This builder now wanted to add touchpoints to this brittle framework of arbitrary rules in order to make buyers exclaim "Wow!" Yet, most of the rules had been established for the convenience and ease of the company. The chance of success? Minimal.

Misunderstandings about touchpoints abound. The real issue isn't so much the number of contacts builders have with customers, but rather the tone they set in those contacts. Balloons and cookies don't make up for mindless policies and lopsided procedures. To show customers they're loved, a company must begin by respecting them. This requires genuine thoughtfulness. It requires evaluating policies and procedures from the buyers' point of view.

Builders need to pay particular attention to what they write and say to customers about processes. Negativity, nastiness, and needless

K. Hovnanian Homes, and even smaller builders, are delivering paperwork to buyers with visuals and pictures attached. When buyers make selections online, they receive a 3-D image. Whirlpool Corp. has a great site where clients can build a virtual kitchen. Kohler does the same thing. Pella offers a similar service for its customers. Clients can go online, select products, their colors, styles, and exterior and interior options, then build them on the Pella Web site. Using the information, they can visit any Pella dealer to buy what they've specified.

Using a Web site takes the instantaneous to everlasting. And the mark of a great Web site is ease of navigation. Just look at The McCaffrey Group's site, www.mccaffreygroup.com. It's effortless to navigate. If your Web site doesn't make the process easy and stress-free, it can become a stressor. The Web can be a great tool when it's managed properly.

THE 5% SOLUTION

Our superintendents do a great job managing the construction process, don't they? And they're beginning to understand that they need to be customer-conscious. They complete 95 percent of the job well, but it's the little things wrapped up in the last 5 percent which make buyers go crazy.

Unfortunately, our project leaders often have the attitude of the person in a comic that I show at nearly all of my presentations. The text reads: *I can only*

complexity must be distilled out of processes and paperwork. Once a builder creates a reasonable, balanced framework, company personnel require training to effectively present these steps to buyers. This often includes taking the time to explain reasons for the way things are done. Developing the ability to draw buyers' attention to benefits from the process is better still.

At home orientations I often hear a common instruction about appliances: "Your kitchen appliance warranties are from the manufacturers, so if you have problems with them, call the manufacturer instead of our warranty department." Technically, this is correct, but this statement ignores the impact of the information on the homebuyer. Listening from the customers' side, one hears: "Don't bother us." Consider an improved version, which includes reasons and benefits: "Appliance manufacturers want to hear the details of your concern directly; this helps them understand what's needed. They also want to set a repair appointment with you without the risk of a third party entangling the details. So if you have a problem with an appliance, contact them directly. Here's the number that's in the use and care booklet they provide. It's also in your homeowner's guide. But please alert us, too, if you don't mind. We'll make a note for your file. If you run into complications, it helps that we've got a record from the beginning." Does that take more time? Just a bit. Does it leave a better impression on buyers? Undoubtedly. Is it worth the effort? Absolutely.

Drill through your touchpoints for such details. When you've corrected all — or most — of these, then you can think about cookies and balloons.

please one person each day. Today is not your day. Tomorrow doesn't look good either.

Communication and people-pleasing are the watchwords of the construction process. Mirman, of Eliant, says planned surprises of the *Yee-Haw!* variety are good but communication that keeps the buyer informed about construction status (without the buyer asking) is as good or better. He suggests a builder-initiated contact at least once every two weeks. Because buyers don't expect this, they're delighted when it occurs. And, it can have the fastest and most direct impact on satisfaction scores, particularly on the question about keeping clients informed of construction progress. Mirman says if sales people keep a log showing they've called buyers once every two weeks, in 60 days the score on that question — keeping buyers informed — goes up.

But remember, it's not just when you communicate, it's also what you communicate. At Rosenthal Homes in Rockville, Md., when Emily Rosenthal calls customers for a draw payment, she doesn't call it a draw, she calls it a progress payment.

So when Emily calls a customer and it's time to write a check, she says *OK, we've finished framing. I guess it's progress time! We've made progress!* It's almost a celebration. And she gets the money!

For you, that's what construction is all about, completing work and receiving checks. For the client, it's a different story, and that's why the hand-off from sales to construction must be done seamlessly. When construction is handed a new client, they must know exactly who the clients are: their quirks, their personality traits, and their communication style. The pre-construction conference is critical to this hand-off and must be managed meticulously. It is the last point to align expectations before the work begins. If expectations aren't aligned, there will be miscommunications and lost opportunities all the way through warranty.

The person who runs the conference has to be a master communicator, detail-oriented and disciplined. This is the last checkpoint before the surgeon opens the patient. After the first cut, you can no longer decide whether or not to do it. The buyer must be prompted constantly, asked if they feel comfortable with the information or need additional clarification or examples. People often won't say they don't understand, so the questions must be framed carefully.

Any preconstruction conference lasting less than 90 minutes to two hours is the kiss of death. You are building value in this step. You must go over the plans and expectations, your policies and procedures, the cabinet layouts, electrical outlet placement, and so on. Define things like "start date." What goes on behind the scenes before the work really begins? What are the contingencies for six weeks of rain or extremely bad weather? Material shortages? What are the backup plans?

Once construction begins, the job site should be kept clean from the moment anyone steps foot on the ground. Remember, this is a hallowed site. This is someone's home. Respect turns into trust and trust turns into loyalty and that's what you need. Most people don't eat lunch in the living room and dump the trash in the middle of the floor. Everyone on the construction team must have respect for the home. One little thing can kill the trust you've built.

As part of your initial sales presentation and pre-construction conference, you need to explain the process for changes, and the timing of those requests. Change requests are inevitable in most companies. So, define the parameters of how you deal with them. You need to put procedures in writing and reinforce them throughout the sales and construction process. When people know what to expect, it's easier for them to comply and it becomes less of an issue when problems occur. The language should be easily understood. As Carol Smith recommends, instead of "we only allow," use the phrase, "we openly accept up to and including."

THE LANGUAGE OF LOVE

Rick Montelongo, president of Montelongo Homes & Remodeling in San Antonio, trains his team in "Montelongo Language," to avoid "fear-inspiring terms" from the first phone call. If he says "we're going to tear out your kitchen, demo everything, and break up the concrete to run water lines," he knows he's using fear-inspiring words. He doesn't use words like "contract" or "price." It's "proposal," and "total investment." They don't "pitch" a deal, they "present." Trash is "debris." A Dumpster is a "debris container." A salesperson is a "design representative."

Remember, the language of *Love*. You can't have a power play. This is an alliance. In written language, *documentation*, in body language, *attitude*. It's all about setting a realistic expectation and solidifying that expectation throughout the process.

Remember it is the tiniest things that make clients go absolutely off their rockers. And at the moment when a buyer is highly emotional, that's also when they are the most vulnerable. It is precisely at those moments that we often ignore their sensitivities, when, instead, we need to pay attention to them.

The same sort of visual process map that Al Trellis developed for Westbridge Homes could be used to explain change requests to your client rather than just saying "our presentation book has copies of all the documents." These are crucial issues for builders to overcome — anticipating these types of bottlenecks. These are not new complaints. They come up with customer after customer. Instead of patching or correcting repetitive problems as they occur, we need to go back and correct the root cause of problems, with the entire change request process.

During the process, you will always have the question come up: *I wonder, if I change this, how much will it cost?* Often it takes seven to 10 days to get an estimate for the changes. In custom home building and remodeling, it's difficult to speed up the process. So set expectations, right up front.

THE FINAL YES (OR NO)

Like change requests, the closing process is a volatile and sensitive step. Yet this is a place where you can really layer on the *Love.*

Usually there's a meeting to sign off on the acceptance. This is the final time for the buyer to say *yes* or *no.* The sheer number of documents they'll be asked to sign will blow them away. Most never read them even if they're provided in advance. They've got two inches of paperwork and half of them are written in legal terminology that the average layman wouldn't understand. Then you have a notary acknowledge that the buyers have read and understood everything. Even this tiny thing, this notarization of the documents, can be emotional for buyers.

Some numbers might be different than they expected — the amount of the mortgage, the payoff amount, or the expressed interest rate — these catch people by surprise, even though your sales consultant covered this possibility nine to 12 months ago. What's the matter with buyers? Can't they remember anything?

Meanwhile, you're taking them out of their comfort zone, their current home or apartment, and putting them into a foreign environment. They'll spend a week in a place where nothing is in order. There are 1,001 details to manage. When is the garbage picked up? Where are the community mailboxes and the mailbox key? It can be exciting, but it's cumbersome and exhausting. Any inconsistency is magnified tenfold. Not only are they living out of boxes, but some of the things they paid a tremendous amount of money for don't work — a cabinet pull, a switch, a latch. One little thing can blow their enjoyment out the window.

In 2005, before she left the company, Lois Cardinale began developing a customer care department for Centerline Homes, the dominant home builder in Coral Springs, Fla. Her job was to use fresh eyes to bridge the gaps between customer expectations and the construction delivery system. Before the home was ready for the buyer, she inspected it and made recommendations for final touches. The satisfaction reported on customer evaluations rose dramatically. Many national builders do this, but for a company that builds a few hundred homes a year, it demonstrated a commitment to customer care, and loyalty. What Lois did was important, but the only way her program worked was if everyone in her company was committed to total quality. Her step was important, but totally dependent on everyone else. Lois couldn't fix the problem. She was just another pair of eyes. She was looking at the home through the client's eyes. It was her team that had to deliver. And they did.

Homeowner orientations are designed to educate a customer about their home, train them on all the mechanicals, and show them all the ways they can enjoy and maintain their home. If the orientation is handled effectively, then the buyer is prepared to deal with maintaining the home rather than expecting it to be maintenance free. In a way, it prepares the buyer for the closing process, because it's not a fun part of the experience — of course that has something to do with signing 250 documents. I'm exaggerating but you need someone to constantly monitor these documents and all the steps of these final phases. A personal assistant would work well here as a last stop-gap measure, although it's not the entire answer because they wouldn't have adequate authority.

As my colleague Carol Smith notes, management must commit to delivering complete homes. That doesn't mean just stating that

commitment at monthly, quarterly, or annual quota intervals. This means that construction carries out this commitment in tangible actions that eliminate the details interfering with a complete and clean delivery. Then and only then are you developing best practices. But it begins by instilling in the entire team a clear vision of a complete and clean home.

Once you've arrived at that point, you get to cement the relationship, and ensure that delighted referral. Hogan Homes in Corpus Christi, Texas delivers homeowners personalized picnic baskets with sandwiches, soft drinks, paper plates, and plastic utensils so they won't have to cook on the first night in their new home. Another company hires a chef to deliver gourmet meals. Another puts a bottle of Dom Pérignon in an ice bucket with two Waterford crystal flutes in the master bath. I often suggest delivering the keys attached to a sterling silver Tiffany key ring bearing the charm of a home. Anything in that blue box has got to be good, no? You align your brand of service with Tiffany's. Clients love it. Another appropriate gift for upper-end buyers is a Mont Blanc pen. Hand it to them as they are signing documents and then when they hand it back, say, *no, keep it, it's to remind you of this special moment.*

Yee-Haw!

FOREVER YOURS

 Lemons are usually used for a garnish, but for one dissatisfied buyer, garnishing the front lawn with 10,000 of them became a way to seek revenge on a builder the buyer believed had created the problems in the house. As Paul Cardis, CEO of AVID Ratings wrote in *Professional Builder*, the homeowner dumped the 10,000 lemons in his front yard and left them there to rot. Then he erected signs calling the house a lemon, and contacted the media, which descended on the property. The public relations damage was huge. If only the mechanical problems — which may not have been the builder's fault — had been fixed after the homeowner's first call. A similar case occurred in San Antonio, when a disgruntled owner posted dozens of signs strategically leading from the entry of his community right up to his front door. The signs read: *Follow the signs to our disaster built by _____ Homes!* To add insult to injury, the signs were posted the first evening of the builders' annual Parade of Homes event.

Warranty service is the most highly publicized phase of the home building or renovation process and often generates negative press for the builder, says Cardis. Most lawsuits and conflicts occur after closing. Customers are happy until warranty issues arise and then there's this huge backslide. It's normally caused by differences in expectations.

The homeowner has written the last check and the check has been cashed. There is nothing to hold over the builder's head. In many cases, litigation or turning to the media are the only avenues left to the buyer. Unfortunately,

some people believe that it's the only alternative they have.

Yet, if you've developed a relationship during the process from sales to production to warranty, you're not creating a new relationship for warranty service. And warranty is about many tiny things. If construction is about the last 5 percent, warranty is about the remaining 1 percent. Fear is a powerful emotion and drives the buyer's behavior at this stage of the process. When people feel powerless, they react in unmanageable ways. They're scared. Once again, everything they've heard and read about builders reiterates the fact that, *yes, I'm going to be left out in the cold.*

You have to keep telling them; no, showing them; no, *proving to them,* throughout your processes, that you provide safeguards for the buyer. In required meetings, you need to introduce them to the players on your team. Define their responsibilities and how you will address their concerns. Address warranty issues in your frequently asked questions section on your Web site. And address how they are resolved because it's not a perfect process. There have been challenges. Yes, even at your company. More will arise. But buyers are more tolerant if they're forewarned. When we catch them by surprise, we create havoc. Most surprises at this point aren't good. Pleasant surprises, over and above what's expected, are so important. Remind them when you exceed your own requirements, because clients don't always remember.

Our industry has moved beyond basic quality issues. We know how to build it right. For goodness sakes, we're even building "healthy" homes today. It's the human element that continues to disrupt the *Love.*

What if the project manager or superintendent who was on the job every day for six months sent a letter and connected with the homeowner? A Hogan Homes superintendent told me that if he was driving through a community and saw a former client unloading groceries, he'd stop and get out of his truck to help and say: *Hi, I've been driving by your house for months now and have been meaning to stop by to tell you the landscaping is gorgeous. I love what you've done with the yard.*

Typically superintendents drive through a community with their blinders on — *if they see me they'll flag me down. They'll have an issue.* But research shows that if you initiate contact, the number of callbacks is minimized. By teaching homeowners how to maintain their homes and enhancing specific touchpoints addressing homeowner maintenance, and putting in place post-move-in contacts, you can reduce callbacks. One builder that implemented a proactive call program reported moving from 75 open calls each month to 25 open calls each month, according to Martha Baumgarten at Eliant.

So every customer contact won't create a problem. Stop and say hello!

The Hogan superintendent who said hello reconnected with the buyer and reminded them: *I made the right decision building with Hogan.* He turned an ordinary moment into an extraordinary touchpoint!

Make buyers know in their hearts that they won't be abandoned. Add to the trust you've developed by making sure customer care personnel and your trades always deliver on promises. Deliver the right response. This isn't just about completing every item on the completion list — note the vocabulary. Again, words have to do with how we perceive things, and the attitude we have. Punchlist is a derogatory phrase. You don't punch out a house — you complete a home.

It's all about getting it right, quickly, and doing it faster than you've promised. It's reasonable that the homeowner expects this to be done in one visit. After all, your contracts don't say you'll get it right *eventually.* "Right the first time" often determines the homeowner's satisfaction with the service process.

The first time you hear a concern, why not stop what you're doing and resolve it? The second time they call, they'll be irritated. By the third time, they're ready to kill you. This could be a $500 item or only a 30-cent item! It's *not* about price. It's about genuine caring. It's about trust, respect, integrity, and *Love.*

John Laing Homes uses an inconvenience payment policy to compensate homeowners whenever trades personnel no-show for an appointment. Laing back-charges trades $200 for the no-show, and often reimburses the homeowner for a missed day of work. Other builders offer extraordinary Web sites to buyers and homeowners, providing maintenance information, records of options and customized selections, appliance serial numbers and more helpful information. Would this exceed your homeowner's expectation? *Yee-Haw!*

NO GAMBLING WITH LOVE

Emotional experiences that touch our hearts and go to our basic needs can be built into our processes, even our homes. But the truest route is through our people. We need to teach our teams to constantly appreciate customers, and when we can, we need to hire those gifted with this innate sense of appreciation. Why? The future of their jobs and our companies literally depends on it. We'll explore that loyalty-giving connection ahead.

Thinking of that connection reminds me of a Las Vegas speaking engagement at a hotel that clearly had seen better days. Forgive me, but I stay in many hotels

— this one lacked nearly every amenity essential to me. But when I walked into an off-the-gambling-floor ladies' room, there was a restroom attendant in a uniform to greet me! The restroom was spotless; there wasn't a drop of water on the vanity. The attendant handed me a clean, fresh towel for my wet hands. She thanked me for visiting her hotel, and she beamed with pride when she said its name. She was thrilled to have her job. And she made everyone who entered her little oasis feel good about going to the hotel's restroom.

There was no tip jar, but I wanted to give her a tip anyway. My goodness, this woman worked at this dated, old, smoky hotel and she was the sunshine in the place. No one taught her that. She made you feel that she appreciated you *being there*.

Loyalty is rooted in something you can't always put your finger on. Sometimes it's just *there*. It might be a name or a logo or a product, and your mind envisions something about that name or logo. Your mind immediately sends you a signal that *this feels good* — that it *is* good. But the best way to build loyalty, as Miss Sunshine in Las Vegas proved, is with people. I'd go back to that dump just to see that woman's smile.

If you nurture loyalty, it never disappears no matter what mistakes you make along the way, and you'll make them — by George, you'll make them.

But because you've layered in the emotional honey of love, you'll have no worries. And your loyalty points will keep your *F-350* charging right to your next client's home.

NO QUESTIONS ASKED:
HIGH SATISFACTION = PROFITS

Preliminary studies show customers who had a consistently good experience make builders and remodelers more profitable.

LOVE MODE

If you are searching for the loyalty Holy Grail in this book, uniting wildly referring customers to soaring profits, this is as close as it gets.

While both reports are preliminary, and their authors suggest more time is required to fine-tune and mine the data, early conclusions clearly tie satisfaction and loyalty to profit. It's a fact: Builders and remodelers scoring higher in customer satisfaction command higher prices and are among the most profitable in the business. Buyer satisfaction allows these companies to predict lower future warranty costs and higher future revenues and profits. Customer satisfaction can be a leading indicator of future performance as measured by higher referrals, revenues, profits, and lower warranty costs.

It pays to **Love**.

Customer Satisfaction — Effect On Referrals

An 8% increase in:	Yields this % increase in number of referrals:
Satisfaction with sales,construction, customer service (30-day survey)	+21%
Satisfaction with loan and closing processes (30-day survey)	+8%
Satisfaction with home quality (11-month survey)	+21%
Satisfaction with customer service (11-month survey)	+16%

Two separate studies produced similar results. One relied on financial data from 5,000-plus customers of John Laing Homes. The data was supplied by Eliant and Laing, a $1.6 billion-a-year homebuilder. It was developed by researchers working with Kenneth A. Merchant, Ph.D., chair of the Leventhal School of Accounting, University of

Source For Chart Data: *Are All Nonfinancial Performance Measures Created Equal? Evidence on Customer Satisfaction and Employee Satisfaction Measures from the Homebuilding Industry.* A preliminary study of more than 5,000 home sales over seven divisions of John Laing Homes by the University of Southern California, Leventhal School of Accounting.

Customer Satisfaction — **Effect On Bottom Line**

An 8% increase in:	Yields this % increase in ...	
	Revenues	Operating Profits
Satisfaction with sales, construction, customer service (30-day survey)	+19%	+28%
Satisfaction with customer service (5-month survey)	+13%	+17%
Satisfaction with home quality (11-month survey)	+17%	+13%
Satisfaction with customer service (11-month survey)	+8%	+13%

Southern California's Marshall School of Business, Los Angeles. The other survey was compiled by GuildQuality, an Atlanta-based customer satisfaction and market research firm catering to about 500 builder and remodeler clients.

GuildQuality, relying on 224 surveys from 15 top-performing companies, learned:

- **Happy Clients Mean Higher Profits.** When homeowners are satisfied with their remodeler, referrals and profits tend to go up, and stay up. The top five performers recorded an average gross profit margin of 40 percent, with average customer satisfaction ratings of 97 percent. Meanwhile, the bottom five performers recorded average gross profit margins of 29 percent, on satisfaction scores averaging 92 percent.
- **Unhappy Clients Push Margins Down.** When customers are unhappy, they don't refer, and margins on those jobs are considerably lower than average. GuildQuality found that the gross profit margin on jobs of remodeling clients who would recommend the company to a friend was 35.6 percent, versus 24 percent for those clients who would not recommend the company to a friend.
- **Poor Performance Kills Margins.** A remodeler's premium — how much it charges in comparison to competitors — is closely related to the quality of service, but profitability of each job is not dramatically influenced by the experience unless the customer has had an extremely bad experience. In other words, satisfaction may not affect profitability on an individual job. But it affects the strength of the brand, the recommendation rate, and the premium for perceived value. If you're not consistent in doing a great job, you can't charge a premium.

Geoff Graham, GuildQuality CEO, says certain issues can influence satisfaction more than others: Communication, construction quality, schedule, and completion lists were high on customers' priorities, and the customer experience was critical. "Unquestionably there's a correlation,"

Customer Satisfaction — Effect On Warranty Costs	
An 8% increase in:	**Yields this % decrease in warranty costs:**
Satisfaction with sales, construction, customer service (30-day survey)	-24%
Satisfaction with customer service (5-month survey)	-29%
Satisfaction with home quality (11-month survey)	-29%
Satisfaction with customer service (11-month survey)	-17%

Graham says. "Remodelers with happier customers make more money. Anecdotally, we can say they can charge more and are probably better run." If a remodeler has a 98 percent recommendation rate and always does a good job, the profit margins will be significantly better than remodelers who do good jobs and whose clients are only generally happy.

Nationally, the average recommendation rate among remodelers is about 65 percent, according to GuildQuality. The remodelers they surveyed had an average recommendation rate of 95 percent, with the lowest performers in the upper 80th percentile.

The USC study demonstrates the relationship between home buyer satisfaction and experience, and home warranty and profitability. With greater satisfaction, referral sales go up. Lower marketing costs would follow. USC learned that customer satisfaction is created differently at different points in the homebuyer's life-cycle. These aspects included satisfaction with sales, construction, customer service, the loan and closing process, and home quality, when customers were surveyed at 30 days, five months, and 11 months. Satisfaction contributes to future financial performance by increasing customer referrals and reducing warranty costs.

The USC study's early results show:
- **Satisfaction Up, Revenues And Profits Up.** An 8 percent increase in satisfaction with sales, construction and customer service, surveyed at 30 days, yields an increase of 19 percent in revenues, and, 28 percent in operating profits.
- **Home Quality & Customer Service Boost Referrals.** The same increase in satisfaction with home quality at 11 months yields a 21 percent increase in referrals; a similar increase in satisfaction with customer service (also at the 11-month survey) yields a 16 percent increase in referrals.
- **Customer Service Decreases Warranty Costs.** An 8 percent increase in satisfaction with customer service (5-month survey) yields a 29 percent decrease in warranty costs; an equal increase in satisfaction with home quality at 11 months also yields a 29 percent decrease in warranty costs.

The USC researchers hope to explore why after a certain level of satisfaction (ranging from 65 percent to 95 percent) profits turn down — and whether it's too expensive to attempt to satisfy every customer, all the time. The researchers hope to break down the population surveyed to determine if the satisfaction-performance relationship depends on type of home (first move-in vs. move-up, for instance), and whether this relationship was affected by boom times or downturns.

GuildQuality's sample was drawn from members of Remodelers Advantage, a Laurel, Md. consulting firm specializing in advising remodeling companies. The companies share equal definitions of gross profit and they allocated costs, if not identically, similarly.

Dick Bryan, John Laing Homes' former vice president of customer care, says working toward satisfying customers can help cut costs in other ways, too. By hiring a third-party inspector to examine window installation, roofing, framing, drywall, and concrete work, and cooperating with its insurance carrier, John Laing was able to add a third look to its own and its insurance carrier's inspections, with the goal being fewer complaints. While the third-party inspector is an investment, at about $1,400 per house, Laing's insurance premiums have dropped by at least 40 percent over six years, while its liability rate dropped 55 percent to 8 percent, according to Bryan.

John Laing Homes proved that keen customer service not only increases profits, it decreases the cost of insurance. Its insurance premiums have dropped by at least 40 percent over six years.

Bryan said the inspections prompted the use of better quality materials, further lowering service requests. While most builders reported up to 15 complaints per home, Laing dropped to one or two, enabling it to keep fewer warranty staff. And, by not handling as many service requests, they save even more.

So John Laing Homes proved that keen customer care not only increases profits, it decreases the cost of insurance. In California, there's a 10-year liability period during which time a builder is liable for structural defects. Lawyers have, in the past, organized class action suits against builders to pursue claims. John Laing was told by its insurance carrier, Zurich, the largest national carrier for builder policies, that it had the lowest liability rating of any builder in the country, Bryan says. It's no coincidence Laing is ranked Number 1 by Eliant in homebuyer satisfaction.

LOVE  CHECK

Help 'Em Yell *Yee-Haw!*

Are you giving clients a chance to yell *Yee-Haw!* because of your interactions with them? Here's how to exhilarate clients:

✔ Speak Their Language

Lose the jargon. They're not "in the business." When sharing technical data, use pictures. Clients don't know what a K164-NF9 faucet or handle looks like, or what a double-lever, single-handle fixture is. Show a picture and they get it. How many times have you said, "we use six-panel Colonist doors?" Or, "we use finger-jointed studs." Tell them, no — *show them* — why finger-jointed studs are superior engineered building components, and don't carry the opposite connotation. Show them how structurally sound and square construction dramatically improves the look of finished surfaces. A highly skilled drywall contractor can't fix a bad frame any more than you can build relationships on meaningless words.

✔ Connect Constantly

Don't assume because you know what's going on that they know. One of the biggest complaints I hear from homebuyers about builders: *You guys were all over me until I gave you a check, and then I never heard from anyone.* Meanwhile, you're waiting for a permit, you're waiting for plans to be approved, you're waiting for client selections. But clients can't read your mind. Tell them what to expect, even when it's up to them to make decisions. You're still doing something, and clients need to *know*.

✔ Connect Easily

Ask clients what mode of communication works best. If they prefer email, email them. Do this early in the relationship. Have them rank their preferred method — email, fax, office phone, home phone, cell phone. If it's by phone, ask for the best times. Establish parameters. If you're in the office between 7 and 8 in the morning and then back at 4 p.m., tell them emails past 2 p.m. won't be answered until the next morning. Ask: *What works best for you?*

✔ Speak In 'We'

You're the buyer, I'm the builder, let's keep it straight. No! You're a team. It's always *us*. Help your team understand and adopt that concept in their hearts. The sales consultant shouldn't refer to "the builder" — *they* are the builder. Trade contractors, not "subs," are part of the team. It's not, "the superintendent," it's "your superintendent." Many sales consultants say "the builder has been in business 10 years." No, "*we've* been in business 10 years." Any language you use to build this circle of continuity — your relationship — is important.

✔ Respond Quickly

Establish parameters on what is timely. If clients have a question and we're busy and know their question isn't critical, we assume we can get back to them later. But to them, it's critical. Scott Sedam, president of TrueNorth Development, says if you allow a customer to go into a weekend with a concern or unanswered question, it'll screw up the client's whole weekend. Their myopic view is on that issue. We see it another way. Most customer concerns, in the builder's opinion, are minor product or process concerns. But to the customer, they're deeply personal. Wouldn't you respond quickly to someone you truly *Love*?

✔ Make Business Seamless

Educate your customer about processes and business principles. Help them understand how to work through this relationship. Every builder or remodeler has a unique process. Make yours seamless. Clients should never have to jump through hoops. They should never have to ask more than one person for the answer. This is a training initiative **(See Chapter 5)**. Teach your employees to be sensitive to this. Most organizations see themselves as a triangle — administration at the top and sales and construction at the bottom corners. But clients should see a circle, with everyone talking to each other.

✔ Lose The Loops

Limit your use of pre-programmed machines or services. Constantly look at how you can make this connection more personal. Eliminate endless loops when people call. Ask clients to leave their number twice to avoid miscommunication. Change your message periodically because warm and fuzzy might not be so fuzzy anymore. Remember: you need to speak the language of *Love*.

✔ Go Farther

Do something unexpected. When promising delivery dates, set yourself up for exceeding the delivery date. Instead of setting the schedule so tight that it will take an act of God to meet it, under-promise and over-deliver. Michael Woods, a luxury custom builder in Fort Worth, Texas, sends every document by courier, even things that don't require urgent attention. Sure, he could use the U.S. Postal Service, but he values the human connection. No one expects that level of care. The cost is nominal but the value is unbelievable. *Talk about a Yee-Haw!*

CHAPTER THREE

LOVE SELLS

BUT IT'S ALWAYS SUBTLE

Why have I been so successful selling and servicing clients? I never tried to find a miracle cure. You shouldn't either. *There is none.*

Over the past 20 years, I've sold hundreds of new homes — from $80,000 entry-level homes to $3 million estates. I was never smart enough to dream up something miraculous or magical to guarantee these outcomes and I'm no smarter today.

But when I was selling, I had the street smarts to do simple, subtle things that touched people's lives. Those simple touches helped close sales, and those sales led to more sales. It was a cascade caused by miracle-free hard work and deliberate attention. No one likes to be sold, but most people love to buy. I didn't *sell*. I *helped* people buy.

My friend, successful author and speaker Myers Barnes, who encouraged me to write this book, shares my philosophy of selling subtly and folding love into the sale in ways that guarantee *referrals* — actually *real buyers* — from at least every second person who builds a home with you. Yes, for every two sales, you can win a referred client-turned-buyer. Sound miraculous? Not a chance.

Barnes would never call it love. But like me, he believes the marriage between the product and the process, between the delivery of the home and the salesperson's follow-up is sealed by a commitment that the delivery nearly always leads to a referral. "If the process is bad, even if the product is good, it's *all* bad," says Barnes. The process must include a relationship and the relationship gives life to the referral. This is why the sales portion of the relationship is so important in generating passionate referrals, trophy clients, and clients for life. As much as 37 percent of the value the customer receives comes directly from the person with whom they're doing business. *Yes, 37 percent.* And that person, at the start, in nearly every case, is the salesperson. The relationship the salesperson initiates for your company has little to do with your product.

HEART OF
THE MATTER

What to take to heart from this chapter:

- A client's first meeting should be vividly remembered, like a first kiss.
- Chart expectations and touchpoints to map the route to trust.
- Be consistent, communicate, take a pulse.
- Sell value, not price.
- Build trust by doing what you say you'll do.

But don't kiss all the people goodbye who make your quality home or renovation possible. This just means that everyone who provides service in your company — not just the salesperson, but *everyone* — needs to know that it's the value they add personally that makes the difference.

Just look at Starbucks, Rolex, and Tiffany & Co. and you'll begin to understand why some companies can charge more for their products. These companies and their products provide and offer a distinctive value. You can get coffee, watches, and silver charms cheaper elsewhere, but there's something that draws customers to these brands. Why? With each of these products, it's how you *experience* the purchase. It's about how these products — and even their containers — make us *feel*.

YOUR DISTINCT ADVANTAGE

Did you know that the average U.S. company loses half its customers every five years? Think about that. *Half our customers every five years.* What's worse is that we lose half our employees every five years. Do you think there's a correlation? With turnover we sacrifice consistency. There's nothing dependable at our company. No one really knows what we're about. And yet, by maintaining our consistency, we can become the Rolex of our markets by becoming as reliable, as predictable as a luxury timepiece.

In most cases, high-value products are high-value because of the people who sell and service them. Your people are your distinct advantage. There are other ways to add value, and I'll explore them, but the best route is through your employees. Your people need to know there's value in everything that goes into providing a home. There's value in not just following up, but in *following through*. There's value in being committed to no surprises — we're professionals, right? If you can't keep a commitment, speak up. Communicate. Best-selling author and speaker Brian Tracy, in his book *Eat That Frog!*, quotes Mark Twain as saying, "if the first thing you do each morning is to eat a live frog, you can go through the day with the satisfaction of knowing that that is probably the worst thing that is going to happen to you all day long." Mike Humphrey of Houston's David Weekley Homes calls it *Bad News Fast*. Get it out and get it behind you.

We start creating this value through communication in the relationship, and the company representative who typically gets the first crack is your salesperson. Make sure your salespeople understand everything that goes into preparing for a sale. Their up-front needs assessment, the discovery, has got to be good. When you skip steps in a great sales process, you move the buyer into the *I'm being sold* mode instead of the *I get to buy* mode. Almost 80 percent of the buying decision is based on 20 percent of the product's features. So discovery is important. Once you know your client's hot buttons, you can focus on the most important issues.

When I recently bought a car, the salesman didn't force me to look under the hood. I assumed there was an engine, and he didn't make me listen to it or look at it because he knew I didn't care. If someone isn't interested in the insulation factor, don't talk about it for 20 minutes. Talk about the grain of the cabinets or their storage capacity. Talk about how many suits, dresses, or shirts the closets will hold. Don't tell them about the concrete's PSI — they'll assume it's to code or it wouldn't pass inspection.

I'm not talking about bonding here — as Barnes says, bonding is worthless. Bonding is a substitute for essential selling skills, it's a false relationship. Find the common ground: "Give me the result of the home," Barnes says. "Forget the bond. Go for the result."

Selling is about message consistency. Consistency in what everyone in the company tells the customer. How they meet and greet. How they demonstrate your homes. How they overcome objections, which, as Barnes observes, are really requests for more information. Clients aren't saying our homes cost too much, they're saying, *justify why I should pay more*. When they say they don't like one model, they're really saying, *do you have something else?*

Selling means listening. You should listen 95 percent of the time and talk 5 percent. I say forget the bond, *go for the pulse*. Reach out and see what gets your customer's blood racing, and what calms them. Turn good experiences into great experiences. If you follow a process of discovery, commit to the delivery, assess needs and motivations; sell value not price, map and exceed expectations, and build critical trust, then your customer's loyalty will sustain your brand. When clients start tattooing your logo on their biceps, as Harley-Davidson's customers do, you'll know they've abandoned logic and made an emotional connection to your product.

What's the reward for that emotional connection? Let me tell you. If I could prove to you, with sales expert Myers Barnes at my side, that relationship building, consistency, and communication bring in one referral sale for every two homes sold, would you do exactly as I suggested? Why not? Oh, wait — it's too much work? That's selling. That's customer care. Investing time and effort into a relationship is the only way to reap rewards from the relationship for life. You'll need to connect, re-connect, connect, and re-connect. To win exponential results, you must connect exponentially. You *never* let go. We get so hung up trying to find the miracle cures that we fail to see the simplicity of the referral sale, right before our eyes, like a rug at our feet. *This is the crux of this book!*

It's not brain surgery. *You have to create emotions within the personal connection.* You must constantly respect the homebuyers and the people who want to renovate their homes. Never lose the perspective of their unique situations. You need to refuse, as a salesperson, to become jaded. You should never think: *I've sold **so many homes**.* You must resist a creeping mindset that's callous to the buyer's needs, and refuse to be insensitive to their emotions and fears. Their fears are real. And to stay in tune with them, each sale must be like your first, every time. You need to get excited with them, *every time*.

Customers *feed* on perception and emotion, says Gust Nicholson Sr., formerly of Engle Homes/ TOUSA. "My people have to be emotional, and perceiving," he says. "They have to move their hands a lot. They have to show emotions on their faces. When a customer starts reading the emotion, and the perception of you starts to change, you're starting to get dopamine, some adrenaline running through the veins of their spirit, soul and body."

That wins the customer over. There's energy in the air — the room is charged with it, and they're caught up in it. These new emotions coursing through their veins drive out the post-traumatic stress Nicholson says every buyer brings from previous experiences with builders and other companies with whom they've done business. They should leave your office, he says, *three feet off the ground.* "When they leave, they are totally stratified with their experience." Yes, he says *stratified* because they shouldn't just be *satisfied.* You should send them skyward, into the stratosphere. Going out the door, they should feel like they did after their first kiss. Remember that?

Roxanne Musselman says because people arrive with baggage, you need to discover and work through their issues with them. Say that you understand how they're feeling, and that your previous buyers, Joe and Lisa, also went through the same things. And they felt the same way, but found that after going through the process they were happy in their new home, and *you were happy to help them work through their issues.*

Don't take this the wrong way. Working subtly toward your goals by consistently connecting and communicating, doesn't mean you can't *sell.* Never be afraid to ask people to buy. Worst case, they walk out. It won't be the first time, or the last. But if you don't ask, your client won't buy. Once you're confident you've provided them enough information to make a good decision (without overloading them), you'll feel comfortable. Once you have a match, you've got to ask. It's your job — just do it.

One of the greatest books on closing ever written is a children's book, *Green Eggs & Ham,* by Dr. Seuss, Ted Geisel. Sam-I-am uses 14 different closes to get his "client" to consider eating green eggs. Most salespeople give up after a second time. Yet the buyer's 'no' only establishes what they don't like. Provide an alternative. To think that someone has 14 alternative closes is unbelievable. Master closers do that. If the buyer truly is a buyer, all they're looking for is someone to hang in there with them and help them see it's the right thing to do. Maybe trying green eggs with a goat is what it takes. I use that book in training all the time and clients are happy to make it their own to remember the ABC rule — *Always Be Closing.*

Kids are the greatest closers in the world. Just watch them. They have no fear. In sales, we're inhibited by our fears, and the greatest fear is someone telling us no — so what! It's not like you haven't heard it before. Children can't accept no at face value. If kids did that, they wouldn't get to do anything. They have resiliency. They hang in there. They wear you down.

So ask. But don't trample your buyers in the process. Make that proposal — *here I go again* — with love.

WAS THE BUILDER HONEST & TRUSTWORTHY?

*A home is not **where** you live your life, it's **how** you live your life.*

Isn't that a wonderful quote? Myers Barnes could have a tag line in the making. He adds: "It's not the most significant financial investment of your life. It's the most significant *emotional* investment of your life. Where are life lessons learned? *Home.* Where are marriage lessons learned? *Home.* And child-rearing lessons? *Home.* Home is everything you're going to associate with it."

Rx FOR THE EXTERMINATED SALE

What to do when buyer's remorse becomes Red Hot.

LOVE STORY

Buyer's remorse is a deadly disease. I'd estimate that remorse kills at least 20 percent of first-time homebuyer deals. In a down market, it infects many more. One California builder told me at the end of 2007 that cancellations affected as many as 70 percent of new home sales. The cancelled sale figure would be higher if we as sales consultants didn't hold our clients' hands. Sure, getting the buyer's name on the contract is easy; the tough part is keeping it there. And we have a duty to keep in touch with that buyer even after the cancellation — after all, in many cases it could have been for reasons beyond their control.

As Roxanne Musselman notes, buyers are bombarded with messages after they sign a contract — literally paralyzing them. As I write, the media is paralyzing buyers when mortgage rates are in single digits. Roxanne recalls selling homes in the early 1980s with mortgages at 17.5 percent interest — *that's* when people logically shouldn't have bought them. She also remembers how one buyer was talked out of buying her home by an exterminator fumigating her apartment! He told her it was crazy to buy a house in the current market. So unless you help buyers overcome the noise of people questioning their purchase, and grow a relationship with your client, you're not going to be their first call when they re-think the sale.

Regardless of market conditions, people continue to live somewhere

If you understand that a sale is deeply rooted in experiences and that you need to tap emotions before locking in the sale with logic, I can change your perspective. Selling a home is about building trust, energy, and emotion. It's about follow-through, not follow-up. Results build trust. Trust builds love. *Consistency* builds love.

We need to start lifting our focus from the things we're making to the person for whom we're making them. From the project to the owner of the project. Is it Job #1403 or the Nelson's new media room? Is it Elevation C or Burt and Maggie's dream home? Don't those little changes in wording make it more emotional? There are six emotional motivators that drive our purchases and choices. These motivators often overlap. That's because our needs aren't all created equally. We have basic needs, base-level requirements of the companies we buy from. We have satisfiers, which don't create allegiance but put smiles on our faces. And, we have exciters and delighters, which give us such unexpected value that they affect all future buying and referral behavior. There are also *dissatisfiers* that are based on universal expectations, such as clean jobsites or courteous employees. We don't get credit for avoiding *dissatisfiers*, but if we don't meet these universal expectations, they will fuel anger or dissatisfaction.

The six emotional motivators are: desire for gain, fear of loss, comfort and convenience, security and protection,

and that somewhere is usually a home. People don't stop living because of economic fluctuations.

It gets back to touch. Did you know there was a study done by a doctor who visited patients in their hospital beds? When the doctor sat and held the patient's hand while asking questions instead of simply asking questions while standing by the bedside, the patients thought the doctor had been there twice as long, when in fact the doctor had been there the same length of time.

Touch is powerful. It can salvage sales. Tom Peters says we wildly underestimate the power of the tiniest personal touch. I know this first-hand. I have a simple technique that helped me sell more homes to first-time buyers than any other. Its simplicity may make you shake your head in disbelief, but it goes to the heart of what it means to be a 20-something buyer strapping on 30 years of debt and all the responsibilities of homeownership, in a marketplace drowning in bad news.

I'd get the call at 10 o'clock at night from the lady of the family: *Beverly, I don't know. I don't know if we can go through with this. We're second-guessing our decision! We're feeling really nervous. I mean, **30 years**!*

Me: *Did you take the "Buyer's Remorse Antidote?" You have to take those pills as soon as you start feeling symptoms. Look, you've made a good decision. You've made a great decision. When you feel the first signs of second-guessing your best decision, take two. When the symptoms don't go away, take two more. And when they still won't go away, **take the whole bottle**. It's OK. When you run out, call me. I'll give you more!*

pride of ownership, and satisfaction of emotion — this last one prompts gifts of jewelry, flowers, and vacations. It's centered on others and helps us gain love and appreciation. But you can see how all of these emotional motivators affect the new home purchase. Look at the expectations the buyer brings to your door. All the more reason to meet and exceed them, time after time.

Buyers want companies to consistently surprise and delight them — and these motivators come into play. How can we see these more clearly? The best way is to map your client's expectations. Just as Al Trellis mapped his client's building process **(See Chapter 2, Page 41)**, you should map your client's expectations of your company and its trades. Clients today make more decisions in a month than their grandparents did in a lifetime. Any tool you can provide — visible or behind-the-scenes — that makes their homebuilding or renovation experience easier — creates a deposit in your *trust account*. You need lots of deposits to win passionate referrals.

Consistently exceeding expectations isn't a matter of lowering expectations, it's keeping them realistic, says Martha Baumgarten of Eliant, so that you beat client expectations 90 percent of time. It's not about sand-bagging buyers, it's about knowing what your performance is *today*. Do you promise warranty items in 48 hours, when it's taking two weeks? If sales hears 48 hours, it's 48 hours. That unreality

At the contract signing, I had given her a bottle filled with Good & Plenty candy. If she walked in the next day after the 10 p.m. call, and said *these aren't working*, I'd give her Red Hots, and over laughs, and hand-holding, I'd reassure her some more. I made up labels that looked like prescription labels and in block letters typed "Buyer's Remorse Antidote."

This lightened buyers' fears. It created a sugary emotional connection and sweetened their second-guessing of what they considered a life-long commitment. At the contract signing, I'd say, *you know when you get a sore throat, you don't want to wait until it's strep, you get to the doctor when your throat's scratchy. That's what these "pills" are for — they head off infection.* We'd laugh … until the late-night call.

Buying is scary, especially buying a first home. A young couple, each 23 years old, who've never signed their name to anything for a 30-year stretch is thinking, *Jeez*, I'll be a grandparent by the time this is paid off! But if you anticipate their emotions, they can move on.

Holding a client's hand is all you can do. Help them understand the emotions they're experiencing. You can't cure them of their fears. Inoculate them to the experience.

Paul Cardis, CEO of AVID Ratings, believes you can't remove remorse with inoculations, but you can reduce it. If you don't address it, it can simmer, he says, and you end up with lower satisfaction scores.

Clients need to work through their fears. You can give them the chicken soup or the Band-Aid that feels like it's the sure cure. It's a psychological boost.

becomes an internal standard. What if sales said 10 working days, escrow was telling people 48 hours, and customer service says 30 days? Can you see how these messages reduce trust?

Perhaps no one is lying, but there's confusion. It comes down to everyone saying the same thing, without variance. It's consistent messaging. Baumgarten says an expectations inventory gives builders the tools to consistently deliver and help front-line employees make the same promises. "People have to be accountable for one another and for what they say," she says. Your mapping becomes a playbook for expectations, which you'll use when your staff meets to review the standards.

Baumgarten sees how people consistently fail on this front when she reads Eliant's customer satisfaction surveys, particularly responses to the question: *Was the builder honest and trustworthy?* If construction shows only 60 percent satisfaction on this question and sales shows 90 percent, the problem isn't with construction. It's more likely with sales since they have a relationship with the buyer. But this much is certain: the "honest and trustworthy" issue contributes greatly to a client's willingness to refer, because there either is or isn't trust in these relationships.

Karen Silvernail, of Hogan Homes of Corpus Christi, Texas, when selling homes, and demonstrating her models, calls them "honest models" — what they see is what they get. Everything isn't either an option or an additional

Sales doesn't have a lock on this technique. You can do it throughout the home building or remodeling process. Tom Riggs of Riggs Construction & Design of Kirkwood, Mo., addresses client meltdowns on his jobs right from the pre-construction conference, when his salesperson pulls out a kit that contains gag gifts targeted to the job's many points of anticipated stress. The kit includes stress balls, Post-it Notes, ear plugs, a dust mask, and fast-food gift certificates. This kit wins smiles from clients when they receive it, and again when they need to yank out one of the items in a meltdown moment. "Sometimes there's a real problem, and if that's the case, we take care of it right away," Riggs says. "Most times, it's an emotional feeling that just needs to run its course. The best way to help is to listen."

Maybe all this sounds hokey, but let me tell you: My antidote made me more money than I could say grace over. It helped me understand the human reaction — that it's OK to be scared. That's all people want: understanding. So hold their hand! It's the perfect antidote.

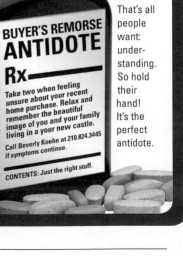

BUYER'S REMORSE
ANTIDOTE
Rx
Take two when feeling unsure about your recent home purchase. Relax and remember the beautiful image of you and your family living in a your new castle.
Call Beverly Koehn at 210.824.3445 if symptoms continue.

CONTENTS: Just the right stuff.

cost item. She sets expectations from the beginning. When a prospective client is marginally qualified and focused on closing costs, she doesn't push options and make the homebuyers feel bad. She won't push high-end countertops and optional $25,000 lighting packages. She knows some builders outfit models with amenities that are highly desirable, and then, market the model as an all-inclusive product when it isn't. Buyers brace for this. Silvernail tells them to relax — *what you see is what you'll get, it's all included in the price.*

We, as sales consultants, have to take responsibility for this discovery process during our presentations. Sometimes the baseline product is best for our customers. They can finish out the basement later, if that's a $30,000 option. Be sensitive to buyer needs and market conditions. But don't cut prices.

Trust-building starts in sales.

Winning Unconditional Trust In Sales
How Different Expectations Affect Trust

Expectation ...	When You're Performing Well, Your Buyer Is ...	When You're Not, Your Buyer Is ...
Universal Expectation	**... Ambivalent**	**... Disillusioned**
+ timely return of calls	— no gain of trust	— major loss of trust
+ warm greeting and inquiry	— no gain of trust	— major loss of trust
+ total customer focus	— no gain of trust	— major loss of trust
When builder fails to set expectations:	**... Satisfied**	**... Disappointed**
+ polite, never short	— low gain of trust	— medium loss of trust
+ messages between divisions aren't conflicting	— low gain of trust	— medium loss of trust
+ speak well of competitor	— low gain of trust	— medium loss of trust
When builder sets expectations; under promising and over delivering:	**... Delighted**	**... Dissatisfied**
+ personal tour	+ major gain of trust	— high loss of trust
+ offered bottled water	+ major gain of trust	— high loss of trust
+ empathetic questioning	+ major gain of trust	— high loss of trust
+ prepared to deal with children during sale	+ major gain of trust	— high loss of trust
+ honest throughout process	+ major gain of trust	— high loss of trust
+ demonstrate knowledge and availability of home features	+ major gain of trust	— high loss of trust

SOURCE: ELIANT, WWW.ELIANT.COM.

Even the simplest expectations, if left unmet, can cause a buyer to be dissatisfied. Note that for universal expectations, such as the timely return of phone calls, you won't gain trust for completing the task as expected, but you will suffer a major loss of trust for not completing this task.

DELIVER ORDINARY, THEN EXTRAORDINARY

Any time a client feels that you've failed on a promise, it's a dissatisfier. Any time you kept them in the dark, said no, didn't offer them options as alternatives, or they felt they weren't treated fairly, it's an issue of trust.

If you inventory your expectations and align them with the client's, you can systemize ordinary and extraordinary touchpoints — trust deposits — within these expectations. Each delivery on an expectation has to be crafted in such a way that it becomes a great experience. The contract signing, the design appointment, and the pre-construction meeting create moments with buyers and opportunities to deliver.

When mapping expectations, consider using at least eight steps, as Eliant recommends to its clients. Mapping should include all the steps listed in the charts on pages 73 and 74.

Lots of builders inject fun stuff into their building experience — post-closing parties or barbecues — but that's icing on the cake. Baumgarten says none of these should begin until the required and ordinary touchpoints are functioning. Before the red carpet and bows on the front door, builders need to accomplish what they've set out to accomplish. All the ribbons in the world will be meaningless if you've failed to make each interaction meaningful. Barbecues don't make up for a mediocre experience.

The number of touchpoints will vary, builder-to-builder and market-to-market. Baumgarten has seen some companies with as many as 120. But key touchpoints might number only a dozen. For instance, the initial design appointment — how is it scheduled? Who schedules it? What has to happen? Who's there? Who drops by? Each of these steps must be mapped out, along with the benefits to both the buyer and builder. Baumgarten estimates that less that 10 percent of builders do this; they simply don't understand that doing so can make everyone's job easier and improve the interaction with the client thus creating passionate referrals.

Baumgarten's experience with multi-divisional builders is that they are reluctant to impose this process on their divisions, since they are lucky to get even one division to adopt it. They face the "not invented here" or "our market is different" mentality. Sadly, for those folks, these principles are universal — they apply to every market. Customer service needs are universal. Yet, for many, that's difficult to accept. Buying into and executing this process takes time.

A Playbook For Expectations
Your clients know what they expect — shouldn't you?

Details. The details of the expectation.

We help the buyer understand our quality in a down market, so that they can purchase on value, not price.

The Message. What we communicate to clients about the expectation.

Our salesperson thoroughly explains the home's features, particularly those that are differentiators from the competition, and including those offered as standard that the competition sells as premium features.

The Messenger. Who's responsible for communicating the expectation.

The salesperson, reinforced by the team.

The Occasion. When we communicate the expectation.

At the walk-through and at contract signing. (Additional times could be considered.)

The Activity. What we do to fulfill or exceed the expectation.

We reinforce the value points in any communication with the client, making the communication sound natural, not forced.

The Standard. What our performance standards are for the expectation.

All value points we have over the competition, including items such as heat shielding, reflective insulation, specialized window glazing, unique plumbing, and any other feature should be listed and pointed out to give reasons why the buyer should choose us over another builder.

The Company Result. What we expect when we fulfill the expectation.

Higher trust, good questions, a client more inclined to be in love with the home and neighborhood. Fewer cancellations, due to price shopping.

The Client Result. What the client expects as you fulfill the expectation.

The buyer gets everything they've seen, including options they select, and that the options perform as they have been described. Additional value might come if more time is spent with them as they select customized amenities.

SOURCE: ELIANT, WWW.ELIANT.COM.

In mapping the result of two sample expectations in the sales process (on this page and the next), note that while the expectations are set by sales, they're reinforced by the team. It takes time to thoroughly map all expectations, but once you have this "playbook," expectations must be periodically reviewed to insure that they're being delivered as planned.

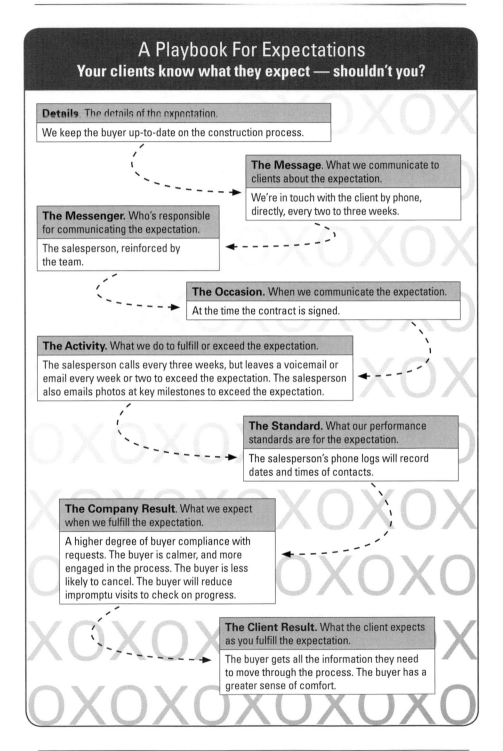

A Playbook For Expectations
Your clients know what they expect — shouldn't you?

Details. The details of the expectation.

We keep the buyer up-to-date on the construction process.

The Message. What we communicate to clients about the expectation.

We're in touch with the client by phone, directly, every two to three weeks.

The Messenger. Who's responsible for communicating the expectation.

The salesperson, reinforced by the team.

The Occasion. When we communicate the expectation.

At the time the contract is signed.

The Activity. What we do to fulfill or exceed the expectation.

The salesperson calls every three weeks, but leaves a voicemail or email every week or two to exceed the expectation. The salesperson also emails photos at key milestones to exceed the expectation.

The Standard. What our performance standards are for the expectation.

The salesperson's phone logs will record dates and times of contacts.

The Company Result. What we expect when we fulfill the expectation.

A higher degree of buyer compliance with requests. The buyer is calmer, and more engaged in the process. The buyer is less likely to cancel. The buyer will reduce impromptu visits to check on progress.

The Client Result. What the client expects as you fulfill the expectation.

The buyer gets all the information they need to move through the process. The buyer has a greater sense of comfort.

At best, it could take six months for a builder's team to thoroughly define 12 touchpoints. That doesn't mean progress will be deferred while they deliberate, but it takes time to completely recognize the touchpoints for what they are. A builder may realize they are "over-touching" at some points and neglecting other points. Once people realize what they are doing and what they need to do, results improve dramatically.

Reviewing its process this way, a builder can easily plan optional or extraordinary touchpoints in order to efficiently connect with the customer. There's no reason for four people to communicate with the buyer on the same day about almost the same thing. You don't want four batches of cookies delivered at once, or to create gaps in customer connections, or to bombard the client with information. Reviewing expectations and touchpoints makes certain that you close gaps and get clients the proper information at the right time so it sticks and is relevant.

Brian Binash, partner of Wilshire Homes, a company building about 750 homes a year in Houston, San Antonio, and Austin, calls expectation touchpoints "set points." He says they set a client off, good or bad. For 25 years in home building and about four years as president of Wilshire, he has tried to help his salespeople avoid negative set points and use positive set points to engage the customer.

Guts To Love

Engineering An Affirmative Experience

BY CAROL SMITH

From setting expectations at the point of sale to warranty service, there's a process builders can use to dissect every detail of the experience for homebuyers. I call it, and have trade-marked it, Experience Engineering®. The term engineering is appropriate because it captures the level of detail required, the precise planning, the cohesive nature of the components, and the idea that all the parts must function together.

Through engineering experiences, a builder ensures that the essential repetition of information occurs without traditional harping on rules and limitations. When the inevitable questions arise to which the answer must be no, wise builders are prepared with explanations of what they can do, or what they offer, instead of focusing on negatives. Roughly 85 percent of the time, the words *no, not, can't, won't* are unnecessary in buyer communications. The soft no — a no without using the word — is a matter of *attitude* and *habit*.

First, your staff must notice where no's appear. A paper sign taped to a plywood cover under a toilet lid that says "no public restroom" sends an unfriendly message. A new sign reading "restroom available in the sales office, thank you," sets the same limit with a hospitable tone. Precise training, rehearsal, and sometimes brainstorming are needed to develop a repertoire of responses that enforce limits without offending.

Wilshire's sales counselors (note the ear-friendly title) explore the client's interest in energy efficiency. If it's one of that client's set points, they share how the company is one of the most energy efficient home builders in Texas, and perhaps, the nation. They show how what is done with windows and behind the walls can save money, and is good for the environment. Wilshire uses paints with low volatile organic compounds (VOCs), and formaldehyde-free products. Wilshire's HEPA home filtration system is the same system that's used by hospitals to keep their air clean, filtered, and fresh. "There are things we do that you don't see," the company tells its clients.

Michael Strong of Brothers Strong of Houston also runs Greenhaus Builders, and has discovered differentiation points that build on buyer expectations when he sells their environmentally friendly homes. Younger homeowners respond to different satisfiers than their parents. "You can throw out key words in the course of a sale and see what people latch onto," Strong says. "If they love windows, you might talk about your energy efficiency. If they push flooring, talk about your low VOCs. Make it part of one long sentence and see what gets their attention — was it *healthy, environmental,* or *energy efficiency?*"

The same goes for universal design. If you're sensitive to a buyer's current and future needs for a home that's easy to live in, not just if life has dealt them a

When salespeople introduce the builder's limited warranty as part of their presentation, the foundation is set for other staff to follow up with details. The superintendent can mention company quality inspections at the preconstruction meeting. At the frame walk, a company rep points out quality techniques used inside the walls, then mentions the long-term maintenance task related to it. For instance, when describing soon-to-be-installed insulation, the rep might mention the buyer's task to ensure that the insulation remains undisturbed after the attic's mechanical systems are serviced. In this way, over and over, personnel subtly establish the separation of builder's and homeowner's responsibilities.

Orientation is the next chance to describe how to use the home's features, the builder's warranty commitment on each item, and the homeowner's maintenance responsibilities. By the time the rep gets to this last topic, they've given so much positive information that the customer willingly accepts their role in caring for the item.

Warranty representatives continue the effort during inspections, educating homeowners with tips and shortcuts while further shifting care of the home. Managing communication details here requires a different mindset, a new energy — a real passion and commitment. The return on investment is this: Homebuyers have realistic expectations. Customer service is all about balancing expectations with performance. This requires buyer education at a level unheard of at any time in our history, and it involves teamwork and planning — from the sales hand-off onward.

challenge, but for ease-of-use as they grow older — then roll-in showers, wider door jambs, grab bars, lever door handles, accessible storage and cabinetry are all items that help create touchpoints along the way.

John Maasch, vice president of sales, marketing and customer relations for Veridian Homes in Madison, Wisc., has found that addressing the right touchpoints varies by culture. Madison has many residents of Indian, Latin American, and Japanese descent, says Maasch. Salespeople have to be attuned to how close they get to a person or whether they physically touch them at all. Through basic principles of *Feng Shui*, they've learned that even simple elements of rounding a driveway or sidewalk can make a difference for some customers. That the way the stairway aligns with the front door, which way a home faces, or how certain cultures pray at particular times of the day all make a difference. Veridian salespeople share what they call "Whale Done" stories at sales meetings (this was prompted after they read *Whale Done! The Power of Positive Relationships*, by Kenneth Blanchard, Thad Lacinak, Chuck Tompkins, and Jim Ballard). The salespeople **P**ractice, **D**rill, and **R**ehearse their customer interactions to make their messages clear and consistent in sessions they call PDR.

Wilshire's BUILD program helps sales counselors deal with buyers in many different situations. In the homeowner manual given to buyers when they sign a contract, Wilshire spells out expectations — indicating which responsibilities are the buyers, and which are Wilshire's. Clients are taken through the pre-construction walk, and shown how a home is situated on the site. They learn about change requests and the home-building processes. When the slab is laid, during a "slab party," the homeowner's name is put on the jobsite sign. With cold soft drinks, Wilshire personnel and the buyers stand on the slab and take pictures, the first of many taken throughout the process to create the photo album given to the buyer at closing. Prior to the closing, the buyer learns about the warranties and how to resolve problems. Their service rep stops by and gives them a tool box and gifts — touch-up paint and caulk among them.

Humphrey, of David Weekley Homes, says his salespeople fill out an internal customer information sheet that is shared with the superintendent and customer service rep addressing how the customer defines quality — explaining to the customer that *the better I know you, the better we can build this home for you.* This way, too, they can set and meet expectations. Those expectations then meet the definition of quality. Humphrey says one of his personal expectations and pet peeves is when carpet is installed too early. To him and some of his clients, carpet is like a piece of furniture — he wants it new, not shampooed after a final trades visit. "We have to know that stuff about our customers," he says. "If we make the delivery generic, we miss some people. For me, to hold carpet a day or two to delight a customer, that's a no-brainer."

All these steps combine to involve the buyer emotionally in the home, and help them feel appreciated. Every employee builds these expectations and contributes to touchpoint excellence. I will share more related ideas in Chapter 4. These ordinary and extraordinary experiences build on each other, and create the powerful emotions tied to a well-delivered home.

THE TRUE VALUE OF CONNECTING

Do you see how so much of expectation building is about communication? And that it's only when a customer understands, through communication, how a specific product or service fits within their lifestyle choice, that it's possible to get full price?

People stop doing business with us not because they're dissatisfied with price or craftsmanship, but because they're dissatisfied with how they were treated. Or, with how we communicated with them, that they've been caught by surprise, and never felt they were kept up to date with progress on their project. How we provide service isn't a set of rules, it's a *feeling* — it has to come from within. As customers, we have to buy into it, we have to think it, feel it, believe it, taste it, smell it, touch it. As employees, it has to be a part of who we are. It has to grow from an understanding of the philosophy or principle of serving our customers, rather than "a policy somewhere." Employees don't buy into a policy, they buy into a principle.

Remember Rick Montelongo of Montelongo Homes & Remodeling in San Antonio? He established his own language for things like price (total investment), contract (proposal), and salesperson (design representative). Every week he reviews with his sales staff the psychological tendencies of buyers. He covers body language, how to mirror and match that language, and how to get clients to love his company. He teaches them to watch their pitch, pace, and power when talking, and how to use their eyes and hands, even their breathing. Watching a client's eyes is vitally important, he says.

You need to pay attention to details because the customer always does. The difference between middle-of-the-road mediocrity and screaming success is delighting customers, not just satisfying demands. How can you do this? One way is by building a database to track customer preferences. Tracking preferences helps you know how to react quickly. Interact with clients on their calendar, not yours, and know that everyone has their own distinct calendar. If you're attuned to it, you can make communicating easier across the board. Then you can measure and improve real customer satisfaction instead of perceived customer satisfaction.

Roxanne Musselman believes that from the time the client signs the purchase agreement until they sign the closing papers you must be their best friend — whether their transmission conks out, their son goes to college, or they have a baby — helping them through those events will determine whether or not they make it to the closing table. And without a relationship, there's a good chance you'll lose the buyer before they close. Everything that changes in their life can keep them from closing on that home. That's what's hard about new home sales — it's not a Monday through Friday, 9-to-5, 40-hour job. It's a 24/7 thing.

Communicate formally and specifically on the client's terms. Respond to their compliments and complaints. Thank them for telling you about problems. Indentify problems, correct them, and reclaim your lost customers. Every buyer has expectations of what will happen when a problem arises. What actually happens is the most important driver of long-term profitability and loyalty. So for those reasons alone, attend to your customers. Make it happen.

It's only when you understand all the elements that guarantee a referral after a sale that you can grasp the beauty of Myers Barnes' method to bring in a referral sale for every second client who purchases a home. His methods are supported by Eliant customer satisfaction research that shows how small, medium, and large builders can improve customer satisfaction by keeping clients informed. Look at this data from Eliant, spanning just over two years:

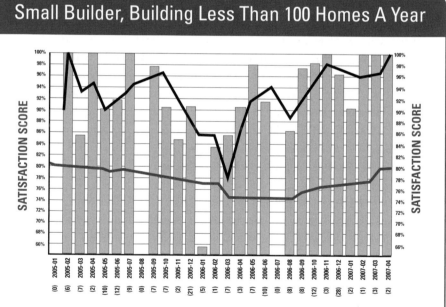

Small Builder, Building Less Than 100 Homes A Year

SOURCE: ELIANT, WWW.ELIANT.COM.

Make the purchase experience a peak experience. Keeping the client informed of construction progress without the client having to ask affects satisfaction scores (noted at left and right). This chart tracks a little over two years (noted on bottom) , along with numbers of surveys returned (in parentheses). This small builder's results — a three-month running average — are noted with the black line as compared against the industry average (gray line). Clearly informed customers are happy, referring customers.

Myers Barnes' method begins after the contract signing. Tell the client that you have a "customer care day" once a week. You'd like to contact them once a week, on the day they suggest, to answer any questions they have about the home you're building for them. Say you'll be in touch with the superintendent, the lender, and the title company, and you'll know the answers to all their questions. If it's a five-month building cycle, they'll hear from you 20 times. You'll take a weekly progress photo of their home and email it to them. They'll see the foundation being poured, the framing being finished, and drywall being delivered. On move-in day, say, *I'd like to bring you lunch, if I may — how many people will be there? Great, six?*

If you've made 20 calls (and calls from the client don't count as contacts), have taken 20 pictures, and brought lunch, do you stand a chance of winning referrals? You bet. Wouldn't some of these calls head off problems that frequently get to a flashpoint and hinder a referral? Count on it. When you drop lunch off on move-in day, ask, *have you been satisfied with our service? Can I ask one favor of you, please? If you know of anyone looking for a home, or considering a home, would you feel good about recommending me?* The answer will be yes, for some clients, because psychologically they'll feel the need to return the favors you've provided with your attentive service. But Barnes' method isn't over. After the move-in week, send a card — *Welcome to your new home! Happy Anniversary!* Then, send cards on six non-traditional holidays, perhaps family birthdays.

Or, create what I call "Happy Nothing" days. We want to stay in touch with buyers not because we expect something from them but we want them to feel valued, appreciated, and yes, sometimes even loved, on any day at all.

Add up those contacts — 20 calls, 20 photos, lunch, seven cards over a year — surely that creates a relationship. Surely, you'll get a referred buyer. Why? You've connected. You've lost the identity of "builder" and become human. See, there's no magic to this — it's all hard work. Have you ever had a buyer who said, *you keep me so up to date, I'm sick of it?* Neither have I.

But there must be a marriage between the delivery of the home and the salesperson's follow through. "It doesn't matter if you've had 20 contacts, and 20 photos, and lunch at the end," Barnes says. "The bottom line is if the delivery is horrific, the punch is eight miles deep and the experience is bad, you're never going to get a referral, no matter what type of relationship you have. There has to be a commitment to that delivery."

Certainly you can see how this service creates value. That's why you sell value, not price. That's why you are in the service business, not the homebuilding business.

FORGET PRICE, SELL VALUE

The more you charge for your services, the greater your perceived value. Research by GuildQuality of Atlanta, which I shared in Chapter 2, would seem to indicate this — that the most profitable remodelers have the highest satisfaction scores. Of course, in down markets, this philosophy gets constantly challenged. We have an obligation to our buyers to help protect their home values. If they see what we sold them, and we're willing to negotiate with the next buyer, what precedent is set? We've destroyed trust. If that buyer negotiates price, the buyer before did, too. If they see the person who gets the best deal is the best negotiator, what message does that send about your credibility and belief in your own value. There are so many ways to sweeten the pot other than cutting price.

"It's unwise to pay too much, but it's also unwise to pay too little. When you pay too much all you lose is a little money. But, when you pay too little, you stand a chance of losing everything because the thing you bought is incapable of doing what you bought it to do. The common law of business balance prohibits paying a little and getting a lot. It just can't be done. So, when you deal with the low bidder, it's wise to put a little aside to take care of the risk you run. And, if you can do that, you can afford something better!"

— **JOHN RUSKIN, ENGLISH PHILOSOPHER**

Say you're $40,000 apart from the house down the street, and you've made clear the difference in your product. Sometimes you have to break the difference into increments. What is $40,000 spread over a 30-year mortgage? About $1,333 a year — $111 a month. That's $3.70 per day. For $3.70 per day or for the price of one Starbucks latte, someone can get the home they want. Ask: *Are you willing to sacrifice one cup of coffee a day to get the home you like?* If you relate it to an everyday expense, buyers will see it for what it is. And how many people ever really pay off their mortgage anyway? People usually move every seven to eight years.

If you improve value instead of cutting price — price will have no emotional component. Price is price. But total value has many emotional elements attached. I always share with my speaking audiences a quote by John Ruskin, Victorian poet, artist, and social revolutionary: *It's unwise to pay too much, but it's also unwise to pay too little.*

Economies change — but housing will always be the best investment. You have to help buyers look beyond dollars and see *enjoyment*.

But even that is not enough. You can't sit on your laurels and expect the parts surrounding your deal to take care of themselves. Regardless of any difficulties in the mortgage industry, there are still awesome loan programs. But we can't be order takers and simply refer buyers to loan agents. I used to pre-qualify buyers at my desk, using a hand calculator. *We can't lose our ability to service the sale.*

The best remodelers in the business base pricing on a 42 percent gross margin. To some degree, remodelers need to have the courage to charge what they're worth. Builders and remodelers have to have systems in place to deliver on their high-value promise of delivering high-quality products on promised dates, in a complete condition, ready for move-in.

While satisfaction surveys are meaningful and published consumer assessments of your company will be looked at by buyers, people really don't give a hoot what other people think. The builders and remodelers who do the best at earning top dollar are the ones who are best at developing relationships. That skill is worth a premium. So charge it and stick to your guns when you sell. Isn't supporting your value better than defending your price? Defend, and people get defensive.

Musselman says salespeople selling against a builder down the street who's cut prices $40,000 need to educate buyers that it's because the builder put false value into the home by raising margins, limiting construction, and slowing the sales pace — all giving false values. As a competitor who's not lowering price, the salesperson needs to justify the position by providing a value offering. It's not good for the consumer to buy today at one price and then the next client receives either a $50,000 discount or pays $50,000 more. What happens six months later, when buyers are transferred to another state and have to sell their home? And what if, at that point, homes in the community are selling for $20,000 less than they paid? "Paint that picture," Musselman says. "If you buy in a neighborhood where the builder doesn't hold the value, you don't know what's in front of you. When you buy in a neighborhood where the builder sustains value, you're protected. If you buy where a builder cuts prices, you're playing 'let's make a deal,' and sometimes that works in your favor, sometimes not — are you a risk taker? If this is the biggest investment of your life, how lucky do you feel?"

Musselman says it is possible to stay firm on price in *any* market. She recalls selling against foreclosed homes in the 1980s when her homes were twice the price of the foreclosed houses. She had to be confident and secure in her price and value. It was something she personally believed. A home that was new, clean, and not surrounded by five other foreclosed homes was worth the money. She helped buyers feel comfortable paying twice the price ... and sleeping soundly at night.

But all of this requires relationship building, she notes. The more time you spend with buyers, the more they will share with you. Musselman says studies used to say *your kids wanted quality time with you*. No, they want *all of your time — they want* **quantity.** The same holds true for customers. When you give them all of your time, any time they ask, they believe you, and believe *in* you. "That opens doors for painting pictures for them. They can see you are going to help them in the long run," Musselman says.

She believes that the love I write about in this book is a product of these relationships. She is so good at what she does, providing value and service, her clients are going to love working with her. It's not her goal, but a product of the relationship.

I reviewed a wonderful mystery shopper tape Hogan Homes shared with me. Kelea Piper, then a sales consultant at Hogan's Rockport, Texas community, was in her early twenties and had been involved with the company for about six months. She was green and growing and hadn't rusted out. A woman buyer walks in and says, *well, what are the prices out here?* Piper calmly responds, *prices begin in the low $140,000s, and range to the low $200,000s — does that work within your budget?* The buyer says, *what are you willing to take? How much will you negotiate?*

Piper's face went blank: *Not at all, absolutely none. We never discount anything, goodness gracious, no.* Her look read: *Are you kidding? Do you realize who you're talking to? We're not Kmart. We don't have to defend our price.*

Once you adopt the posture of defending the price, you're lost. And Piper was selling homes like hotcakes, in 2005. She was selling on the buyers' first time out when everyone in the company was telling her you can't sell on the first time out. She was convincing people the product was so exceptional, they'd better buy. Because if they didn't, prices were going up next week. *I don't know what the price will be tomorrow, but I know this: It will be higher than today.*

Why should we defend price, when all our products — new homes or remodels — traditionally appreciate? Sometimes we can't raise our prices fast enough to keep up with what values are. Just look at the Florida and California markets in the past five years. Values were quadrupling and then the spigot was turned off. We forget how to sell value, when prices appreciate at extreme rates. When prices stabilize, we have to make buyers see this is a great value proposition. Buying a home has to be based on more than making or losing money. What is the price of raising your children in a beautiful environment? What is the price of having stability and your kids becoming friends with your neighbor's kids? We forget how to tie value to enjoyment.

When prices are appreciating at astronomical rates, the cost equation makes sense. But as market conditions change, we can't rely on an equation with numbers in it that make everyone go, *ah-ha!* What is it worth to know you have people living around you who are familiar with your routine and if you don't pick up your newspaper that day, they start worrying about you? Value has to be equated to lifestyle and enjoyment.

Piper would never think of cutting prices. She exudes confidence and feels good about her company's position in the market. Her attitude comes first, her communication skills follow. As a salesperson, you have to increase your value by doing things yourself. You have to study constantly. No one will ever know all there is to know about sales. We, as managers, have to invest in education, training, and in understanding the importance of following through.

It's not just calling customer care to tell them your client has a problem so they can call the plumber. It's learning that the plumber will be there tomorrow afternoon, and then calling your client to tell them he's coming. It's not taking the word of the customer care representative that the plumber is coming. What if the plumber's truck gets a flat tire and then the next morning they promise to come, another emergency arises? You need to keep your client informed. That's follow-through. That's not letting it die until the homeowner is satisfied and everything happened *as it was promised*. Follow-through warrants a higher price. I know that as a buyer, once I call you, and you stay on it until it's done, constantly keeping me in the loop, it's worth more. Buyers rarely say *you kept me so up to date I'm sick of it*. They always say, *I don't know what's going on. I'm waiting here and no one has shown up. Why haven't you called?*

Education, like follow-through, is highly valued by buyers.

There's a company called Americus Diamond in San Antonio that educates people about diamonds, not necessarily to have them shop at Americus Diamond, but to help them select a quality diamond, learning about inclusions and blemishes. The message they send is if you go into a jewelry store, you need to be educated about what you're looking at, because it's possible even the person selling the diamond won't have this knowledge. We'll educate you in the terminology, so when you make your purchase decision, you're informed and you'll feel comfortable. They're not concerned about this sale but all the sales to come.

Are we teaching our clients about our homes? Are we making the purchase decision easy for them? A strong, dominant brand is rooted in owning the terminology, defining the terminology, and plastering the terminology on everything you have. Do you share your history with clients, showing them how it provides peace of mind? Don't tell them what you do that's different from the competition, share with them why your process and products deliver a distinct advantage.

Education builds trust. Trust and honesty go hand in hand. Honesty is living up to things both spoken and unspoken. Many things in remodeling and homebuilding are implied. When someone says *don't worry about it, we'll take care of it,* the client hears: *I don't have to worry about it at all.* But what's the parameter? Don't say things like that if you can't live up to them.

Salespeople constantly say, *we offer a one-year warranty that covers every-thing in the first year. Don't worry about it, give us a call, we'll take care of it.* That's way too open-ended. If you don't add the word *limited,* the customer infers it's unlimited. If you don't explain the homeowner's responsibilities, they assume they're yours. FCB Homes of Stockton, Calif. does an incredible job throughout its process to make homeowners better understand their responsibilities. One activity is a homeowner maintenance seminar at the local hardware store. This creates responsibility but also completes a circle of trust — trust in the fact that FCB "cares for us."

Trust goes back to your principles. You won't get trust out of a customer if you are not trustworthy. Make sure you quote the right prices and build trust into your documents from the client's first contact with your company. Through

LOVE mode

A Love-Hate Story
BY ROXANNE MUSSELMAN

Building a relationship with a Realtor, to me, is critical to new home sales. In retail, it's said that a business can only survive with repeat clients. I believe that in order for on-site sales agents to recognize the benefit of referral sales through Realtors, the Realtor must be treated as their repeat customer. If you use Realtors, your referral rate should be 50 to 75 percent, and you will be able to sustain your market share in good times and bad.

The National Association of Realtors says 85% of home buyers use a real estate agent during their search for a home. It makes no sense to spend your time chasing 15 percent of non-Realtor business because you hate the thought of paying a 3 percent commission. Missing out on 85 percent of all home sales is a hard way to do business. The easy way is the referral way.

Builders turn to Realtors when the market is bad. Then, when it's good, they don't want to pay commissions, so they neglect or outright ignore the Realtors. Don't be a fair weather friend! If you want to sustain a homebuilding business, you need to be consistent in good times and bad. Continue to court Realtors even when you don't need them. The Realtor *is* your repeat business. They're your referral. If you sell directly to clients, chances are they're not going to buy another home for at least seven or eight years. If you sell a home through a Realtor and do a good job, you each step you build trust, and put it in your trust account. Those pictures of the job site you take to email your client, they build trust, too.

Eliant notes how builders win trust, not by meeting universally accepted expectations, but in those moments when they exceed expectations. The best way to gain trust, or lose it, is when you set expectations and exceed (gain trust) or fail to meet them (lose trust). It should be our universal mission to treat every customer in such a memorable way that when the transaction is complete, the customer tells someone not how *good* it was, but how *great* it was. And, that they would be missing something very wonderful indeed, if they did not do business with us.

There is no such thing as *middle of the road. So don't ride the line.* Jim Hightower, in his book of the same name, wrote: *there's nothing in the middle of the road but yellow stripes and dead armadillos.* No one wants to buy from a middle-of-the-road company. They want someone who is knowledgeable, real, and warm — someone they can trust who makes them feel good about what they are doing.

So be *memorable.* Map your expectations. Map your client's expectations. Know what your competitive differentiators are, as a salesperson and as a company. Communicate well. Whatever you do, don't make price your differentiator. Value your true worth, and sell subtly, through the quiet, firm touch of your people.

could see the Realtor tomorrow … and again, a week later. When those folks start bringing you one qualified prospect per month, you have a relationship. They like you. But if they eat your special grand-opening hot dogs or donuts and don't bring in clients, there's no relationship.

Give your best Realtors VIP treatment. Share your research findings, if you do market research, and data on why you're building in a particular area. You will help real estate companies grow their business by sharing. We keep too much of this information secret for no reason. Shared, it's more likely Realtors will educate clients with the ammunition needed to sell out your community. They're not just selling your product or specifications sheet, they're selling a whole market area and why you chose to build there. OK, they might also use that information in their resale business, and you might account for only 5 or 10 percent of their business. But if you have 10 to 20 Realtors as business partners, they can bring you as much as 100 percent of your business. Set up a commission structure so on-site agents win the same commission whether someone walks in with a Realtor or not. Some builders pay less because there's a Realtor commission but that sets the Realtor relationship up for failure since the on-site agent doesn't want to earn reduced commissions.

All builders have a Realtor program, but few have a broker liaison responsible full-time to work with the Realtors. This position keeps the folks happy who are providing you up to 85 percent of your business. When your company takes time to staff an employee, that sends a message that you care. Yes. It's sheer overhead. But how much is 85 percent of your business worth?

LOVE ✓ CHECK

Discover Me, Sell Me, *Remember* Me

If you're selling subtly, never let the relationship become "transactional." In other words, I should never be *buying* from you. Think of your best experiences when you bought something meaningful. Did you ever feel *sold?* Keep it personal and it's easier to return to a client and ask for a favor, like a referral — wouldn't you do the same for a friend? Here's how to keep *me*, your client, in sight, and not the sale:

✔ Prepare Yourself

Selling or remodeling homes requires knowledge. Know your product, company, offerings, unique selling proposition, your competition. Once you've mastered that, prepare for your client, so that the experience isn't disjointed. You shouldn't be running laps to the copier. You're prepared. Your client benefits. You don't waste time. No one has more time than they need, especially buyers.

✔ Welcome *Me*

Personalize your presentation to *me*. Build rapport. Don't use a script or a canned presentation. Discover me. Get to know the *real* me: My family, my wants, my desires, my likes, my dislikes, my *loves*. Remember, I am the only one you're working with now.

✔ Match My Needs

Offer me what's right for me. If you have 15 plans, I'll buy one, so help me zero in on what fits. Don't make me look at all 15. Match my needs to your offerings, and begin by narrowing down the choices. The more the offering is aligned with my needs, the easier it is for me to make a decision. The more it appears that what you're offering was my idea anyway, the easier it is to make a decision. It becomes personalized, and therefore, emotional. If it becomes obvious that what's best for me isn't what you have, advise me to go elsewhere. That's a love connection and leads to referrals — even without a sale.

✔ Embrace My Objections

The only way to come to agreement is to handle and embrace objections. Yes, *embrace* them. Respect them. Answer them. Be honest and sincere when you tell me whether this is the best thing to do. Always remember the final decision must be good for both of us. If it's a lopsided decision, the love connection is lost. Trust is broken. Then it becomes transactional. It's not two people doing business. We've become a purchaser and a seller. Never make your client feel that way.

✔ Ask Me To Buy

Be confident enough in our relationship so that you can confidently ask me to buy. Care enough about me to hang in there until I buy. Don't make me ask you. Don't fumble — carry me home. Love me enough to ask uncomfortable questions: Are you ready to buy? Tell me, *we've thought about this thoroughly, now I think it's time to make a decision, don't you*? Remember, they deserve to be asked to buy. Because, after all, if you're confident this is the best decision for me, you'll gently force me to do it. Because it's a huge decision. The biggest reason salespeople don't succeed is that they get to the closing and fail. You don't want to be perceived as pushy. But be humbly confident: "I'd be doing you a disservice today if I let you walk out without making a decision. You've thought about it and thought about it — *now* is the time to act."

✔ Celebrate With Me

Let me know immediately that I've made the right decision. I should feel good about it. This is after you receive your earnest money and have the client sign the offer. Immediately say: *You guys should feel so good! You made the absolute best decision you can make. Let's celebrate.* Go out for a latte. It needs to be more than, *whew, we got through that, OK, now let's schedule the loan application appointment.* Make it a point to be festive. *Let's go meet your new neighbors! I can't wait for you to meet Joe, your project superintendent. You're going to love him. If you don't mind, let me call Joe and see if he can stop by. I'd like to have you meet him before you leave this afternoon.* Walk out onto the property. Have them jam a "sold" sign into the raw earth. Take a picture. Out on the dirt, look at their plans again: "It will never look this way again. Your home will be gorgeous here."

✔ Don't Forget Me

Never treat me as a past buyer. Don't let me drop off your MIB list — your list of *Most Important Buyers.* I will always be an MIB, so treat me like one. Remember: *I am a client for life.*

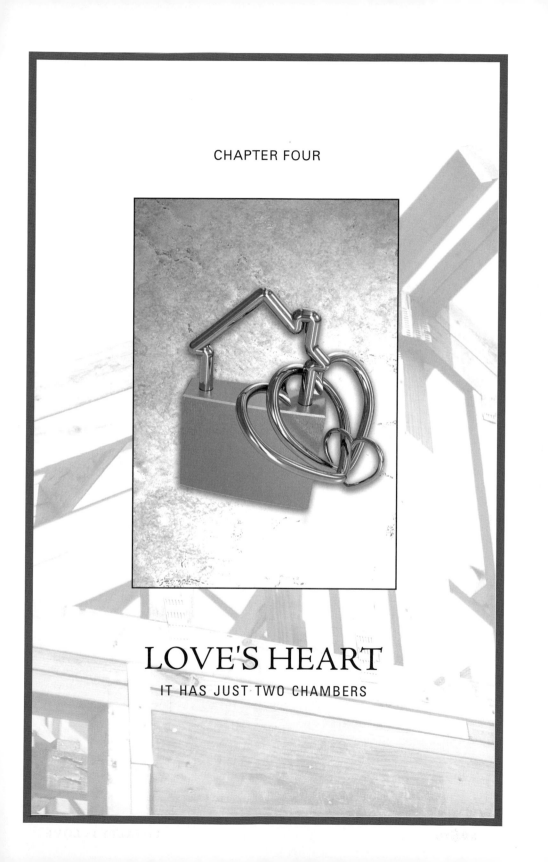

LOVE'S HEART
IT HAS JUST TWO CHAMBERS

Caring doesn't mean "giving the store away," and it doesn't mean trying to make everyone happy. People have to be happy on their own.

Aren't you delighted to read that? Caring isn't synonymous with astronomical costs. Those are the words of Richard Staky, region president, Colorado, John Laing Homes, an organization that, for years, has topped customer satisfaction indices and in 2007 was named one of *Professional Builder's* top three best workplaces. The company scored highest in employee satisfaction with opportunities for personal development, and this came at a time when the drop-off in home sales forced many builders to cut employee rosters by half — or more. John Laing has reduced staff, too, but employees tell the company they're happy with their jobs and trust senior management's leadership.

Staky's observation recognizes that customer service springs from the place you create for **employees** — even if you're selling fewer homes than you did three years ago. It's recognizing that while customers come first, **employees** make up the other chamber of the heart that keeps loyalty alive. You can never forget **employees.** You can't breach the trust they have in you as the leader of a great company.

Like most forward thinkers, Staky knows that homebuilding is about relationships, and that making people happy in these relationships starts with the hiring decision. "We look for honest and true people," the John Laing executive says. "People who care, who are responsible. That puts them in a good position in situations when things are tough.

"We're not about making people happy," he insists. "It's a byproduct of what we do, and not the main goal. We try to create a great experience for people, because in the process of building a home, a lot can go wrong."

In 2005, John Laing Homes' Denver division won another award from AVID Ratings (then NRS Corp.) for the highest customer satisfaction ratings in North America. AVID asked homeowners: *Did you feel like the homebuilder cared for you?* Every John Laing homeowner said they thought their builder did, indeed, care.

HEART OF
THE MATTER

What to take to heart from this chapter:
- Client trust mirrors the trust employees have in company leadership.
- Trust employees to put their personal stamp on your process.
- Build trust from the hire.
- Care isn't intuitive; training makes it natural.
- Make *every* employee a customer experience champion.

Caring. How do you get your customers to *feel* that? There's only one way and you hired him or her last week. So what can you do to help this new employee make your customers feel that you care? Does it cost money? Does it require leadership? Or, does it demand *imagination?*

CEO Larry Webb, Staky, and their colleagues at John Laing Homes use lots of the latter. They have no secret training program. They use pre-hire assessments to hire caring, reliable people, and they provide constant training, coaching, and opportunities for role-playing customer interactions. They measure and reward employees when their communities reach a 90 percent satisfaction score on their customer surveys. That happens often for Laing, formerly one of the largest privately held homebuilders in the U.S., now part of the largest real estate development company in the world, Dubai-based Emaar Properties.

But it happens on a smaller scale, too. FCB Homes, a 150-home-a-year builder in Stockton, Calif., follows similar principles, relying heavily on its team to build and map customer expectations to guarantee delighted clients who refer over and over again. In litigation-happy California, where lawyers aggregate homeowners to sue builders using dubious claims before home warranties expire, FCB, having built more than 3,000 homes, is one of the few builders that, through 2006, had never been sued by a client.

That's because FCB has built trust that customers see as care. In fact, they'll call FCB when they receive one of those sue-the-builder letters — before they call the lawyer. And that allows FCB to approach all past customers in their community, to ask: *Is everything OK with your home?* They *care*.

Steve Petruska, COO of Pulte Homes, says he learned this principle in the early to mid-1990s, when his Las Vegas division began understanding that "we fall in love with customers … and they fall in love with us."

FCB, through rigorous training, at the height of the market, when its homes were being sold by lottery, began to help employees understand that the company culture wasn't really product-driven even though it appeared that way. It was customer-driven. This was a difficult mindset to accept when so much of what they did dictated to customers what the company wanted. It was hard to accept that you no longer chased customers off jobsites, but handed them a hardhat and welcomed the chance for interaction, in spite of any potential liability issues a raw site might pose. FCB moved from barely helping customers "win" a home, to a place where every employee "sells" a home and cheers the latest sale. This, in a market that tightened FCB's ranks from 90 to 45 employees. Employees now know their attitude toward customers is independent of market condition. And perhaps, that attitude and interest create their own economy — an economy of loyalty.

WE ARE THE CHAMPIONS

FCB began its internal evolution during a fragile, but ongoing trend in home building — the advent of the Customer Experience Champion™, a title trademarked in 2006 by Eliant to describe a determined, perseverant individual that completes its CEC training and certification program. As of this writing, I'd estimate that as few as 40 companies employ CECs (with variations on that title). The evolution is fragile because in a down economy, this position is at risk.

As Carol Smith notes, this job is unique in that its responsibilities cut across departments and functions. Company owners establish how much authority and influence over departments this position has. Veteran employees need time to adjust to sharing their authority with this new professional. People can grow defensive and feel second-guessed. So this person's ability to build healthy relationships while working with a variety of personalities and egos is critical to their success. They're a bridge. A cheerleader. A coach. Most importantly, they're process neutral — they have no allegiance to any one department's methods, but see only the customer through a humble, servant's heart.

What a great job!

It could be said that the customer experience champion model has roots in the late 1980s when Pulte Homes Chairman Bill Pulte and then-CEO Bob Burgess hired Scott Sedam to work on quality and customer service issues and provide organized bench-marking of other industries to improve standards of quality and customer service at the company. As COO Petruska notes, Pulte Homes was getting big and wanted

to manage growth without losing the ability to touch its customers. Then, in the mid- to late-1980s, David Weekley Homes became one of the first big-name builders to publicly announce that it was independently surveying buyers and analyzing questionnaires to tweak customer systems and processes.

Dick Bryan, the now-retired vice president of customer care at John Laing Homes, openly acknowledged "customer experience" as a core corporate philosophy in the 1980s. Through the likes of Weekley, Laing, and Pulte, it became a model few could follow, but many would try to imitate. Today, John Laing Homes has customer experience champions in all nine divisions, although it gives them the title of customer care vice president. Bryan was the first formally recognized Customer Experience Champion™ for a multi-divisional company, says Bob Mirman, Eliant CEO. David Weekley Homes' vice president of sales and marketing also contributed to the historic evolution of this position.

Everything Bryan did while at John Laing Homes was about holding employees accountable and setting expectations for the customer experience — from the way employees dressed, to how he got them, in the early 1990s, to wear hospital surgical booties over their shoes when they entered a customer's home. "I thought he was nuts," Mirman says. "I didn't think he would get anyone to do it. But he wanted to show the customer they cared about the home as much as the customer did." *He wanted to build trust.*

Out of that history, too, came Martha Baumgarten, the prototype of the Customer Experience Champion™ at Shea Homes, another care leader. Although Baumgarten didn't hold the title, she performed many functions of today's CECs: She got each department to analyze its processes through the customer's eyes, and then, to work together to focus on the experience and refine these processes. She does this now as vice president of customer experience management at Eliant, consulting with builders. At Shea, and at these other true leaders in customer care, service is no longer something that comes post-sale. It's in the sale. It's in design. It's in production. It's in warranty service. It's in trade contractor and supplier relationships. It's in *everything they do*.

These days, Grand Homes, of Dallas, a multi-divisional builder, employs Missy Jones as its champion. M/I Homes of Columbus, Ohio, counts on John Kluba, a director of customer experience, to make certain departments work together to deliver exceptional service in M/I's Midwest region.

Richmond American Homes, an M.D.C. Holdings subsidiary in Denver, Colo. and one of the nation's top builders, has counted on Ted Wickenhauser, its vice president of national customer experience, to oversee customer experience managers in all 12 of its divisions. Richmond American has seen key customer satisfaction measures climb every month over more than two years as it focused on the *experience* of building a home. Mirman says he has never witnessed such a meteoric rise in these key satisfaction measures.

But isn't that what happens when you tap the power of people? When you lead the change and offer the best care? When you express pride in

LOVE mode

Trust On The Frontlines

Shea Homes' Buddy Satterfield builds an open, trusting, serving environment, from his trade partners on up.

You can't build a superior home in wind and rain, in 115-degree temperatures, with wood that twists and nails that pop using 40 trade partners, and keep the homebuyer delighted. Or can you?

Every builder, even those making strides in customer care, laments that the service mindset can only be taken so far — it stops at their concrete, framing, plumbing, electrical, drywall, and HVAC trade partners.

It doesn't have to be that way.

In the Arizona division of Shea Homes, trusting his people *and* his trades, Buddy Satterfield, division president and chief executive servant (you read that right), has built a culture of service that extends from the trade partners right to the top.

The roots of the program reach back to the early 1990s. Shea ramped up too quickly and delivered homes that took too long to build and rarely exceeded customer expectations, Satterfield says. But as the company adopted total quality management, process mapping, flow charting, zero-defect deliveries, and the concept of using measurement to build faster-better-cheaper, it rolled out principles that changed the course of its business. In 1993, only everything your employees do? When you tap their ingenuity and reward a common goal?

Everyone makes a difference. And, everything is built on relationships, says Mark Sanborn, author of the international bestseller *The Fred Factor*. He believes the marketplace is starved for people who are *interested*. He means people who are keenly aware of other people's needs. Customers' best interest is the connection they have with your employees, what they share in common. The premium you charge for your service represents the value you create within that connection. The relationship provides a way to differentiate and connect.

So during bad cycles, Staky sees the opportunity for his people to spend more hours nurturing client relationships. In bad times, FCB knows from its Eliant surveys that what they call evangelical customers refer an average of six to seven potential buyers, double the referrals of less satisfied customers. So FCB *drives at* exceeding customer expectations to create these evangelical buyers. They'll weather any storm.

We can't always control our product. We can control and excel at owning relationships and help our people better understand these experiences and processes. This way, they can create trust with clients — what customers see as "care." Such care will carry homebuyers through problems, whether they're caused by product failures or communication snafus.

13 percent of its Arizona homes were zero-defect delivered, as measured by customers, says Satterfield.

In 1995, Shea discovered Stephen R. Covey's *The Seven Habits of Highly Effective People*, and through the efforts of trade and training adviser Paul Kalkenbrenner, they became aware of how to use the language of Seven Habits to transform the division. The seven habits include: taking responsibility, beginning with the end in mind, putting first things first, thinking win-win, seeking first to understand and then be understood, working in teams, and seeking balanced self-renewal. Shea introduced its 150 employees at the time to the book's concepts, and then trained facilitators to help them learn the seven principles even better. "There are inherent benefits in having employees teach each other," Satterfield says. "There's more accountability, buy-in, and commitment." The initial course takes 24 hours; Shea holds refresher courses annually.

Soon after employees were trained, Shea brought the message to its trades. "They learned a critical success factor is the relationship," Satterfield says. "And if we can get their people to open their eyes and ears, to be receptive, beginning with the end in mind, taking care of first things first, thinking win-win, they could see that either we both win, or we don't work together." It's a marked contrast to what the trades have come to expect.

As our markets continue to tighten, some builders in Shea's territory have said that unless the trades cut their invoice prices by 16 percent, they would lose bidding rights on future jobs.

Doing so creates bonds for life. Think of the hard times you've been through with your spouse or family — aren't you better for it?

I hire employees with manners and common sense, and you can train them to communicate and act in ways that not only help them avoid conflicts, but prevent situations from escalating beyond *your* control. With the authority to act, a better understanding of your corporate DNA, and a solid indoctrination into the company's culture of care, they'll be able to leave their fingerprints on these relationships and slowly create, for you, a client for life, a promoter that hitches onto your corporate DNA.

That's why great employees, next to great customers, create the heart of love, and that's why employees should be your first clients. Loyalty's foundation of trust is built on these fingerprints, on all these customer interactions. Mike Benshoof of SMA Consulting of Orlando, Fla. reminds me that *you're only as good as the person dealing with the customer at that point in time.* Customer experience champions put external *and* internal clients — not houses — first. Let me share how you can improve the odds that those moments are peak moments: Begin with training and carry it through to your company culture.

After all, to be trusted is more valued than to be loved. You might love someone, but still not trust them. But if I trust you and have faith in you, I trust that you'll deliver my home, no matter

BUDDY SATTERFIELD (LEFT) WITH CHUCK HASKINS.

Chuck Haskins, owner of the 600-employee Haskins Electric of Phoenix, Ariz. serves all the major builders working in Arizona and parts of New Mexico. Haskins says it's nice to work with Shea because the trades have a say, and aren't brow-beaten. About 200 of his employees have been through the *Seven Habits* training, and it has helped the trade partners, especially with each other. "A lot of us have become good friends," he says. "If there's a problem on a Shea job with a framer, I call Jim Younger, who owns the framing company, and he says he'll get on it. He does the same for me."

In actuality, the training has ended up helping all the builders in the market as these habits extend to other jobs.

By developing a better understanding of the big picture, Haskins says he's able to balance dramatic swings in his workload, and the corresponding pressures on manpower. Instead of working on 300 homes in one week and 200 the next, for instance, he calls up the plumbing subcontractor owner and asks if his guys might work ahead of their plumbers, with the lack of proof. And the level of loyalty your customer feels will directly mirror the level of trust employees feel with you, their CEO or manager. You can't have clients who love you unless your employees love you. How do you create that bond?

SEE THE UNSEEN

Tim Kane is president of MBK Homes Southern California, historically one of Eliant's top builders in customer satisfaction rankings. MBK's Japanese parent company Mitsui & Co. is one of the oldest and largest publicly traded companies in the world, one that Kane likes to note existed before the  Mayflower landed on Plymouth Rock. In a more contemporary vein, Kane likes to share a video with his audiences that shows white-shirted and black-shirted basketball players repeatedly handing off a ball as they juke around a room. He suggests that viewers count how many times the white shirts pass the ball. What most will miss, is the person in the gorilla suit who easily slips into the fray, and, just as easily, exits the room.

Kane says construction superintendents, faced with the same constantly moving mishmash of people coming in and out of their worlds,

the understanding that if they have to pull wires to do their job, no one's charged. "It really helped open up the workflow," Haskins says. "We never did that before."

"Our industry is so steeped in tradition, and a lot of it wasn't good," Satterfield says. "It's a win-lose mentality, much like the world. In America, we are brought up with that. If you have a sports background, there's one winner, one loser. Once you understand the win-win and adopt the abundance mentality, that there's enough to go around — it gives people permission to work in a spirit of cooperation and to do it faster, better, and cheaper." It becomes a language everyone speaks, Satterfield says. Because of the common language, people aren't afraid to step on someone else's toes, and make suggestions, or challenge what each other says — they can say: *Are you really thinking about win-win?*

"It forces people to reflect on their training, language, and skills," Satterfield says. "People have to be brought up to think differently."

Because of less rework, less waste, better cooperation, and quicker completions, Shea was able to control costs along with pricing for customers, and the trades experienced better profitability, Satterfield says.

But the most dramatic, successful number for the division president has been referrals, up from 8 percent in the early 1990s to 33 percent now. And conversion ratios for those referrals mean that one out of every three people who comes in the door becomes a sale. Shea shares these and other customer satisfaction often miss "gorillas," due to what he calls *constuctionitis*. They overlook the obvious details others easily see. Psychologists coined a term for this: *inattentional blindness.*

This is the same reason you miss the dirty *Welcome* mat in front of your quality model home. We miss things because we're literally too close to them, and yet we need to see them in order to meet our customer's standards for the experience and delivery of their home. They always get closer than we do.

Kane understands that you need to create a culture where everyone's eyes are engaged, because that returns bottom-line results. By examining each part of its process through the customer's eyes, MBK discovered that even adjustments in community development affect clients. They found that forward planning was important. If community development didn't obtain permits on time, more permits would be pushed to the fourth quarter. Then, *CRUNCH* — sales, production, escrow, and other departments all had to kill themselves to deliver what they had promised. Meanwhile, accounting discovered that paying trade partners on time actually produced a better quality home. By looking at processes through the eyes of internal and external customers, every department began to see how it affected the experience, and consequently, satisfaction scores.

To further guarantee promises to customers, such as on-time delivery and an *impeccable* (not perfect)

measures at regular trade partner breakfasts, examining satisfaction scores community-by-community and trade-by-trade.

"His commitment to learning, change, and collaboration on all kinds of issues is extraordinary," says Tom Noonan, a senior associate at TrueNorth Development of Northville, Mich. "The other thing he did that was unique, is he turned the organizational pyramid upside down, and took on the mantra, 'if you're not serving the customer, you better be serving someone who is.'"

Satterfield has modeled that behavior to the point that his business card describes him not as president of Shea Homes Arizona, but as president/CES, which he tells people stands for *Chief Executive Servant.*

"As a role model, he has had an impact on his culture, customer satisfaction, and the division's relationships with its trades beyond any builder I've seen," says Noonan. "And his commitment to learning and sharing with his colleagues is extraordinary."

Satterfield says it's not all "lovey-dovey Covey stuff." He takes a real interest in people. Why? Because he understands it boils down to relationships. By the way, the superior home for his Shea division is a lot closer these days. Some 80 percent of Shea homes in Arizona are delivered with zero defects, as measured by customers. In some months, 100 percent deliver defect-free.

"We're far from everything being perfect," he says. "Now, it's part of our culture, striving for perfection, but we're settling for excellence. It's never going to be perfect."

People, working together in trust, make near-perfect possible.

product, MBK decided to hire a *quality assurance auditor*, someone with no construction experience, but who was meticulous and detail-oriented, and who set the benchmark for the company's standard — actually the customer's standard, not construction's. Kane found his perfect auditor — really, his customer service champion — in Felecia Ash, who worked in his accounting department. At first, employees tended to give Ash a hard time during audits. But she took digital pictures, and soon employees began to better understand her points. The visuals persuaded her builders that yes, this crack in the concrete might meet a construction standard, but not the customer's standard. It took three years before the company could meet the bar set by Ash's audits. Kane thinks it's significant that a woman in a male-dominated world can provide a fresh perspective.

Even today, Ash is helping change MBK's culture to one emphasizing service. But it took another set of eyes, eyes that saw *all* the gorillas in the room. Ash focused differently, and with a relaxed view could see what was really wrong.

While it's interesting to look at change in customer care culture through the eyes of those fine-tuning it, it's also worthwhile to share the perspective of those who stared into the abyss — and didn't blink. Grand Homes, for five consecutive years, found itself dead last in J.D. Power and Associates' Texas rankings. Although it employed Eliant to gauge customer satisfaction, it didn't leverage the results by sharing them with employees, says Missy Jones, Grand Homes' relatively new corporate customer experience champion. That habit would change. "To get off the bottom of J.D. Power, we had to face the fact that the majority of places we found we were lacking, were in the emotional connection with the customer," Jones says. During the same period, Grand produced only a 64 percent satisfaction rating on Eliant surveys covering courtesy, trust, communication, and looking out for the homebuyer's best interest, hardly a worthy result.

CEO Stephen H. Brooks didn't find it acceptable either. He hired a customer experience director and champions for each of the company's four divisions, and kicked off a contest in September 2006 that offered this challenge: Score 90 percent or better on overall customer satisfaction and you'll get a bonus. He had Jones and her colleagues trained through Eliant's programs. Jones began to see results and, of the four divisions, hers produced the highest satisfaction scores. But the downturn prompted challenges, and by April 2007, the director and CEC positions were eliminated in a downsizing that reduced total employees from 360 to 270. Jones, however, was promoted to corporate customer experience champion.

"I work with the divisions, the departments, corporate, and executive management — I have my hand in every cookie jar," she says. Jones works closely with key people within each division disseminating information and exciting employees about the role they play in producing the customer experience while delivering 650 homes each year.

The initial challenge improved the company's overall satisfaction rate. More recently, a year after Brooks' initial challenge and after months of effort by Jones, it saw overall satisfaction scores rise to 83 percent. The CEC says she was able to do this by helping her teams concentrate on the weakest points in the J.D. Power survey: on-time delivery, jobsite cleanliness, and proactive homeowner communication. One division vice president didn't immediately buy in and remained at 64 percent in overall satisfaction, but after flat numbers for six months, he had an epiphany, and finished at 87 percent. At last check, he was leading the company at 91 percent. "He does not want to lose," Jones says.

Jones worked with management to develop a structured bonus off of its Eliant surveys' "would you recommend?" question. Individual goals were based on how construction communicated with the homeowner on project progress. The program later evolved into a team approach based on an entire community's satisfaction scores. "We hold the people who work in the community responsible for creating peer accountability," Jones says. Communities compete against each other.

But corporate incentives aren't all that motivate them. Employees in lower-performing communities see others receiving bonuses, and understand what's possible, Jones says. Much has been done to boost morale, including get-togethers like chili cook-offs and have-fun-at-work days that create a tightly-knit workforce — all created by a culture committee that plans in-house events. After an internal survey revealed employee dissatisfaction, staff was given more vacation days, more holidays, and a lower threshold to enter the 401(k) plan, among other benefits. "It's gratifying to see people come together and be happier," Jones says.

MBK's Kane says that while it's difficult to measure customer satisfaction on a balance sheet, and accounting sees customer satisfaction as an expense, he believes that to win results, a widespread culture change is the only solution. He believes that tying satisfaction scores to incentives is a two-edged sword — are you paying for higher satisfaction or better scores? So MBK doesn't pay score-based incentives, but many companies do, or pay a portion of their employee rewards based on scores. I'll examine the advantages and pitfalls of these programs in Chapter 6.

Meanwhile, at Grand Homes, each community has a leader trained in improving the experience, and builder, sales, and warranty service reps make up each team. Jones says the group leader is the most influential role model. She works with them on how to handle customer conversations and how to praise employees. She develops required

WHEN THE BEST IS THE WORST

LOVE STORY

Help your most skilled workers align their attitudes with their abilities.

A client of mine, selling 500 homes a year, had its processes down cold. They were learning how to handle customer concerns and were teaching their trades to do the same. The company sought a stronger mindset and attitude of cooperation to anticipate construction challenges.

They hired me to meet with one of their top superintendents — let's call him Bobby. He was a big bear of a man. Sarcasm was his sharpest tool. Even though he built his company's best quality homes, he had more customer complaints than any other builder. When customers complain over and over about something, you know they're telling the truth.

Bobby saw customers as obstacles in his path, instead of *the* path. When I first started talking to him, he couldn't fathom why he was being counseled. He was the lead superintendent, the *best*. He rarely had cost overruns.

If your superintendent needs this, you're in trouble.

touchpoints, and scripts the *who- what why-how* of each conversation. The team uses a spreadsheet Jones developed to help them fulfill their touchpoint obligations to homeowners. It takes them from the contract signing through the first year of home ownership and beyond. Trigger dates change colors when actions need completion. The team receives reminders before tasks are due.

Jones reviews reports weekly with community leaders to provide accountability. The accountability piece is critical, she says. Yet, when there's a glitch, everyone thinks they're the exception to the rule.

What makes it gel, Jones says, is that she works at the right hand of the CEO and her regional manager. President Joe Vastano, hired by the company from David Weekley Homes, backs her accountability, too. "The buy-in from him is in his blood," she says. She meets daily with management to review problems. If she has to "call people on the carpet," she does it herself, or through the CEO or division managers. There's a written system for disciplinary action: If someone doesn't perform to standards, then there's a trial period followed by termination.

CEO Brooks is investing in training modules on customer satisfaction that Jones holds routinely. Brooks knows his company could never be all about the customer unless it is all about employees, first.

His scheduling was impeccable. His work was technically correct. *He was breaking production records.*

The problem was Bobby's attitude and responses. Even though this was a difficult conversation to have, I had to lay it out, directly and distinctly: *Bobby, you've been here 19 years and you're about to lose your job if you don't lose the attitude. Your manager said he's going to give you one last chance. Unless something changes dramatically and quickly, you're no longer going to be part of the team.* Bobby literally saw things in black and white. Besides being sarcastic, he could be callous. When asked about the air conditioning, he'd say: *I'm not an AC expert, are you?* Or, *If you don't like the way I'm running the job perhaps you shouldn't have bought a home from us.*

The chewed-up pencil in your superintendent's ear falls into the 5 percent category — we complete 95 percent of the job well, but it's the little things wrapped up in the last 5 percent that make buyers go off their rockers.

While he saw everything in black-and-white, most customer issues are in the gray area. He followed policy to the letter of the law, instead of working within guidelines. I had to help him see those inconsistencies. I told him that we can't demand anything of the customers. We need to ask and share things. He countered that a client can call with a "horrible emergency" and when he goes out to see it, it isn't an emergency at all. *Well, it was to them.* I told him that he made too many snap

START AT THE TOP

As you can see, trust starts with a passion for the customer at the top. As a speaker and consultant, I see this everywhere I go. It has to be known from the CEO down: *The customer matters.* Bill Frey, vice president of customer care at John Laing Homes, tells me that when Eliant delivers their automated customer satisfaction results at 2 a.m. on the 10th of the month, CEO Larry Webb is at his home computer, analyzing them. Why does the CEO of a $1.6 billion company do this? Other company executives also interrupt a good night's sleep, at 4 or 5 a.m., to check the latest surveys. Clearly this organization doesn't want to lose *more* sleep than it has to over customer care. The passion starts at the top. It's interesting to note that Webb used to be a soccer coach, and he uses a distinctive coaching philosophy to motivate his company to lead the industry in client satisfaction.

Culture and leadership also make it work at M/I Homes, says M/I's John Kluba. "They personally believe in it and have shown they're willing to take on the associated costs to make it happen." As a champion, he doesn't have direct contact with customers, just like a coach doesn't have direct contact with the spectators. But what he does in "practice" helps frontline employees entertain and excite homeowners. "The homeowners aren't our competition.

decisions, instead of thinking first and acting later. *Frankly, Bobby, you're a poor listener.*

As I talked with him, a curtain came down behind his eyes. *It's happening right now, I said, you're doing it. You're shutting me off.* I gave him examples of better words he could use, how he could be cooperative instead of demanding, and how he could have a solicitous manner, instead of an insistent one. I suggested he lose the chewed-up pencil tucked behind his ear that he often handed to clients when he needed them to sign paperwork. *Clients are accommodating, but why would they want to touch a pencil that had been in your mouth and tucked behind your ear over and over again?*

Bobby also realized he could joke around with very few customers. It's good to be happy-go-lucky, but you have to be careful. You have to get to know customers before you launch into that vein. You have to find out how people like to communicate, and then communicate with them in that style. If you're serious, you can't go wrong, because spending their money is serious business.

Bobby took my message seriously. *He changed.* You might not think so, but that chewed-up pencil falls into that last 5 percent of things that we fail to do well, when we do 95 percent right. As does the questionable bumper sticker on your plumber's truck, parked in front of your client's new home: What do those poorly-chosen words say to *your* customer?

They are the crowd watching the team play." And in the end, he says, the team models its coach's behavior.

Pulte Homes, which, like other builders, underwent a massive re-organization on the turn of the market, moving from 14,000 employees to about half that many, has had to rely on the strength of its leadership to motivate and instill pride, because more traditional incentives have been curtailed, says Peter J. Keane, senior vice president of operations. "Our hope, and what we've seen, is that our employee retention rates remain strong," he says, "because employees want to work for a company that feels it is doing right by the customer."

Keane says the "pride factor" keeps employees engaged, and Pulte always tries to celebrate success in relation to its goals. The company gives its divisions platinum, gold, and silver awards based on the customer satisfaction scores compiled by Morpace Inc., of Farmington Hills, Mich. In the past, Pulte provided their customer relations employees with compensation incentives for outstanding monthly customer relations scores. "There's never been a 'pay-for-the-score' in that incentive," Keane says. "It's more of a rallying cry for the team." Part of Pulte employees' bonuses correlate with how well their communities score on internal satisfaction surveys. Employees strive for a consistent delivery process to reach the end goal of repeat-and-referral business, rather than simply achieving scores.

If your company culture is ingrained and customer-centric, it permeates everything you do. It's a chromosome you have and you can't remove it. If it's not there, it's apparent. Yet, it's subtle, driving behaviors.

The reason, Benshoof says, that Destination Homes of Layton, Utah has come so far so fast — from 30 to 250 homes in a few years, is because President and CEO Brad Wilson, a former American Express executive, understands the importance of training employees to delight customers through their experience. As builders or remodelers who live and die by customer satisfaction show — John Laing Homes, Shea Homes, Pulte Homes, and smaller companies like FCB Homes and Riggs Construction & Design — it takes a leader to create trust in the workplace, to allow it to live and grow, to foster training initiatives to refine it, and monitor the ways it's effective for customers. This includes trade partners, who, for some builders, are indispensible.

Kane of MBK notes that in the Western world, *to serve* has a different meaning than in the Eastern world, where serving is an honorable endeavor. He's right, American building companies and their leaders don't realize that superior customer service is an attitude of service that starts at the top. It's a compelling desire to be different by serving at every level of the company.

GROW AT THE ROOTS

So how does this culture of service filter through every department? Much of it has to do with giving people authority and rewarding their initiative.

A corporate and customer experience manager in the northwest shared the story of a company receptionist who had a natural gift, besides just her way with people: She knew how to arrange flowers, beautifully. She voluntarily put her own fresh-cut bouquets in the company lobby. It wasn't long before the company, after publicly recognizing her, took on the expense of providing the flowers. We need to appreciate employees like this thoughtful woman.

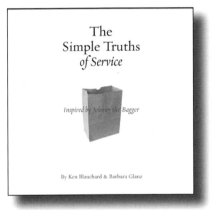

The
Simple Truths
of Service

Inspired by Johnny the Bagger

By Ken Blanchard & Barbara Glanz

For more insight into where I'm heading with these ideas, visit www.barbaraglanz.com/johnny for the beautiful story of "Johnny The Bagger™," a grocery store clerk with Down syndrome. Johnny was made famous by speaker and author Barbara Glanz, who with Ken Blanchard shares his story in their book, *The Simple Truths of Service*.

Without cost, this young man changed the culture of his grocery store by giving customers more than they expected, and proving that everyone — everyone — in your organization can make a difference and create memories and experiences, enough to motivate customers to come back.

After hearing Glanz speak, Johnny told her in a note that he liked what she said but didn't think he could do anything special for customers, adding, "After all, I'm just a bagger." Then he had an idea. Every night after work he'd come home and find a "Thought for the Day." If he couldn't find one, he'd make one up. When he had a good one, his dad helped him make copies off the computer. He cut out each quote and signed his name on the back and brought them to work the next day. When he finished bagging, he put his thought in the bag.

A month later, the store manager called Glanz, saying, "You won't believe what happened. When I was making my rounds today, I found Johnny's checkout line was three times longer than anyone else's." But when he tried to get people to slide over into new lanes with new cashiers, no one would move. They said, "It's OK, we want to be in Johnny's lane — we want his 'Thought for the Day.'"

One woman told the manager that she used to shop at the store once a week, "But now I come in every time I go by." A few months later, the store manager called again ... "Johnny has transformed our store. Now when the floral department has a broken flower or unused corsage, they find an elderly woman or little girl and pin it on them. Everyone's having a lot of fun creating memories. Our customers are talking about us ... they're coming back and bringing their friends."

Johnny's spirit of service spread, not because of any major company initiative, or program, but because Johnny, the bagger, chose to make a difference. What a simple addition, from his heart. Great service comes from the heart, but we need to give our employees the authority to help us build cultures to inspire the innate desire of people to make customer experiences extraordinary. [†]

So what's the lesson here? How many potential Johnnies do you have on your team? And what are you doing to nurture them?

"It's not trying to force someone to be someone they're not," says Tom Riggs, of Riggs Construction & Design of Kirkwood, Mo. "It's understanding the importance of the client and the client's happiness." He told his 20 employees that he had withdrawn $600 from the bank in $50 bills, and one of them would receive a fifty every time he said "Wow," about something extraordinary that they had done.

One project manager, when he learned the owners of the home he was remodeling couldn't decide where to put the dining room table and light, cut plywood to the size of a table and set it on sawhorses with two candles and chairs from the kitchen. He positioned a droplight where the fixture would go and it helped the client make their decision. "Wow," Riggs said when he heard the story — and gave his PM a fifty.

Another time, Riggs received calls from two homeowners, raving about how clean the neighboring Riggs jobsite was, and how, if every builder could keep their sites that clean, there'd never be a problem with infill construction. "Wow," Riggs said, and dispensed another $50. But then, that project manager turned around and gave the $50 to the laborer who really made it happen.

[†] © Barbara Glanz Communications, Inc. 2006. All Rights Reserved. Reprinted with permission from *CARE Packages for the Workplace—Dozens of Little Things You Can Do to Regenerate Spirit at Work* (McGraw-Hill 1996) and *The Simple Truths of Service* (Simple Truths 2005); www.barbaraglanz.com.

That's when you know you have a working culture of service. And that's when it's working top to bottom, side-to-side, and inside out.

Your frontline is going to see your service gaps. Your teams need to buy into the changes and see the benefits, not just for the customer and the company, but for their own position. When people contribute, they participate. They get fired up. I recall the story of a construction manager who took over a community from a superintendent whose service was less than exemplary. At that time, it was taboo for construction mangers to communicate directly with homeowners. Sales was the primary contact until the close of escrow, when customer service took over the relationship. But this CM wanted to connect with the customers. He inherited abysmal community satisfaction scores and wanted to find a way to invigorate his homeowners. He started popping in on customers during contract appointments and they enjoyed meeting their builder. On the jobsite, if they came by, he'd grab a hardhat for them, and take time to chat. His satisfaction scores rocketed from 60 percent to 90 percent. He helped his company grow, at its roots, because he *cared*.

BELIEVE IN EACH OTHER

But it's more than an individual initiative; it's the team believing in each other, trusting each other.

If management believes in this stuff and is fanatical about it, you can't help but catch the disease. You'll catch the virus of care and constantly spread it. It will infect every person on the team, and the team is only as good as the individual players. You can develop this by job rotation, or cross training — letting everyone experience other jobs for a day, or by developing process flow charts that show all the steps in the delivery of a home and all the people who touch the process. If they're living in just their own little world, they'll never know how important their part is. Receptionists have to understand how their phone demeanor — or their carefully arranged flowers — affects everyone's day.

Teamwork can be a challenge at any company. The processes and desires of the sales and construction teams often clash, but your customer experience champions can help them see each other's perspective. Part of the problem is a lack of communication, and their conversations are more operational than strategic and proactive. Help them understand that they need to communicate answers to these questions: *What are the buyer's hot buttons? What does sales need to know to prepare their presentations? What does customer service need to know about that buyer and what they didn't like about the process?*

After a market shift, your team will be leaner and focused on their workload. Executives will want salespeople to sell and close as soon as possible. But because there is a smaller workforce, the resources to clean and prepare a home for a walk-through, based on the adjustments identified during the orientation, might not be as readily available as they were before. So your construction manager has to have every confidence in the sales team that it is not setting unrealistic closing dates and inflating buyer expectations. The manager must know that sales understands construction is pulled thin and doesn't want the customer relationship damaged by a missed clean-and-prepare date. If priorities change and the buyer pushes the close-of-escrow back, the two departments have to be in constant communication. These situations can improve the relationship and their trust in each other. Your construction manager will know the sales consultant isn't going to "stick it to him," and, they're not going to get stuck.

Creating a team that believes in each other might require other tactics, as well.

Petruska says that some years ago, Pulte Homes launched a diversity program to create an environment of inclusion. "So, no matter what it says on your business card, or your rank in the organization, you'll feel like you're at a place where you belong," he says. Research shows, he notes, that people become engaged when they are *included*. Buzzwords at Pulte include *discretionary effort*. "We choose how hard we work," Petruska says. "No one controls our productivity, other than us. If people feel included, have input, and are appreciated, their desire to give discretionary effort is exponentially higher than if they are unengaged."

That's why it's so difficult to measure individual productivity. If we work together, support and nurture our people, we'll learn to believe in each other — and we'll grow.

ALLOW A TEAM VISION & MISSION

Belief in each other starts with vision and mission statements developed not just by management, but by the entire organization. I've heard it said that companies whose employees, suppliers, and trades understand the company's mission and goals enjoy a 29 percent greater return than other companies.

It takes more than rewards or monetary incentive to achieve that. When I was at Texas Instruments, we had productivity improvement programs. There was a suggestion box for people to turn in suggestions and every suggestion was carefully considered. You didn't have to hold a certain status or position for an idea to be implemented. If it was worthy, it flew. It was an organic way of incentivizing, with no monetary reward attached. It made you feel good, and therefore everyone was always thinking about improvement. A lot of people got on that bandwagon, even the woman who soldered one wire on a circuit board all day long.

When we have strategic planning sessions in good companies, they often don't include everyone on staff, only upper management. Why is that? That's not where the best ideas come from. Even the cleanup crew guys have plenty of ideas. They see everything, from the ground up. But if they've never been groomed or solicited, their *job* is all they do. They keep their mouths shut.

There are three definitions of quality service — the company's, the employee's, and the customer's. Rarely are all three the same. The only way to find out is to ask customers and employees what they consider quality service to be. And then, write it down, say it out loud, study it, re-work it, and check it to determine whether it depicts your understanding and feelings. Then, make sure you can deliver what you attest.

Guts To Love

Customer Care Isn't Intuitive

BY CAROL SMITH

Through assessment, employee involvement, and genuine respect for customers, you can create satisfying care connections with your homebuyers.

My new client was shocked when they discovered that their homeowner satisfaction ratings were in the low 60th percentile. Searching for answers to explain why customers weren't more favorably impressed, even though they built great homes, prompted their decision to hire me to conduct an assessment.

For these assessments, I usually spend a week visiting the homebuilder's communities, observing their employees' interactions with buyers, and interviewing personnel, from the front line to office staff. To prepare for my visit, the builder forwards copies of everything the homebuyer sees and reads, from sales brochures to warranty documents. In reviewing these materials, I often find opportunities for improvement. That happened in this case, and my on-site visits confirmed my preliminary conclusions.

In the assessment report, I outlined several steps to improve homeowner satisfaction: Develop and master the use of a well-written homeowner guide; plan and conduct meetings with homebuyers throughout the process; and then, train and coach personnel in how to cover these basics in a

A CEC tells me her company never saw the gorilla in the room, never totally focused on the customer and found discrepancies in what employees thought they were doing for the customer and in what executives thought everyone was doing as a company. An internal employee survey revealed this disconnect. Employees learned satisfaction scores weren't consistent with how they thought they were carrying out operational responsibilities. They also scored low on the survey question: *Does my immediate manager demonstrate a strong customer focus?* The survey showed that everyone could do more to please customers. Employee training followed that helped define the customer experience. As they better defined the experience, they also tracked satisfaction results, compared communities within the company, compared their scores with peer companies, and shared community results with the team. They saw the truth in the adage: *Whatever is measured is improved.*

Whatever is worth measuring becomes part of your vision and mission.

The best service philosophies are the shortest and simplest. Carol Smith suggests: *We promise to deliver to the customer 100 percent of what we promise, on time, in good condition, and with a smile.* Not complicated, but extremely powerful. What could you do to kick that up a notch?

Remember, quality workmanship and products are simply your cost

hospitable and professional manner. The company's response was gratifying. Executives immediately set up two task forces with representatives from each department — sales, production, warranty, administrative, etc. We worked together to outline agendas for each task force. One group developed the homeowner guide. The second defined an appropriate homebuyer meeting schedule for each product line: single-family and townhome.

Climbing from 60 to 90 percent in satisfaction rankings takes a team effort.

After two day's effort — one with each task force — I was convinced they understood their tasks. Their enthusiasm and commitment was apparent. Between meetings, each task force discussed key points and gathered ideas from their respective departments — effectively providing the entire staff with opportunities to make suggestions. Their sincere respect for customers combined with the pride they took in their company quickly translated into a simple but effective system for working closely and more effectively with homebuyers. The group preparing the homeowner guide had a multitude of materials that needed to be gathered and reviewed. It made their job seem monumental. Dividing the materials by phases broke the project into more manageable chunks. Progress was slow but after a few hours, the group developed a system and momentum increased. One person compiled final decisions, often making note of specific wording for the final homeowner guide.

of entry into the marketplace. You must go beyond this threshold. Once you've defined your service philosophy, determine who in the company needs to know about it. How will you get the word out? How will you test throughout the organization for understanding and buy-in? Even the greatest philosophies die unless the entire team buys in. And don't forget your trade alliances and partners.

Your training program has to educate from the start and reinforce the message of your vision and mission throughout the tenure of the employee. Training requires commitment, manpower, budget, and time. It has to be a part of the company culture and part of your strategic plan. Great performance doesn't just happen, even at the top, or even with those who are most educated.

Start with what you want your culture to be and how to get there. It has to be woven into your strategy throughout your process. It has to be deeper than *we build 2,000 units a year and this is how we build them*. It has to be more like: *These are the type of people we hire, and this is our hiring, recruiting, and training strategy to get them on board with our culture, to delight the customer every time they encounter them.*

We have to be aware of what's important, and we have to develop a plan of action to address every need. What is your hiring and recruiting practice? What results have you achieved so far? If you're not getting

At the end of the day, we planned the next four meetings, three hours each, a week apart. The homework assignment between sessions would be for each task force members to read the next batch of customer literature and mark it with their suggestions or questions.

Meanwhile, the meetings task force debated how many meetings to recommend. Should single-family and townhome communities host exactly the same meetings? Was a frame tour necessary in a townhome community? Could group tours be offered to save staff time and give buyers an opportunity to meet future neighbors? How should they proceed with (typically out-of-state) buyers who were unable to attend these meetings?

These and many other issues were analyzed. At first, it seemed everyone had differing viewpoints, but they kept returning to the fundamental goal: increasing homeowner satisfaction. That goal anchored their thinking. Again, progress began slowly, but momentum increased as the group established a systematic way of debating points and arriving at a conclusion. Occasionally, they sought direction from upper management. Their scribe furiously recorded the ideas, prepared minutes, and circulated them to the group the next business day.

Again, at the end of the day we scheduled the sessions the task force estimated were needed to complete its tasks. Their homework assignment was to interview everyone involved in each one of these proposed meetings for ideas and cautions. The task force chairmen would share insights and the right results to improve customer care, experience, and trust, where are the clogs in the system?

If people are our greatest asset, why do we spend so little time on this part of our business? Everything you do depends on the early steps. The end results are only as good as what you put into the beginning. Do you test your employees for their attitudes, values, skills? Do you ask behavioral questions or just general ones? Behavioral questions will give you insight into how people react. Are your candidates telling you they can please only one person a day? How can you recognize that?

Is your corporate culture people-oriented or skill-oriented? We need to be both. You're looking for people who can create an *experience*, not those who say *that's not in my job description.* Remember "Johnny the Bagger™." The person with a service attitude says: *I'm not sure who's responsible for that, **but I can find out.***

Is your service process fun and enjoyable for the customer? If not, why are you doing it the way you are, after all, they're the ones paying the bills.

COVER THE BASICS

Perhaps you are beginning to understand why as much as 37 percent of the value customers receive comes from the people with whom they do business. Your people are your point of differentiation. Your employees are your company. Your competition

conclusions; they'd copy each other on all materials that were developed.

I returned to my office confident this group was on its way and that great things awaited them. The work took roughly three months. Once new homeowner materials were complete, we held training sessions to increase the comfort level among all the personnel involved in the new service initiatives. The sessions also helped them understand the strategies behind the initiatives. Support staff — from purchasing to accounting — most had never spoken to a homebuyer — joined us for the training to ensure complete alignment throughout the organization. Our educational training took on an aura of celebration. We recognized members of each task force and introduced the results of their efforts. We planned follow-up coaching sessions to reinforce new concepts and techniques. The task force volunteered to do this; members wanted the new tools to succeed and they wanted to discover any missed details for future system improvements.

The anticipation and excitement was almost tangible. A few skeptics withheld their approval, laying the groundwork for a later, "I told you so." I advised them to wait and watch.

Within six months, the low 60th percentile ratings climbed to the high 80s. Within a year, they were over 90 percent, and still climbing. Today, they're first in the J.D. Power and Associates rankings for their region. They've held that spot for several years. The secret was simple: Educate and communicate in a hospitable tone, but mostly, act as if you like your customers.

can copy your designs, improve on your processes, undercut your prices, and perhaps even match your quality. *What they can't replicate are the attitudes of your people.*

We work in an industry where our assembly line is an open forum. "The homebuilding industry is one of the only industries where the consumer has the ability to walk the assembly line each and every step of the way," says Todd Booth of Prestige Homes of San Antonio. "They can inspect the assembly of their purchase at each and every stage."

It's critical to have people working for us who can withstand tight scrutiny. *As far as builder credibility goes, every negative is believed and every positive must be proven.* Sorry, but that's the nature of this business and the heritage we've created for ourselves. Know then, that your people can decimate the balance in your trust bank account with:

+ **Indifference.**
+ **Over-promising.**
+ **Avoiding the truth.**
+ **Not listening.**
+ **Not following through.**
+ **Delivering a poor quality product.**
+ **Being disorderly** — *either in personal habits, on the jobsite, or in the office.*

We build the mightiest walls with language. Do we tell customers *what they have to do?* Do we use phrases that contain the words: *That's company policy?* Do we use phrases that blame or make assumptions? All of these build walls keeping out trust. Service is a *feeling* and an *attitude*, not a set of rules. So instead of saying NO, your people need to try saying, as Carol Smith suggests, "What *we can do* for you is …" or *"your options* include …" or, "may *I suggest …."*

The biggest trust builder is skillful communication. Good communication doesn't just happen. Remember how we learn: 55 percent from how we look when we speak; 38 percent from our tone as we speak; and just 7 percent from the words themselves. So just by looking at you and hearing you speak (not necessarily what you say), I'll determine more than enough for me to even continue our conversation. Verbal communication goes right to the heart of trust. "The real art of conversation is not only to say the right thing in the right place, but to leave unsaid the wrong thing at the tempting moment," wrote Benjamin Franklin. So many times, it's better to keep our mouths shut, no?

Put your employees in charge of communications and have them communicate well. List the top 10 disputes you regularly face and see what answers you

can come up with to resolve the situations. Nearly 95 percent of the problems we have with customers are communication related. We're not building a shoddy product, it's that we're not covering the basics. I need to make this point again because the entire framework rests on basics. Technology is a wonderful tool, but it doesn't replace human interaction. For instance, customers hate voicemail — they can't talk to anyone and can only leave a message. They want an *answer*. And they want that answer by the end of the day. And does *end of the day* mean 3 p.m.? 5 p.m.? Or, late at night? It becomes *that* intricate.

Why do you think John Laing Homes has a 15-minute response time, across the board? If any customer calls with a complaint, the employee must respond in 15 minutes, by phone or to the front door. If you're in a meeting or with another customer, your coordinator or secretary responds. And, further, you are required to meet and go over the request within 24 hours.

What peace of mind! John Laing raised the bar — *over 10 years ago*. Can you afford to promise your customer anything less?

Other basics that build trust include:

- **Proper Dress.** Yes, it's *this* basic. How you look affects your communication effectiveness with clients.
- **Etiquette.** This goes beyond manners. How do we behave in front of customers? I can't tell you how many of my clients have asked me: *Can you just show our employees how to improve their behavior?*
- **Personal Organization.** If my home folder is on the dashboard of your truck, in a big pile, I'm concerned about that as a customer. If you take notes on a piece of drywall, that affects my trust. How we present our organizational skills to a customer is very important.

- **Time Management.** Do you organize what you say? Do you value my time as a customer? If you value my time, you'll be organized whenever we meet.
- **Body Language.** Watch your stance! Observe your expressions. Listen to your voice. Pay attention to your appearance. Smile! Maintain good eye contact. Gesture appropriately. Look in the mirror for practice. It's this simple, really.
- **Conflict Resolution.** People stop doing business with companies because of breakdowns in communication — not because of price or quality. Do you hear, *no one ever does what they say they're going to do?* Or do you say, *I got it, I got it, no problem, it's taken care of,* and then don't write it down? The customer is thinking, *Yeah, I'll bet you do. You've got 10 jobsites and mine is the first stop. What happens when you get back to the office at 4 p.m.?*

Most conflicts have to do with listening skills, and as an industry, we've been poor listeners. Why? *We're usually too busy talking.*

THE MARKET REFINES THE EXPERIENCE

Fine-tuned customer service, accentuated in a down economy, will weed out the weakest companies, predicts Benshoof, of SMA Consulting. "If you're a company that can't survive 12 to 24 months in a bad market, you're probably not going to survive anyway. Service is a systemic issue. Look at David Weekley Homes — it grew during a downturn. NVR grew during a downturn. This was in the late 1980s, early 1990s."

I predict we're going to see the same things happen over the next five years. The best of the best are going to pull ahead and gain market share.

NVR Inc., the parent of Ryan Homes, among other companies, and David Weekley Homes, are still using the market shifts to their advantage. It's probably no coincidence that Weekley was one of the first to measure key performance markers throughout the company.

David Weekley Homes is still doing this. During the 2007 downturn, they hired two senior managers to start building attached townhomes in its active markets. The first attached homes will be built in Dallas. Other markets might include Denver; Raleigh, N.C.; and Hilton Head, S.C.

Benshoof says companies like Weekley and NVR take advantage of shifts in market pace and get better and better. "They developed better systems, got their people better trained, and made sure they had the right people on the bus. When the market is soft, it's time to grab good employees. In good markets, companies get complacent with their employees. They were getting away with murder. They were doing the job but in tough times you have to have 'A' players.

"Production and custom builders say the public companies have an advantage — they have the cash, and the land positions. And yes, look at the 10-Ks and you'll see Toll Brothers has cash reserves that will last seven years. But the real advantage they have is their HR department. They hire better, do personality profiles, and teach their managers to hire better people. Those better people still have to be trained and trained again."

One CEC I know recalls the day her company had 152 people on a priority waiting list for a home in one of its communities. But times change, and through training, employees saw that they could still make a difference, even if there were no waiting lists. "We see how the construction manager builds people's dreams and how salespeople can build a level of trust with a customer even if they've never built a home before," she told me. "The support we provide can make it so much easier."

"Builders have taken a long time to understand the customer service revolution, but finally that revolution is bleeding in, in a good way, from other business sectors," she adds. "We've taken longer to catch up, but changes in the market are forcing our hand, making it a requirement as opposed to a 'nice to have', just to differentiate yourself."

Bleeding in is an interesting analogy. Because to those who don't understand the service culture and how to win business when others aren't, the past year or so has felt like a lot of bleeding.

CLOSE YOUR EYES

There's no question that trust takes years to develop. But to be a company for the future, to get in the game, trust is critical. As author Harry Beckwith of *Selling the Invisible* wrote: *Quality and service gets you into the game. The relationship **wins** the game.*

My sense is that if you step back and consider what happened in the 1980s with warranty service, and compare it to what is happening now with customer service, or customer experience, we will soon see parallels. In the 1980s, no one cared about warranties. Then, homeowners sued big builders for major issues affecting the integrity of their homes. Then, everyone got on the bandwagon. Who would think *not* to have a warranty program today?

Don't you see the same thing happening, prompted by the economy and the buyer, who can now say: *The heck with you, you're not treating me right, or providing what I need — I'll go somewhere else.* Don't you think that this consumer awakening is going to prompt the same sort of changes in customer experience that we saw with warranty experience in the 1980s?

You bet.

How long can the consumer go on expecting to be treated like a doormat?

There will always be winners and losers in the housing market. People will either close their eyes and give up, or close their eyes and trust their greatest asset next to their referring customers: *Their very own people.*

"The winners will be the smart operators," says Staky, of John Laing Homes. "The people who create a great experience for their customers. Those are the organizations that are curious, measure what they do, have the data, and know what to do with it. They'll put it to use when things are slow, to become more focused on getting better results."

And better results to Staky mean better relationships, more referrals, and more — well, I'll let him say it this time ...

"*You've got to put yourself out there, take a risk, **stretch** yourself. And that's a lot like love.*"

LOVE ✓ CHECK

Don't Bust The Trust

How do you avoid busting the trust and encourage an open, trusting workplace? Open a "trust bank account" with employees to build their confidence.

✔ Get Off Autopilot

Employees have to understand their role in building trust. They have to think "people," not "product." Their communication skills directly relate to the trust the client feels in them. This isn't just a way of thinking, but how they convey thoughts and attitudes. So many times, we're *unconsciously incompetent*. Body language, looking at the ground, smirking, wearing an offensive T-shirt, smoking a cigarette, stamping out a cigarette on site — these directly affect the customer's experience. Perhaps, no one has brought these things to your employee's attention. We don't know what we don't know. We need to get off autopilot and do the right things unconsciously.

✔ Build A Trust Team

How does each employee's actions affect team members? Does everyone have true, human respect for each other? Do they value all abilities and contributions? Everyone has to believe they're on the right team with the best people. If they don't, this conveys, unconsciously, to customers. If sales reps don't believe what they're offering is worth the price, they can't sell. If employees have good relationships, they're protective, and sensitive to their affect on other people. They talk to each other, and not just when they're forced to. They're looking for opportunities to elevate their team, and are willing to share credit. When you can hand a fifty dollar bill to a project manager or superintendent as a reward for a neighbor's comment on their clean jobsite and that project manager gives the $50 to his laborer who made it happen, you'll know you've achieved your goal.

✔ Appreciate & Grow

Too often management only interacts with employees when it has something bad to share. But it's important to have everyone connected continually — good or bad. Does your sales staff periodically drop by jobsites to deliver donuts and coffee or ice tea on a hot summer day? I know of a production manager who walked into a company owner's office one day and told him — out of the blue — how much he appreciated his job. The guy almost fell out of his chair. We don't do enough of that. These connections form personal relationships, and those important personal relationships create long-term trust. That's why so many marriages fail — the courtship ends. We get so busy doing business that we forget to be human. Every person, regardless of how unemotional, needs appreciation. Yet we're not taught to appreciate. It extends to our clients. We thank customers once if it's on a flow chart and we have to do it. Was it because we forgot our internal customer, our employee? Your external service is only as good as your internal service.

✔ Invite Innovation

Do we respect everyone's contribution? If we understand how important our role is within a process, it is an awesome experience. We can't get lost in the team. Daily, we have to make each employee aware of his or her contribution. I recall a story of a Disney maintenance employee, riding around in a golf cart, picking up trash on the ground by stabbing it with a sharp stick. "What are you doing today?" he was asked. "I'm selling Disney," he replied. He knew his role in the larger picture — he was a salesman for Disney because he was cleaning the grounds. He wasn't a groundskeeper, he was a sales professional. Everything he did affected how Disney sold its experience. The same holds true for your employees. So don't just appreciate them, give them ways to improve your systems. People have incredible talents, and we, as employers, often never tap into them. If we're given a role, we tend to stay within those parameters. If you say I'm part of the cleaning crew, what role will I play in manufacturing or sales? Probably none … and yet I could have insight on the next best thing.

✔ Provide Tools For Trust

Make it possible for employees to live up to your expectations. Provide the environment to prosper, regardless of economic conditions. Can you imagine being in the shoes of the superintendent who deals with your trades after — based on economic conditions — you automatically discount what you pay them? If you're cutting your employees' ability to get their job done well, not allowing them to prosper, they can't function. Tell your superintendent the price of gas shot up, but you're going to cut his gas allowance, and assign him three more jobs. How can he do it? He has to cut corners. If we want to make sure finishes are meticulous, but we cut his budget, and if the painter can't apply three coats and touch-up, who's going to suffer? There have to be safeguards so that regardless of economic times, certain items will not be cut. How many chief executives' salaries are frozen or cut during tough times? Very few, I imagine. Yet, the day-to-day is more dependent on the jobs in the field than the guy in the ivory tower. Some companies have such a culture, and when they hit turbulent times, they pull people together, and the front line people say, "we should take a temporary salary cut." We have to get away from: "If you want to work here, you'll do it our way." That's OK if don't want a good customer referral program. Unhappy employees will refer unhappy customers.

✔ Trust From Day One

Honesty and trust are built from the hire. You need to share your culture and how you operate as a company from the interviewing process, and it has to be continued throughout the life of the relationship. Employees can't be thrown into the fire only to realize the company is nothing like they expected. They can't hear, "I know we said we'd give you a bonus, but times change and we can't do that now." They can't hear, "you had full control on the job, but you don't now." If in the interview you paint rosy pictures that don't exist, there's no opportunity for trust. It's just like with your customers. If you say you'll call by 5 p.m., you have to call by five. Every inconsistency chips away at the trust. "We have an open door policy here," yet every time you walk by the door it's closed. "Every Monday morning, we have a sales meeting and 75 percent of the meeting is dedicated to training." But, now, you learn that 75 percent of the meeting is a gripe session, and little time is left for training. How does that build trust?

✔ Define Trust

You have to be able to define your customer philosophy and how it filters down to everyone in the organization. Put it in easy language for everyone to understand. It goes back to expectations — if you know the parameters, it's easier to live up to them and understand when you don't meet expectations. "Our philosophy is to provide excellent service." Well, what philosophy is that? Everyone says that. What makes you special? How is everyone able to make you special as a company? How could someone who takes public transportation to the jobsite be doing something special when everyone else has their own car? How do you build up *every* person on staff? There are great people beneath the wings of your companies, but no one sees them — it's not just your trades and people in the field, it's your escrow officer sitting at the back of the office. And you've got to be listening to these people, too. If you never put metrics to trust, how do you know you've got trust in place? Survey your people, your internal customers.

✔ Give Trust, Get Trust

Give your people the authority to say no, especially your front line and sales people; let them tell you this isn't your customer. Regardless of how badly you need a contract, you can't sign someone who's not a fit. If I trust my people to tell me this isn't the right customer fit, they know it's their responsibility to tell me it's a bad deal. This authority goes to hiring, too. Prospective employees need to be interviewed by more than management. They need to be interviewed by co-workers, and we need to listen to their opinions. The person working with me every day needs to have input into the hiring decision. In most cases, after orientation, you might never see the hiring manager again. If you've hired the right person and provided the training to grow in that position, you need to trust them to grow, but you need to give them authority before they can be held accountable.

© 1999 Ted Goff

"The customer you don't like is here."

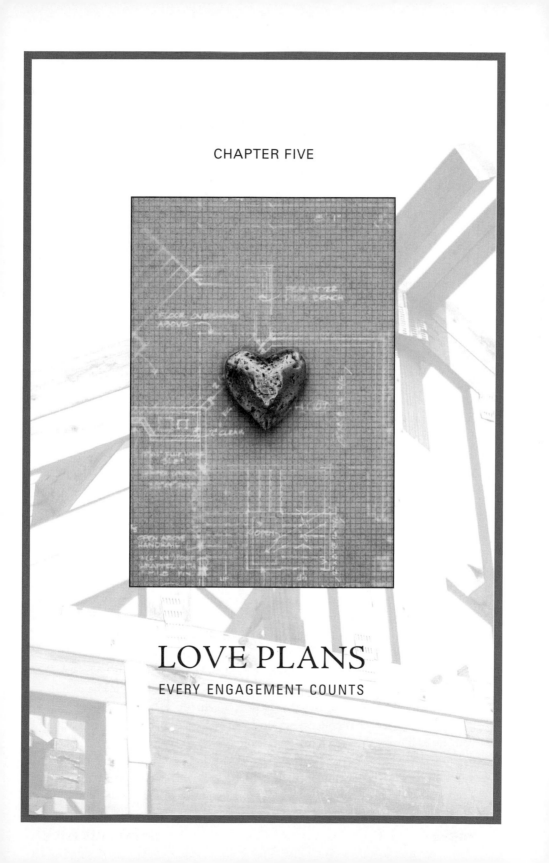

CHAPTER FIVE

LOVE PLANS
EVERY ENGAGEMENT COUNTS

Let me go on record: I know this isn't easy. I don't want you to think that getting the customer experience and customer care processes to operate seamlessly is a walk in the park. It's not. It's the hardest change to engineer. Why? Because you're dealing with dozens, if not hundreds, or even thousands of individual personalities — employees, trade partners, and customers — and you're trying to achieve predictable results.

To roll out any change is difficult, and economic challenges make it even harder. When builders with historic achievements like Levitt and Sons cite "unprecedented conditions" and file for bankruptcy, it's serious. When companies like Pulte Homes, John Laing Homes, and Shea Homes reposition themselves because of market changes their executives see, you know it's serious. Our tough business just got tougher. But, hey, we're tough, no?

The best in the business tell me there are still opportunities to improve and enhance customer relationships. The bottom line is important, but we can't lose sight of what gets us there: our people and our customers. CEO Larry Webb of John Laing Homes won't stop getting out of bed in the middle of the night to look at satisfaction scores when the market improves. The mark of a true leader is consistency and vigilance. Does this fire burn within you? Does it carry through to every one of your people?

"People will look at your book, and say, 'I don't know if that's possible,'" says Dick Bryan, the retired John Laing Homes executive. "*Anything* is possible. I helped make John Laing what it is by hiring and training good people and having the power to make decisions to do the job the way it should be done. I had Larry Webb behind me, wanting to make it happen."

Bryan and Webb know the pitfalls of the "it-can't-be-done" syndrome. In his own words, Webb offered a similar response to Bryan when he came up with seemingly far-fetched customer care initiatives **(See Love Story, Page 135)**. And let's not forget the stamp-it-out syndrome. As an industry, we got so big and busy, and we were cranking out homes so fast and furiously, that we lost sight of how we delivered them. Because of this unprecedented demand, people settled for less

HEART OF **THE MATTER**

What to take to heart from this chapter:
- Planning makes every engagement count.
- Hire employees *willing* to engage, then train them.
- Develop customer care processes that appeal to employees.
- Train and re-train.
- Ask employees to re-invigorate the plan.

service, and we kept our eyes fixed on the product. But as the market shifts, the public is getting what it always deserved — more attention. It *can* be done.

This requires a total refocusing within your company. It requires incredible discipline. And through all these changes, it requires you to choose to thrive, not just survive. You need to make this choice as you juggle all the initiatives necessary to your survival. You can't think that training and re-tooling your workforce to deliver the best customer experience is another weight dragging you down. It's the only way to get back in the game.

To develop the right business model, you can't *stamp them out*. Thank goodness for market leaders who prove that providing exceptional customer care and experience for *each individual client* is the only focus that promises longevity. Otherwise, we'd have other builders and remodelers wondering, *why am I wasting time and money on this stuff?*

The proof is in the referral base of these benchmark companies. When throwing money at advertising stops bringing people to your door, this is where you'll find buyers — from former customers. Don't you think that, with its billions in revenues, Pulte Homes is thankful that 45 percent of those dollars come from repeat and referral business, and that, through the years, it has been able to increase its repeat and referral base from 28 to 45 percent?

It takes time to develop a plan, a program for customer care that can produce such fruit. Prospective clients call me up and ask: *We're not making sales; can you train my people this week?* In a crisis mode, they want the magic pill. It doesn't exist. In fact, magic pill believers usually end up on Eliant's list of builders rated lowest in customer satisfaction.

Substandard Loyalty	
Traits Of Builders Rated Lowest In Customer Satisfaction	
Blinders On	They don't monitor customer perceptions. Why bother? *We know how our customers feel. They tell us all the time.*
Building Biased	They're overwhelmingly product-centric. They see themselves as a homebuilder only, not as a service provider.
Magic Pill Believers	They believe that getting customers to take satisfaction surveys is all they need to do to improve satisfaction. They don't realize: It's not what you find but *what you do with what you find.*
No Leaders	They believe managers will automatically develop customer satisfaction improvement processes. Worse, they think managers should want to do this on their own, without being held accountable. When managers do (but most don't), they feel there's no need to reward performance.
No Champion	They feel it's unnecessary to place one person in charge of customer experience — why bother? The survey will take care of it.
Better By Default	They believe that if they simply get better at their jobs, survey scores will improve. They forget that if buyers' expectations rise at the same pace performance improves, scores will stagnate.
Limited Metrics	They require managers to record and report on metrics for their team's financial, sales, and delivery performance, but not for customer satisfaction or loyalty.
No Rewards	They punish employees for poor survey scores, but rarely provide recognition and rewards for performance gains.

SOURCE: ELIANT, WWW.ELIANT.COM.

So how do I turn sales consultants who earned $180,000 for basically taking orders into employees who get paid $90,000 for working harder and signing half the business? From my perspective, to go back and help people undo bad habits in order to learn new ones is harder than if they had no habits at all.

How do you create, from the beginning, a plan that makes certain you hire right, get company-wide buy-in, train effectively, re-invigorate, and make every engagement count — day in and day out?

It's like Vince Lombardi said — we've got to get back to basics. And like that legendary coach, you need to convey the basics of your tough sport as you hold out to your team the focus of your game: *This, **this** is a football.*

TEA LEAVES NOT REQUIRED

It starts with a vision plan that states your customer philosophy and extends to job descriptions, hiring plans, training plans, and finally, expectations and process plans. It begins before the hire, extends through the new employee orientation, and never ends. Even the most seasoned pro needs training in essential skills like communication, time management (if you can't effectively manage your relationship with the customer, you can't deliver on time), body language, and etiquette.

Guts To Love

Fundamentals For Peak Performance
BY CAROL SMITH

Job descriptions and performance reviews are the perfect place to anchor your service mindset and to make certain employees understand that every engagement counts.

Assuming that employees — newcomers or veterans — understand that meeting your company's service objectives requires their focused effort puts your service success at risk. Yet, few companies include any mention of the necessary behaviors and performance criteria in their job descriptions or performance reviews. You can correct this once you recognize the need, and you can achieve astonishing results.

By connecting the dots, you can create a stronger employee service focus. This need for an employee service focus extends to behind-the-scenes support: accounting, purchasing, estimating, administrative staff, land development, marketing, and so on. Everyone has customers and everyone's performance affects the paying customers, your homebuyers.

To this end, you might add a clear statement regarding service to every

You have to understand the various personalities that are drawn to this business. Love isn't second nature to everyone. You'll need to work with people who don't quite appreciate that perspective — employees who

are head-down, product-focused and people-averse. How do you get people whose tendency is to avoid connections to take ownership of a customer *relationship? This, **this**, is a customer. Look them in the eye.* How do you get them to go beyond that and feel like they're doing it for their company? You'll only be as good as your weakest link. You can try to hire for attitude, but not every skill set you need comes with an ingrained service mindset.

The proof that you're getting somewhere will be when a laborer stops to pick up trash just because it's there, or when a carpenter parks across the street to leave the homeowner the driveway, or when your production

job description: from leadership positions to the newest laborer. Perhaps something like this: *Provide all customers — homebuyers, company colleagues, and all outside business associates — with consistent and exceptional service.*

Now, you need only to define "exceptional service" and you'll have a great starting point. If you have developed a set of Universal Service Guidelines as described in Chapter 1, simply reference those, and you will have defined "exceptional service:" *Be familiar with and apply company Universal Service*

Provide all customers — homebuyers, company colleagues, and all outside business associates — with consistent and exceptional service.

Guidelines to all dealings with homebuyers, company colleagues, and outside business associates.

While you're at it, consider the closely related issue of continuous improvement in products, processes, and service. The *we've-always-done-it-this-way* mindset has no place in a service-oriented organization. The employees who perform a job day after day are in an excellent position to spot opportunities to do that job faster, better, or more economically. They can offer ideas for minor adjustments or sweeping changes and are more likely to do both when you make it clear that such suggestions are not merely welcome, but applauded and expected. So add this sentence to your job descriptions: *Monitor* superintendent stops what he's doing, turns to the customer who's dropped by the site, and says, *How're you doin'?* When they're not just trying to make a good impression, but stepping out of their comfort zone to recognize the presence *of the customer.*

In fact, that's one "word track" behavioral consultant Grant Mazmanian teaches to on-site production managers at his 225 client companies. The CEO of Media, Pa. based Pinnacle Group International is a behavioral assessment and human resources consultant for Fortune 500 firms, and has worked with replacement contractors for 18 years. He develops performance and workforce improvement programs focusing on career planning, communication, and customer service.

These days, Mazmanian gets more calls from business owners who had never considered their employees to be company assets. Owners who didn't realize that their employees would make or break their company, and owners who didn't understand that they could actually grow the company with a better understanding of employee and customer interactions. He's learning from contractor clients that even male customers — it used to be only women — have a strong need to relate to their builder during the job. These guys want access to their home and property as it's built and they want to build a relationship. So how do you train your people to put down the hammer and interact?

work processes to identify and offer suggestions for improvement or innovation in our products, policies, or procedures.

Carry your campaign a step further. Often those closest to processes can overlook opportunities outsiders readily spot. So besides asking employees to offer suggestions, ask them to review homebuyer feedback and communicate with other departments to ensure that they discover all improvement possibilities:

- *Review feedback from customers to identify (1) areas of excellence to preserve or expand and (2) opportunities for growth and improvement.*

- *Seek input regarding the success of your work processes as they relate to, and affect, other departments, your colleagues, and outside business associates in order to discover potential improvements.*

Round out this effort by incorporating selected items from the job descriptions into performance review paperwork. The prominence of these details sends a clear and consistent message to every employee, from upper management to the newest laborer. Imagine beginning every performance review by discussing an employee's progress in their service behaviors, and discussing the significance of the specific suggestions for improvements they've offered. When service and quality are specifically mentioned in these fundamental tools, assumptions give way to action.

And, customer satisfaction efforts reach new heights.

Word Tracks For The Service-Challenged
It's this easy: "Hey, how're you doin'?"

Track 1	*Hey, how're you doin'?* What this achieves for the left-brained production manager who wants to get his work done: It reaches out to the customer without asking, *can I help you?* So while it makes a connection, there's no obligation, and the worker can stop, interact, and get back to work. With this track, you take someone with a "gruff gene," which homeowners sense, and allow them to — for a moment — adopt a different behavioral style that makes the homeowner feel recognized. What most upsets the homeowner is not being seen as a person.
Track 2	*Well, I can hear you're busy. I'll let you get back to your work.* Efficiency-driven administrative personnel covering the phones can use this track to avoid sounding rude, which goes against their DNA. Like the production super, the admin is task oriented, left brained. To make them more empathetic, more sensitive to a customer's needs, requires a right-brained approach. So a few well-chosen words achieve the characteristics they're looking for. The sentence provides them an out, because they're afraid to say, *Hey, I've got to get back to work.* They're customer focused, and want to help people.
Track 3	*Let me write that question down because I need to verify it with the home office.* Like admin employees, salespeople are right brained. This track is geared for the salesperson whose DNA makes it difficult for him to say, *I don't have an answer.* It avoids dancing around looking for an answer, because if he concocts one, the homeowner knows it; this breeds mistrust. For salespeople, it's hard to say, *I don't know.* So writing it down and reading it back helps this right-brained person act in a left-brained way. It's difficult for them to do. But it's critical to the relationship's trust and respect. The minute they lose it, they've lost the sale.

SOURCE: PINNACLE GROUP INTERNATIONAL, SEE WWW.PINNACLEGROUPUSA.COM.

To help employees foster customer-focused and service-friendly interactions, Pinnacle Group International equips contractors with word tracks similar to these samples for a superintendent, an administrative leader, and a sales consultant. Each employee has a "nightmare customer." The production leader's nightmare client shows up at the site with Gatorade for the guys; the administrative employee doesn't want to look rude, so rude customers make the job nightmarish; and the sales rep's nightmare is the customer who asks technical questions for which he has no answers. But employees with these behavioral styles can be taught to adopt a tactic from another style so they can deal with the person they're talking to, and then, are able to return to what they do best.

Mazmanian's formula for selecting the right employee begins by "interviewing the job" — what would it say if it could talk? What are the attributes necessary for the position? You might develop this description: *We need an experienced leader who manages a four- to six-person crew independently, works effectively with administrative and sales staff, and considers customer service a priority.*

Next, the wording of the Help Wanted ad is critical, followed by a telephone interview in which the employer asks situational questions, and an online assessment to uncover the applicant's dominant traits, attitudes, and values. The applicant's attributes should be checked against company-wide assessments to see if the candidate is a fit for this service-centered culture. And, how does this potential employee mesh with the supervisor and team?

Ad-writing is an art in itself, and crafting ads to attract only the candidates who are a fit takes practice. Instead of writing **ability** to *deal with the public,* you write **willingness to deal with the public.** Top-notch production people may not be able to do that task, but they can be willing. As we saw in my work with Bobby in Chapter 4, an excellent production superintendent may lack right-brained interpersonal skills because of his finely-tuned left-brain characteristics. But, they can learn — *if they're open to learning.*

DICK BRYAN: AT 68, STILL LEARNING

LOVE STORY

How a well-dressed man can revolutionize a company, and quite possibly get an industry to see that with a suit and tie, the sky's the limit.

I'm just talking here …

Employees at John Laing Homes know what it means when the freshly-cologned Dick Bryan uses that phrase. Bryan, the retired vice president of customer care known for his impeccable grooming habits and perennial suit-and-tie, uses those words often when he teaches customer care values. He's not *just* talking. And employees aren't *just* listening.

Listening well is an art form Bryan perfected in his nearly 20 years with the company — listening to the customer. It's why some call him the housing industry's *Father of Customer Service.*

One of Dick's secrets (besides his 300 suits and 450 ties) is that he never

KYLE SIBLEY, LEFT, AND DICK BRYAN, WHO *ALWAYS* LOOKS COOL.

PIT BULLS & NO B.S.

HELP WANTED
Office Manager

XYZ Contracting, an established and growing company, seeks an assertive office manager to efficiently control three office administrators and six field managers. Must be a "hands-on" individual who will "roll up their sleeves" and "get the job done" — no matter what.

Pit Bull Personality A Plus
View duties and responsibilities at www.xyz.com/officemanager. $40K-$60K, depending on experience. Excellent health plan, 401(k), profit sharing. Send resume with cover letter explaining your qualifications to pitbull@xyzmail.com.

If you want a manager who's a straight shooter, you might write in the ad, *No B.S. Manager Wanted.* It'll say something to some that it won't say to others, Mazmanian notes, and determine if they have a sense of humor. If you're absolutely driven by service, yet haven't gotten there yet with your production crews, you might need a really tough office manager to keep them on target. Mazmanian recalls writing an ad for an office manager with the descriptor, *Pit bull personality a plus.* They set up an email address to respond, something like pitbull@email.com. After all, it was that person who would drive the customer service

stops learning. "I learn every day just by the things I hear and the people I talk to," says Bryan, who still consults with his former employer. "You can learn something *every* day. You never know it all."

Dick's so sensitive about how someone interacts with a client, he's not adverse to offering a breath mint or sticking an air freshener in their car. That's empathy with the customer and a sixth sense of how they're going to experience the interaction. He wasn't beyond telling CEO Larry Webb to shave his goatee, either, when the president tried a new look. At Bryan's retirement dinner, Webb recalled Bryan's form of persuasion when he drove home the point: "He chewed me out the whole time, but it felt good," Webb says.

"Dick wants so much for this industry," says Kyle Sibley of Sibley & Associates, of North Hills, Calif., a John Laing preferred vendor. "If I'm telling him stories about things other builders are doing, or variations from what he thinks is a proper customer response, it's upsetting to Dick, because he feels like it's *his* business … it affects the business he's in."

"They just don't get it," Bryan says of companies putting limits on customer care. He sees their representatives at conferences. "I'll have 25, 30 people walk up to me — 'how do you guys do this? How do you do that?' I've told the same people time and time again. They just don't get it. They don't take time to get it. They listen and someone at a higher level says, 'no we're not going to do that.' And it's a shame."

Bryan came to Laing in 1988, and by his assessment it was probably one back office. <u>One</u> person responded to that ad. When she did, she left the message, *My bark is worse than my bite.* She's the one, the consultant told the owner. The consultant later called the new employee and asked what she thought when she read the ad. She said she didn't. Her husband read the ad, threw the newspaper at her, and said, "Read this. This is *you.*" She was a great employee because she wanted to ensure customer service while dealing with undisciplined production crews.

I might add: Did you ever think of advertising to hire people who live in your communities to find people similar to your clients? Kelea Piper, who sells for Hogan Homes, bought a home in the community where she sells. So she's not only a sales consultant, she's a resident, a neighbor, someone who cares. It takes a special person whose home life becomes an extension of her professional life. But these people are out there. These employees stay connected to buyers and when problems arise, they eagerly work to resolve them.

Resolving problems is a key skill in customer service cultures. And to this end, Mazmanian thinks hiring interviews are sorely lacking when it comes to pinpointing these skills or an openness to learn them. Not only do we ask the wrong questions, he says, we wrongly interpret the answers. For instance, instead of asking: *Do you enjoy working with people?* And then getting an answer to interpret, like, *I have*

of the worst builders he went to work for. "It was a disaster."

John Laing Homes had entered the U.S. market in 1984 from Great Britain. When Laing merged with Watt Homes in April 1998, WL Homes became one of nation's largest privately held homebuilders. Today, WL Homes operates 13 divisions in California, Colorado, Arizona and Texas under the John Laing name. In 2006, it partnered with Dubai-based Emaar Properties, one of the world's largest global real estate development companies.

But back in 1988, Laing had one division. Its CEO, Bob Fritz, followed Deming's quality improvement principles. But Fritz wanted to be like Nordstrom, the department store legendary for service. "He gave me the tools," says Bryan. "He said: 'Whatever you need to be like Nordstrom's, you got it.'"

(May I gently remind the reader: Isn't that what Karen McCaffrey said on the first page of this book — *we're beginning to realize we're retail.* Bryan and Fritz saw it in '88!)

Four years earlier, Bob Mirman founded his firm, Eliant (then known as National Survey Systems). Mirman had 28 builder clients. Out of 28 firms, John Laing ranked lowest in customer satisfaction. Within two years, Bryan helped bring Laing to Number 1. The company has not fallen out of the top three builders since.

At Bryan's retirement dinner, Webb recalled how, not long after he promoted the executive to vice president, he asked: *How can we get better?* At the time, a two-day response to a complaint was considered good; years earlier, to, ask for examples from a previous job: *How did you deal with an upset customer, and what did you do about it?* The interviewee might say, *I never had to deal with that, my supervisor took care of it.* "They're automatically knocked out," says Mazmanian. "They admitted that they don't have the experience to be self-managing, to manage customer complaints at the point of service."

By asking non-theoretical questions, you might learn that the production supervisor candidate, when hit with a difficult question from a client, said, *Please, give me a second. Let me get my clipboard from my truck.* And the candidate continued, *I had to take a breather. That lady scared the heck out of me.* Did you get the clipboard? *No, I picked up a pad and pencil. I wrote the lady's name down and the date. I said, Let's start at the beginning. She started crying all over. I said, Let me write this down. I took all the questions, even the ones I couldn't answer, and told her I'd get back to her by the end of the day.*

"Bingo," says Mazmanian. "There's your supervisor. He didn't like confrontation, had to head to the truck to take a breather, forgot the clipboard, but he can work with it." And Mazmanian suggests learning all this over the phone before candidates arrive for the interview.

If you are looking for an office administrator who goes out of the way to please the customer, you need to ask questions that drive at the "save face factor" as the behavioral consultant calls it — they're finding a way to

requests for service weren't accepted by phone — you *wrote* your builder a letter.

"I know what to do," Bryan told Webb. "We get back to people in *15 minutes.*"

"And I'm thinking: *Is he out of his mind?*" Webb recalls. Bryan suggested giving everyone cell phones. Webb replied: "We can't afford them!"

Bryan replied in a characteristic way he became legendary for: "Don't worry, I got a deal. And we'll put one extra person in the office and that person will call the guy in the field and get back. Webb said: *It can't work.*

"Don't get in my way on this," Webb says Bryan told him. "We're going to do it."

And they did.

"It was revolutionary," Webb says. "It was amazing." And when Laing personnel showed up the next day after the call at the client's home, "it was *miraculous.*"

Bryan also played a part, in influencing Webb's first decision in 1998 after they merged with Watt — to survey every household, with the reasoning, *how would we know how we're doing in satisfaction unless we knew what every customer was saying?* And Bryan helped Laing change to an incentive program that included customer care personnel. It became one of the first companies to take that step.

These steps don't include Bryan's everyday influence on Laing culture, where some personnel are known to be better dressed than their protect the company. *Can you give me an example of a time a customer called when the crew didn't show up?* It's a good trait for this person to make the customer happy and give the customer a sense of security, he says. The candidate says, *well, I told them they'd be there, because they're usually never late, and that I'd find out what was wrong and get back to them in five minutes. Then I called the foreman who said they were getting lunch. I said, 'Cut it out, and get over there right away because I told the customer you'd be there in five minutes.'*

It's a good thing for this person to use the conversation with the customer as a weapon against the job supervisor, Mazmanian says. They're acting assertively, and while they don't like confrontation either, they're creative and spontaneous and good on their feet. There are so many variables in construction and they need to be comfortable with them. But they have to be OK with the "save face factor" — like their guys are *usually never late.*

Roxanne Musselman suggests this question when interviewing sales applicants: *What are the five success habits you practice every day?* Many people have trouble thinking of even one, and if they can't, or don't understand the relevance of the question, they're not your candidate. If someone can't share some of their inborn philosophies for better performance, you're in trouble.

Once your candidate passes the phone interview test, and takes the online behavioral assessment, Mazmanian

doctor and lawyer clients, and the joke is that tuxedos are next. What's uncertain is how Bryan can wear a suit coat and tie in the 125-degree heat of Las Vegas.

While Bryan continues to learn well into his retirement, he says new ideas and programs only work with constant training and communication, from the top. "It's hard to find that type of culture," he says. "The

> "Dick has made us all think that just because this is the way it is, that doesn't mean it can't be different."
> — Kyle Sibley

building industry has a lot to learn. If they would just listen and follow Nordstrom's philosophy."

Sibley says he's always asked when he's working with people who hold similar positions to Bryan's: *How does Laing do it?* He tells them: *Don't skimp on service.* In Southern California, he says, the average homeowner buys another house every 4.5 years. So if you do it right, you can win over the starter buyer and then get them to buy the mid-range home, then the luxury home — if they stay with you.

"Dick has made us all think that just because this is the way it is, that doesn't mean it can't be different," says Sibley of customer service. "If you're passionate about what you do and consider the customer the end-all to what we do, then the sky is the limit."

For Bryan, the sky will always be the limit. Nothing stops how he looks at the home: *From the customer's eyes … and nose.*

When Did You Go The Extra Mile?

ORGANIZATION	Give me examples of how you organize things, using situations from your current or past positions. How many duties do you have to manage and how do you do it?
DEDICATION	Give me an example of when you went the extra mile to make the homeowner happy. What specifically did you do?
COOPERATION	Tell me about a time you had the administrative or sales department cooperate to help you resolve a customer complaint?
INNOVATION	How did you handle a problem with a homeowner in a creative or resourceful way? What happened?
FRUSTRATION	If we're in a crunch situation, we need you to do whatever it takes for you and your crew to get the job done on time. Are you comfortable with those situations? Can you describe a recent example at your current job?
CONFRONTATION	Tell me about a time when a homeowner was very angry with you or the company. How did you resolve the issue?
CONFUSION	Tell me about a time when a homeowner said the sales-person promised "X" and your work order said "Y." How did you handle it?

SOURCE: PINNACLE GROUP INTERNATIONAL, WWW.PINNACLEGROUPUSA.COM.

Situational questions uncover how job candidates react in the heat of critical interactions, or, in situations that demand the best customer care.

suggests a company culture check, aligning the profile of the candidate with the current employees. This sounds like a good idea, however I also would recommend a team interview to see how all the personalities fit together because they have to gel. The more opinions you have, the better it is. How will they communicate with one another? Once the person is on board, the manager won't see them every day, but the people who work with them will.

If the supervisor is a perfectionist and time-conscious while the production manager is a get-it-done and don't-ask-how-I-did-it person, that's a problem. People don't quit the company, they quit their managers, Mazmanian says.

Once they're on the job, they need to be schooled in communication as part of providing customer service. This is true even if they don't see the need to tell the customer they've arrived (at a remodeling project) or are leaving the home — customers need reassurance. It's the connection, Mazmanian says.

Many times, employees aren't getting what they need in their training and need to be told exactly what to do or say, and how to act and behave. For instance, Mazmanian notes that at least 60 percent of homeowners — the percentage of the population that buys auto and appliance service agreements for safety and security — want to know what's happening next. *OK, we'll be back tomorrow at 7 a.m. and, if it's raining, someone will call from the office.*

A lot of times, it's getting people to be comfortable with being more interactive — even if it's just knocking on the door to leave a hang tag that says, *We're here today, and we'll be gone by 4 p.m.* Or, if the homeowner suddenly opens the door, the foreman takes a moment to say, *Hi, my name is Bob and I'm in charge of the crew. We'll be here until 4 p.m. today.*

Many production employees dislike dealing with customers, and will avoid them, Mazmanian says, and he has plenty of stories from all sorts of contractors whose employees ignored customers … *even as they stood in the same room.*

EMBRACING RESISTANCE

So the trick is getting company-wide buy-in to the sort of training that helps people to first see the customer and then interact with them. This requires training, re-training, and using employees to reinvigorate the plan. Sometimes it takes a book to galvanize the team (**See Love Mode, Page 147**).

John Laing Homes spends millions of dollars each year on training, as much as 10 percent of revenues. Its 400-plus page customer and service training manual alone, which affects all departments, contains six sections and a CD. It's used for monthly training sessions, takes a year to complete and when it's completed they begin it again. This is in addition to regular field training, where field employees visit manufacturers to learn about new products such as jetted tubs, or sales program training.

The whole idea behind training programs is to help employees understand all the ways they can make the customer feel connected, because if customers feel good about their relationship, they are incredibly forgiving. And if customers are able to forgive, they are able to trust, and if they trust, they'll last as customers.

A good exercise to get your employees to trust and feel connected is to ask everyone to identify something personal about someone on the team that no one would otherwise know. When you connect with customers, you share a similarity with them. Lots of people know other team member's job titles, but not much personal information. Once your team knows these things about each other, they can tell a customer — *oh, our production leader, John, is a mountain climber, too.* This makes it easier to connect with people who have different personalities and preferences than our own. Job rotations also give team members the chance to better understand other roles. People often get in their own worlds and forget the whole organization. If they better understand how what they do affects everyone, it can make them more sensitive, caring, and trusting.

You don't have to be a huge company to invest in training. Do you remember FCB Homes of Stockton, Calif.? It doesn't share Laing's history of customer care, or its budget, but it started down this road, getting everyone focused on the customer, three years ago. Growing out of recommendations from its expectations or E-team, they developed a touchpoint inventory of their customer interactions, says Dawn Harshman, FCB's customer relations manager.

Expectations training at FCB reviews how to develop customer "devotions" — such as communications, instilling pride, sharing the vision of the company, why an employee works for FCB, why it considers itself to be better than other builders, and so on. When employees talk to clients, they do a better job.

FCB schools their employees in author and speaker Chip R. Bell's seven steps to devoted customers,[†] including:

[†] Adapted from *Magnetic Service: Secrets For Creating Passionately Devoted Customers*, by Chip R. Bell and Biljack R. Bell, SF: Berrett-Koehler Publishers, 2003. Reprinted with permission.

- ✦ **Engagement.** Get to know them. Listen to their needs and wants.
- ✦ **Enlistment.** Make customers feel like owners. Involve them in the process.
- ✦ **Enlightenment.** Make customers smarter. Mentor and teach them. They want to learn.
- ✦ **Empowerment.** Put yourself in the customer's shoes. Seek their feedback and listen to ideas.
- ✦ **Enchantment.** Know children's names, take a personal interest, personalize, and wow.
- ✦ **Entrustment.** Build a trust account — under promise and over deliver.
- ✦ **Endearment.** Keep a positive attitude. Customers keep FCB's doors open.

FCB starts off with a needs assessment for buyers and then breaks out these needs and expectations through each step of the process, noting the customer's expectations and needs as well as the builder's goals and requirements.

A typical needs assessment for construction might look like this:

NEEDS ASSESSMENT — Construction

Customer Needs	Builder Needs
I trust the construction reps.	We complete construction phases without incident and on schedule.
I have confidence in the competence of the people building my home and I understand their roles in constructing my new home.	We incorporate construction options as early as possible to ensure proper integration.
I see a safe, clean, and secure jobsite when I visit my home under construction.	We complete a frame walk with the homeowner to get their sign-off for construction options.
I understand the construction process and timelines, as well as the stages of construction.	We ensure design options are ordered with sufficient lead times.
I can watch my dream home become a reality and I'm excited about what I see.	We control the flow of resources (trades) and materials to effectively manage sequencing and schedule.
I feel I am a part of the process and in the loop.	We work out most of the construction issues by the first phase and increase productivity for the remaining phases.
I have access to my home during construction.	We are 100 percent clean, and have a complete home ready for orientation.

SOURCE: FCB HOMES, SAMPLE ONLY, WWW.FCBHOMES.COM. ELIANT, WWW.ELIANT.COM, ORIGINATED THE TEMPLATE.

Expectations planning helps educate employees on the types of questions a buyer might have; develops consistent answers for employees when questions are asked; and allows some of those interactions to be turned into touchpoints. Nick Guantone, FCB customer care director, says they discovered that the people with the most opportunities for touchpoints were the laborers and detailers in the house. So they equipped them with tracks, similar to what Mazmanian described, answering specific questions. One frequent answer, is: *I don't know, but the FCB Web site provides a lot of answers that might help you.*

FCB maps its touchpoints — whether required, spontaneous or extraordinary, for every construction phase. They remind employees that everything they do or say or don't do or say sets the homeowner's expectation.

They train for key questions:
  + **How often will you call me about the purchase of my new home?**
  + **When will you return my calls?**
  + **How much time will I need to take off for appointments?**
  + **Can I talk to construction?**
  + **When will I be able to move in?**
  + **Will things need to be fixed after I move in?**

And FCB basics:
  + **How can I find out more about FCB Homes?**
  + **Can I trust FCB Homes and its employees?**
  + **Why is an FCB home a good value?**
  + **What does quality mean to FCB Homes?**

Then, they equip employees with FCB expectation notes so they can refer back to the anticipated questions. The expectations documents are always evolving, says Harshman, as different expectations, situations, and market changes prompt refinements. Harshman keeps in touch with customers after the move-in, not only to win their trust and get to know them as people, but to see what else is on their minds.

Best practices FCB has developed include:
  + **Listening.** Really listening to customers by communicating with them regularly. Telling from the inflection of their voices (note the intricacy of this) that they're busy and you need to respect their time. If they share that their daughter swims, do you ask: *What*

stroke? Do you listen to what they say instead of driving right to the heart of what you need from them?

- ✦ **Taking Responsibility.** Seeing a task through and following up. Not passing the buck, but checking and re-checking that issues are resolved.
- ✦ **Continuous Education.** Yes, for employees, but using Chip Bell's suggestion, FCB takes it beyond — to customers, too. How do you educate customers? Through these interactions.
- ✦ **Embracing Resistance.** Dawn Harshman notes some of the worst customers can lead to better future business decisions. If the surveys say the paint can't be scrubbed with a brush, the purchasing department needs to know, and ask — is there a better product?

By creating a chain of care throughout their employee roster, in the past year alone, FCB has seen a 40 percent decrease in customer care costs. Harshman says they actually get more claims on older houses, because those customers weren't effectively schooled by FCB personnel at key points and at the hand-off of the home in what homeowner maintenance and warranty entails for them. Part of the education process now includes client invitations to free homeowner maintenance seminars at Lowe's and incentives include 10 percent off coupons and $50 gift cards.

I have to ask: What's happened to an employees' ability to be thankful? Appreciating customers is a tiny thing to do. Yet this step is frequently missed during training. Carol Smith says one of the things customers want is to be appreciated. It's almost as if: If it's not on a checklist, we won't do it. It's something that should be internal, and developed during their training. How can you train people to be intuitively thankful and appreciative? You have to look for that ability. If it's always me-me-me, that person probably won't be able to appreciate customers for you.

If you suggest to your employees that they occasionally should bring a dozen donuts and hot coffee for the framers in the morning and the first thing out of their mouth is 'how do I get reimbursed for that?,' they don't get it. Not that you should expect people to take money out of their own pockets for the company, but if their first thought is compensation, it's not going to work. Being thankful is a way of being. We need to school people to show appreciation.

As you can see, training your employees is an intensive, exhausting process, and I've barely touched the surface. Getting buy-in requires

lots of encouragement and support. Employers need to help employees identify the strength and weaknesses of their learning styles and it's one of management's jobs to help people discover the benefits of learning. Or better, to understand the benefits of learning from a loyalty perspective: *How will this incremental change in what I do help a customer and add a client for life?*

Training must be ongoing, not a one-time event. Employees need constant feeding, or the love will go away. The biggest inhibitor to great is *good enough*. We can never accept good enough.

We need to look at *incremental* ways to improve the experience.

FANS FOR ETERNITY

How a catalyst can transform a company and keep it winning referrals through fast-track growth.

LOVE MODE

If the book *Seven Habits of Highly Effective People* can transform the culture at Shea Homes, the largest privately owned homebuilder, why shouldn't another book, *Raving Fans,* be able to help guide a $15 million-a-year remodeling firm through the difficulties of growing to $53 million-plus over seven years?

Sometimes you need a catalyst to get you thinking differently about how you understand the customer experience. That's what author Ken Blanchard's book was for Sal Ferro, president of Alure, of East Meadow, Long Island, N.Y.

Back in 2000, Ferro saw the 60-year-old company becoming bigger than the typical remodeling firm. "I read the book, and I thought it should be the foundation for our customer service philosophy," he says. "We had no consistent concept. We had a culture with that type of customer service philosophy, but we hadn't formalized it."

He spent a week at the Ken Blanchard Institute in San Diego, Calif., and learned how to train his people in the principles in *Raving Fans: A Revolutionary Approach to Customer Service.* The book's formula:
- **Decide on a vision;**
- **Discover the specific needs and expectations of customers;**
- **Deliver your vision a step at a time.**

So Ferro re-wrote his company vision statement to encapsulate the internal and external clients and culture he wanted, then posted it on his Web site (www.alure.com).

Although Alure's repeat business and referral rates topped 50 percent, Ferro wanted to maintain that rate through the addition of products and services, locations, and employees. He wanted to maintain production control during this growth. In 2000, Alure employed less than half its current 105 employees. Today, Alure has four divisions selling sunrooms; siding, windows, and roofing; kitchens and baths; basement refinishing; and energy remediation products and services.

In 2001, Ferro developed a system to rate client experience and asked Freda Krackow to head the effort. Krackow does close-of-job interviews with each client by phone, asking about the experience, the value received, and the overall rating they'd give the company. Krackow fits the description of most customer care champions — she's upfront and brutally honest. If a customer says they'd work with the company again, she asks: *OK, what's the next project?*

The company president uses survey data to see how project supervisors and sales reps rate against each other, how departments compare, and to determine a quarter of the incentive pay for those who receive performance-based compensation. (The remaining three-quarters is based on volume sold/completed, profitability, and attitude/personal performance.)

The first training session Ferro developed from Blanchard's concepts was two days long, then he winnowed it down to a day, and now he can complete it in a few hours. He reviews the experience he wants customers to have, reviews customer expectations, then performs role playing with employees, and hammers home how he envisions the *Raving Fans* philosophy as the spirit of the company.

Most replacement contractors subcontract their installation, so they have little control in the field. They also are built as sales organizations, so less emphasis is placed on long-term relationships. Not so with Alure. Ferro has trained more than half his trade contractors in *Raving Fans* philosophy, getting them to work with clients and be more responsive, clean up job sites, watch their language, and dress to fit Alure's image.

He says the company learned to improve communication and to manage expectations. "I always see room for improvement in communications, period." He has outfitted his sales and production personnel with BlackBerrys to allow constant phone and email communication, and staff can document and access client projects online. If a service call comes in, company policy requires someone to be at the house within 24 hours.

Every other month, Alure throws a party in its showroom. Ferro talks about the company referral process and an incentive program for clients that rewards points for referrals based on the size of the job. Points can add up to a Caribbean trip. Employees, too, are eligible for Partner Points, and this past year 50 employees and clients took the trip.

The *Raving Fans* work seems to have paid off: In Long Island, its oldest territory, its repeat and referral rate is 70 percent for kitchen and bath remodeling. Its newer basement refinishing business boasts a 20 percent repeat and referral rate and is growing.

Revelations Ferro had during the culture change:

- *Don't underestimate the power of knowledge.* Once you can rate yourself and keep score, you know what to work on with your people.
- *Understand that the top issue in customer service is communication.* Clients don't complain about quality work. But there are always complaints about indifference, lack of follow up, and failed expectations.
- *Change doesn't happen overnight.* It starts, however, with passion from the top.
- *If you focus on the client during change, it's a no-lose situation.* Always have a sense of urgency and follow-through. Do it, or get to it.
- *You need to be on the customer's agenda.* "We're working for them," Ferro says. "They're paying us to create this dream. If we're on our agenda, we have a tough time exceeding expectations. If we have our people on their agenda, they feel really powerful."

He says the changes helped increase employee retention, and made it easier to recruit. Tying in nicely with his *Raving Fans*-inspired change were alliances with ABC-TV and *Extreme Makeover: Home Edition*. Through the experience of doing major remodels in 4.5 days or less, Ferro was able to add the company tag line, *We go to extremes to fulfill your dreams.*

But Alure doesn't forget the less extreme stuff customers need, either. It has a playroom in its showroom, and parents can watch their children play while they work out project particulars. "If we take care of the customer, everything else will take care of itself," Ferro says. "If we try every day to deliver an experience superior to what they expect, if we strive every day to deliver a raving fan, Alure will be successful into eternity."

That's a long time, but his experience shows extremes aren't necessary to create raving fans. Planning, training, commitment, and hard work are all it takes.

Alure Vision Statement

Deliver a *Consistent Experience* to our customers that is *Superior* to what they expect.

Have a *Harmonious, Enthusiastic* environment where employees at all levels are *Responsive* to our customers' needs and react with a *Sense of Urgency* and *Follow Through*.

Create an environment where *Ethics and Values* are not sacrificed, where we *Listen* to and *Educate* the customer to *Build Value*.

Provide our customers *Great Products*, with *No Hassles and Superior Results*.

ALL 105 ALURE EMPLOYEES HAVE MEMORIZED THIS VISION STATEMENT, PROTECTED BY ALURE COPYRIGHT, AND RECITE IT BEFORE EACH MEETING, SAYS COMPANY PRESIDENT SAL FERRO, "LIKE THE STAR SPANGLED BANNER OR THE PLEDGE OF ALLEGIANCE." IT IS THE COMPANY'S PLEDGE; HE WANTS IT INGRAINED IN EMPLOYEES' HEARTS. HOW MANY OF US CAN SAY THE SAME?

LOVE ✓ CHECK

8 Ways To Plan The Love

To make customer care your mantra, you need buy-in throughout the chain of service. You need to constantly monitor, feed, and celebrate the passion that drives the core culture. How? Let's count the ways:

✔ Start Topside

If company ownership doesn't live and breathe the plan, no one lower in the corporate hierarchy will give it credence. This loyalty can't filter up. As Scott Sedam of TrueNorth Development says, it has to be in the corporate DNA. The corporate vision and mission statements are two powerful initiatives that set performance benchmarks. Those are metrics for measurement. Once you write your service philosophy and have it in place, you have a broad plan of action. Post it to let it work its way into the hearts of your people. Everyone should have access to the plan, including the vision and mission statement, action items, and initiatives. Otherwise, it's just lip service.

✔ Share The Plan

You'll need key players at all levels. Plan for implementation through training provided in weekly sales or production meetings. Inject incremental parts into each meeting. If you choose an action item like — *don't leave any customer concern unresolved for more than eight hours* — it has to be a training objective. Who's responsible for monitoring customer follow-up? What actions are necessary to make sure it's implemented effectively? Who will call the customer? What will they say? How will they document the chat? What reporting systems will see the issue through? This is *follow-through*, not follow-up, and it's integrated into your system. So if training is offered in sales meetings, it's also part of administrative meetings, and construction meetings. *Every* department plays a role.

✔ Get 'Em Involved

You help people see how their piece of the puzzle creates the picture. The sales consultants might not understand how they have anything to do with customer experience when they meet another rep's customer. That customer expects this salesman to understand their problem, or find someone who does. Customers think we actually talk to each other! That's not always how it is, but how it should be. If you have a company logo on your shirt, you should know everything the company knows. You need to help each employee do an exceptional job, regardless of position. It's part of their performance evaluation and job description — total customer care is everyone's job. It's not a department's job. It's too much for one department to handle. You can do that with construction duties, not customer care.

✔ Measure & Monitor

There have to be metrics in your business, something you constantly use to tweak and adjust, part of weekly or even daily evaluations. We monitor profit margins, purchase decisions, designs, price points — customer care is the same. But you need to teach people *how*. Once measurements are in place, make sure employees understand the criteria. We need more assessments of how both customers and employees feel. Is there a sense of camaraderie? A sense of enjoyment? Is there a nurturing feeling within the organization? Or, is something missing? Are people looking for opportunities to enhance the experience beyond what's required? You can't wait until the job closes to figure out if you made money, because at the end you can't ask for more money. *It's the same with satisfaction.* It requires watchful monitoring.

✔ Look For Shining Eyes

In speaking and consulting, I use a wonderful training series based on the work of Ben Zander, conductor of the Boston Philharmonic, and Rosamund Stone Zander, executive coach and family therapist. The Zanders' book, *The Art of Possibility*, helps others understand the assumptions they're making and helps them gain access to "new ways of being." They believe you can invent the story for your life. They suggest that leaders "enroll" people in an idea, and then be relentless architects of the possibility that human beings are. By transforming as an individual into a person living in a connected world, people become aware of all that they can do with others. We lead by making our people powerful. But we don't force anything on them, we simply guide that power. Conductors are like builders and remodelers: They don't create their end product, but they inspire the people who do. The conductor never makes a sound, but produces a beautiful symphony from the orchestra. Zander, so in tune with his players, might suggest to a cellist to sit on one buttock instead of two, to refine the sound coming from the musician's cello. Would you be that sensitive and able to help your employees adjust how they handle your customer care? Owners and conductors get the best from their people. Zander says we need to look for "shining eyes" — a reaction to beautiful direction, and to the spark of possibility in a world where there was none. Dave Herber, construction manager for Denton Homes by Bill Watson in San Antonio has those shining eyes; he's one of the most upbeat, down-to-earth, easy-going, caring, construction savvy country boys I know.

✔ Celebrate The Passion

Let's celebrate the littlest things with our people. Let's stop, in this crazy busy environment we work in, and thank people for doing great jobs. Let's encourage them to tell us what they need from us as well, so we can support them. Zander, for example, gives his musicians a blank sheet of paper to write down what they need from him to perform at their best. We can go beyond that and do things that take our people out of the sea of sameness, and distinguish them. At a recent Pacific Coast Builders Conference, organizers walked around and handed envelopes with $20 enclosed to people affiliated with the conference, such as cleaning atten-dants, room monitors, and information specialists who spread the enthusiasm and energy organizers wanted to display to attendees. The card read: *you've been caught with a PCBC® attitude.* Take that idea and use it with your own employees. Build your people up and remember: It takes 10 *attaboys* to get rid of one *ah, poop!*

✔ Remember The Customer

The customer is the reason for our being. Wayne Gretzky, regarded as the greatest hockey player in the history of the sport, was known for skating to the puck, instead of "trying to make a goal." Don't allow your people to get so absorbed in the day-to-day that they forget the goal, the vision. The vision is the customer. Customers aren't obstacles *in* the path, they're the reason *for* the path. We need to constantly "skate" to the customer. To do that, employees need to know that anything is possible. I recall the movie *Dangerous Minds*, about former U.S. Marine LouAnne Johnson (played by Michelle Pfeiffer) who became a high school teacher in the ghetto. Johnson gave each student an "A" at the beginning of the semester, then told them it's more difficult to *keep* an A then to *earn* it. Do that with your employees. Believe in them. Then, help them keep their stripes by remembering who they need to serve.

✔ Don't Forget Number 1

That's you. Unless you have balance in your life, you can't help other people. Especially in turbulent times, you have to be in your best physical, spiritual, and mental shape. This business is too stressful. It'll kill you. The minute your mind accepts negativity, and buys into the media's tsunami of bad news, you're toast. Watch the criticisms in your head, and watch your criticism of employees. The Zanders say that negativity is deadly. In effect, you take their eye off the goal, and deflate their trust. The leader's job is to take people out of any downward spiral into possibility. Leaders *radiate* possibility. They help people live their dreams, and connect to others. When you are energized, you can accomplish the incredible. When emotions and everything else are in sync, the endorphins are surging. It makes it easier to handle a customer's emotional ups and downs when you first invest in yourself, because that's where it starts. I encourage random acts of *self-indulgence.*

"Sorry, Customer Appreciation Week is over. Buzz off."

LOVE SPREADS

LOVE IS CONTAGIOUS

Experience, not price, will be your differentiator in any market, good or bad.

So how do you define the customer experience, push it to higher levels, and get your best salespeople — your customers — to promote your brand? You have to discover the best way for your company to regularly assess the satisfaction and loyalty of your clients. Or, discover how they're poisoning your brand. But having done the assessment, do you really listen to what they tell you about how to make your company better?

I hope so. Because for the buyer, when a quality decision process is absent, the decision is reduced to the lowest common factor: *price*. Unless you can give the buyer a reason, a quality response for why they should do business with you, decisions fall to the lowest common denominator.

The things I write about aren't price components; they're experience differentiators and emotional connections. Neither experience nor emotion can be aligned with price. So, you need measurement and feedback to back up your value proposition.

When a customer looks to make a purchase, price is one consideration. But if the customer feels good about your representatives, price becomes less decisive and with something as important as a home, this is critical. Why? The quality of your sticks and bricks isn't much different from the builder's down the block. Most builders have quality down cold.

If there's no emotional connection, there's nothing special for the customers to use to make their evaluation. If you're finding sales difficult and you're seeking the greatest long-term antidote to a sales drought, let me tell you: You've come to the right place. You'd better understand what it means to be an *Information-*

Experience company. How do we use information to refine the experience? How do you commit to sharing information with everyone in your company? Changes in your process are driven by the information you receive. Information for information's sake doesn't make sense.

And remember, **perfect doesn't exist**. Take control of what you promise and make sure customers understand what's promised. Once your execution improves, start measuring your process — before you start building; throughout construction; after completion and at delivery;

HEART OF
THE MATTER
What to take to heart from this chapter:

• Love spreads, creating value through an understanding of client experiences.

• Obtaining client opinions should never dull their love.

• Information, used well, spreads love's contagion.

• Seeking client input can push you to higher levels of care.

• Employee attitudes always affect customer loyalty.

six months after completion; a year later; and then every year thereafter, for as long as the homeowner owns the home. Eliant has begun developing annual surveys to be given to buyers for the first *six years* after they've moved into their homes, and it has a program offering builders tips for homeowners on such things as re-sale and remodeling.

I'm suggesting that you survey *more* and listen *better*. Put customers front and center. Get yourself in tune with them. Remember: Absence does not make the heart grow fonder.

I can't do justice to all the evolving customer satisfaction and loyalty assessment services available to home builders and remodelers today. But I can give you an overview and explain what they can help you do. I can share the experiences of those who work in these market segments, and share with you the excitement, reach, and impact these tools — used well — have had on satisfaction and referrals, the foundation of loyalty.

QUEST FOR TRUTH

My consulting colleague Marc Warren of Customer Follow Up doesn't hold back his enthusiasm about surveys: "What a sales tool!" he says. "For clients, what a great way to set yourself apart. You can say: 'We've had problems and we've corrected them.' Clients receive the assurances they're looking for, and see they're not just a number. They see there's a system in place that substantiates customer satisfaction and loyalty — and that you're the company to build their home."

Warren loves to make these points to his builder clients:

+ **Customers Know.** Customers are the best source of business information.
+ **Service Differentiates.** In many cases, the differentiating factor, business-to-business, is the level of customer service. Cost advantages are no longer relevant.
+ **Retention Saves.** It costs five to eight times more to get a new customer than it does to hold on to an existing customer.
+ **Retention Pays.** A 5 percent increase in customer retention equals increases of 25 percent to 85 percent in profitability.
+ **Referrals Beat Ads.** General Electric Co. (GE), found that word-of-mouth influenced customers twice as much as advertising.
+ **Service Up = Prices Up.** Businesses with perceived high customer service can sustain higher prices than their competition.[†]

[†] **Sources:** The Edward Lowe Foundation; the White House Office of Consumer Affairs; the Profit Impact of Market Strategy Report, American Strategic Planning Institute.

LOVE mode

Topping Off On Satisfaction

Once you grab the "low hanging fruit," bigger challenges are in store. How to grab the "top box."

Moving from a 60 to 85 percent recommendation rate is easy, says Geoff Graham of GuildQuality. It's going from 85 to 92 percent that takes significant training and effort.

Alex Saloutos, who has for 20 years built brand awareness, sales, market share, and customer satisfaction, says early gains come from "low hanging fruit" — the obvious problems, like a construction manager who's not communicating with a customer. The more complicated processes, he says — completing the home on time while involving sales, purchasing, estimating, construction and your trades — take more time but produce higher gains. They're the items that drive the customer to check not the second or third box, but the top box — *delighted to recommend!*

If you receive 90 percent of your checks in the second and third boxes and only 10 percent in the top box, no one really loves you, and your referrals won't be strong. But if you can get those second and third boxes to move to the top, you'll see an exponential increase in referrals, Saloutos says.

He sees four fundamental drivers to satisfaction, and they coincide with other expert observations in this book: *Was the home completed on time? Was it 100 percent complete at*

If you don't use satisfaction and loyalty measurement tools, you're losing your best source of information, sacrificing retention and profitability, spending more money to advertise, and aren't receiving top dollar. If you don't use these tools, or use them ineffectively, you'll be unable to help your employees improve what they do for you. You won't improve as a company, or worse, you'll send clients the wrong messages. Over time, you'll destroy your business. In fact, I'd hazard to guess that a large segment of our industry has already done this. I've seen some head-knocking data that convinces me this could be the case.

One of the most intriguing, documented methods for evaluating client satisfaction and customer loyalty to hit the business world in the past decade, largely outside of homebuilding, has been the work of Bain & Co. director emeritus and fellow, Fred Reichheld, author of *The Ultimate Question: Driving Good Profits and True Growth*, and many other books. Reichheld's methods with the Net Promoter Score (NPS) have captured the attention of leading companies, among them GE. Every GE business unit uses Reichheld's methods to measure the number of promoting, detracting, or passive customers they have. Their small business financial services unit, GE Money, shared with me how they use a variation of the system to improve and grow their business (**See Love Mode, Page 178**).

closing? Was it delivered on budget? Did the builder give you good service after the sale?

To achieve higher levels of satisfaction you must align expectations with actual performance, he says. "You have to be honest with yourself and your customer about what you promise and then what you deliver consistently. You have to make promises you can deliver 100 percent of the time." You need to set realistic performance standards. Don't bother telling the customer about them until you can execute those standards over and over again.

Saloutos suggests when looking at opportunities for improvement, you need to assess them using a four-square grid — difficulty versus impact. Weigh the high or low opportunity against the difficulty. Make one improvement at a time, and you'll make better progress than trying to make many changes too quickly.

He suggests that if a builder follows three steps, the company will achieve continuous improvement, particularly if leaders create that sort of culture. "They can't be more concerned about profits this month or this week," he says. "And they have to understand all their drivers of dissatisfaction. If purchasing is picking the electrician who's cheapest, who doesn't show up on time, doesn't do work right the first time, and doesn't do service work, parts of the organization will work at cross purposes."

Steps he suggests:

Measure It. If you're not listening to your customers, you can't measure their satisfaction, or your progress toward improvement.

At a recent Eliant National Round-table on Homebuyer Satisfaction, Bob Mirman, Eliant CEO, introduced the builders in attendance to Reichheld, and his system. Martha Baumgarten, an Eliant vice president, shared information that, fully understood, would just about take your breath away (**See Why Clients Hate Us, Page 161**).

Baumgarten took data from 144,842 homeowner surveys received Jan. 1 through Sept. 30, 2007. Based on gradated responses to the scaled statement *"I would recommend my builder to a friend or family member,"* she developed average Net Promoter Scores at move-in, mid-year, and year-end. She also devised a numerical composite score of those measurements. Eliant's builders, among the industry's most forward-thinking since they know they need to listen to customers, received a composite NPS of 11 percent. This compares to a composite score of 63 percent for the top 10 percent of Eliant's builders. Mid-year scores barely hit 1 percent and year-end scores were only 5 percent.

At 1 percent, for every person promoting your company, you'll have one person detracting, spewing negative comments to everyone they meet. As Mirman notes, that's not a wash. Detractors tell at least four times as many people as your promoters will tell. In other words, from his sampling, we're sliding backward. For every eight people a detractor tells about your company, every promoter tells only

---

Use A Likert Scale. In other words, use a five- or six-point gradated rating system that states options such as unlikely, probably, likely, very likely, definitely.

Listen. Set a standard so that any customer who doesn't check your top box (would highly recommend) gets a visit. Ask these questions: *What could we have done to receive a "would highly recommend?"* The visit needs to be non-confrontational. *What would it take for us to give you a better experience? What could we have done differently?*

Because research firms give their builder clients tons of information, problems can get lost in the mix, he says, and if company leadership says "fix this stuff," and there's 10 questions with bad results, confusion arises. What's first?

"But it may not be 10 things," Saloutos says. "It may be one thing. Or it may not be one of the 10 things that get you into a 'love' situation. It's like the wife who says 'I don't care if he makes my coffee in the morning ... If he wants me to love him he's got to tickle my toes.'"

Ask the customers what delights them; they will tell you, he says.

Often it takes one more step.

You can't get that from a 120-page report and 60 graphs, he says. "Data makes you think, but emotion drives change. If employees can see a customer in a focus group, from behind one-way glass, saying, 'I will never refer you if anyone asks' and they see a face and they see emotion, that drives change."

---

two. But what else can we learn from this data? That we're lousy at nurturing homeowner relationships, especially late in the process — *we love 'em and leave 'em*, as Baumgarten says. Overall, she says, "it's scary to look at this data. It freaks me out."

It looks chilling to me, too.

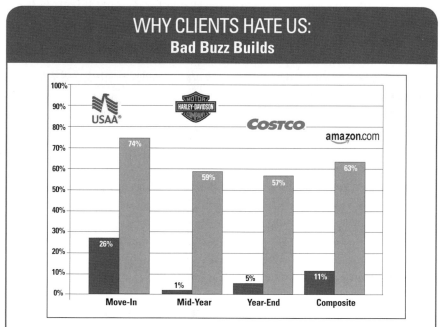

WHY CLIENTS HATE US:
Bad Buzz Builds

SOURCE: ELIANT, WWW.ELIANT.COM.

The average Net Promoter Score of all Eliant builders at move-in (noted in black) is 26 percent, compared to 74 percent for the company's top 10 percent builders (noted in gray). This is based on 144,842 surveys from 224 builders, received Jan. 1 through Sept. 30, 2007. Eliant's top 10 percent builders have scores approaching loyalty leaders Harley-Davidson and Costco (about 80 percent) and exceeding Amazon.com (about 70 percent), but most telling is that 90 percent of builders rank very low on the key statement: "I would recommend my builder to a friend or family member." That figure averages 26 percent, or less. With a score of 26 percent, you have two promoter customers for every detractor. A score of 74 percent means you have about 9 promoters for every detractor.

Ladies and gentlemen, it's time to start getting real about listening to our customers. There are many ways to do this, but with AVID Ratings reporting on 500 builder clients, Eliant reporting on 300, GuildQuality reporting on 500, and a generous estimate giving other market research firms approximately 1,200 more clients, that leaves 435,700 builder and remodeler employers who aren't listening to their customers, or who are doing assessments on their own.

I would agree with Madison, Wisc. consultant Alex Saloutos, of The Office of Alex Saloutos, that only 1 in 20 builders listen to their customers in a formal way. This helps to explain why we, as an industry, are more likely to have detractors than promoters — more people who hate us than love us.

The irony is customers only want a few seconds of our time and then will be satisfied. It's similar to an unwritten rule for parents: If your kids say "Mom!" more than five times, you are required to answer them. In a company, repeated requests irritate everyone, but often the person hearing the customer yell doesn't have the ability or authority to answer. Strict lines of communication prevent an immediate response. We need to change these procedures to overcome such barriers.

To understand your value and begin to sell this value, you have to understand how clients view your company and its processes. The only way to probe these inner workings and their effectiveness is to be in touch with everyone who experiences them. Surveys are the best way to do this. The best in the business, like David Weekley Homes (**See Love Story, Page 172**), learned this years ago, and they've never stopped listening. The best companies even survey their competitor's customers. Surveys define your value and when you create value, you receive less price resistance. If your customers' perception is that you're overpriced, prices slide, and then you're no longer supporting value, you're defending price, or even haggling.

Remember Rosenthal Homes in Rockville, Md., where owner Emily Rosenthal calls customers for a draw payment, only she doesn't call it a draw, she calls it a *progress* payment? She learned that from a customer. He was a marketing executive, and one day, when she presented him an invoice, he said, "It's not a *draw* payment, it's a *progress* payment. When I give you money, you've made *progress*. You're closer to having my home done." See how much we can learn by listening?

See how much *progress* we can make!

Let's explore how to spread this love, and examine potential pitfalls; why it's important to realize that to make progress, we need to listen, really listen, 100 percent.

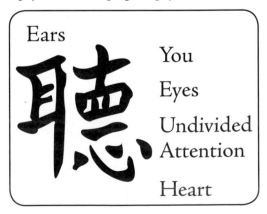

AS THIS CHINESE SYMBOL FOR LISTENING INDICATES, LISTENING REQUIRES USING MORE THAN JUST YOUR EARS.

WHEN YOU KNOW, YOU GROW

Reichheld says most people think loyalty is a joke, and what they really care about is growth. But loyalty and growth are one in the same, he says, because growing companies report the highest customer loyalty. By asking his ultimate question — *How likely is it that you would recommend the company to a friend or a colleague?* — he's able to determine for companies which of their clients will help them grow.

His books are replete with examples of major companies that have used his method to great success. Eliant, working with the University of Southern California School of Business, has done research on NPS and other survey measures tied to profitability and warranty costs. They found interest from their builder clients in a simpler, yet perhaps more effective method to predict growth. Paul Cardis of AVID Ratings says the NPS philosophy is already deeply integrated into AVID systems.

AVID divides customers into nine referral potentials. The categories help clients understand the relationship between the client experience and loyalty. An automated system slots each customer into a referral potential category. While built from Reichheld's principles, the system focuses on home builder issues. An example of the AVID proprietary system is on the next page.

Cardis says AVID's system, by assessing individual customers' referral potential, helps the builders' employees understand how to respond to the customer. And let me add: This is the most critical piece if you want surveys to work within your company — what do my employees do with this information? If they know they have a customer with a high referral potential, it makes sense to invest in that customer. You can efficiently align resources where they will provide the most return. On the other hand, if surveys spot a potentially hostile client, AVID suggests a "SWAT team" response — not unlike that of a police department's response to a threat — to deal with and recover the customer, before they severely damage your organization. (I'll address "hostiles" in Chapter 7.)

Eliant ranks homeowners in the following categories: Evangelical, A, B, or C. It has determined that category C buyers make an average of 1.7 recommendations 10 months after move in, while category B buyers make an average of 3.5, category A buyers make an average of 4.6, and Evangelical category buyers make an average of 6.1. Mirman notes that the only difference for each category is the intensity of the experience they've had during the process. If quality issues weren't resolved, or commitments weren't met, this affects their willingness to refer.

WINNING FANS, ASSUAGING HOSTILES

Categorized Survey Table			52 Surveys From The Last 30 Days (02/10/2008 To 03/10/2008)		
Filter Surveys by:					Page Size: 25
☐😊 ☐😕 ☐😫 ☐😵 | ☐⚠	☐Read ☐Unread	All Communities			Prev Page **(1 of 3) Next Page**
Satisfaction Type	**Alert**	**Name**	**Division** / Date Received	**Community** / Date Closed ▲	**Read Status** / View All
😊 Borderline Loyal		CHERYL CLARK	Sample Homes #1 / 03/06/2008	Saint Helena / 07/18/2006	☐ / View Survey
😊 Avid Fan		PHYLLIS THOMPSON	Sample Homes #1 / 02/11/2008	West Hills / 07/11/2007	☐ / View Survey
😊 Avid Fan		PATRICIA DAVIS	Sample Homes #1 / 02/12/2008	West Hills / 08/16/2007	☐ / View Survey
😊 Avid Fan		HENRY COX	Sample Homes #1 / 03/06/2008	Hamilton Hark / 10/30/2007	☐ / View Survey
😊 Avid Fan		CHRISTINE TURNER	Sample Homes #1 / 02/15/2008	Hamilton Hark / 11/14/2007	☐ / View Survey
😕 Moderately Content		Confidential	Sample Homes #1 / 02/2008	Canton / 12/2007	☐ / View Survey
😊 Avid Fan		HOWARD TAYLOR	Sample Homes #1 / 02/10/2008	Canton / 12/05/2007	☐ / View Survey
😊 Avid Fan		BRUCE WRIGHT	Sample Homes #1 / 02/10/2008	Homeland Ph. 2 / 12/06/2007	☐ / View Survey

😊 Avid Fan

Avid Fans are the ultimate customers for any business. These customers are absolutely delighted and generate the highest value to your company. These customers will provide tremendous ROI by making referrals to other customers and they have an increased tolerance for any mistakes that may have happened during the experience, which makes them most profitable as well. Keep in mind, these customers may have a few items to correct which shouldn't be ignored. They can yield even higher rates of return if their items are resolved. We recommend viewing these surveys for any lower score on the survey and addressing these items, if possible, with the customer.

😕 Fanatical Loyal

Fanatical Loyal customers are less common but nice to have. Essentially, they are very loyal, despite having had a dissatisfying experience. They may have filled the survey out incorrectly, so examine the survey to check the consistency of the results. Most likely, the customers are, fortunately, very loyal and any efforts you make to improve their situations will result in them becoming Avid Fans. We recommend taking care of any easily resolvable issues.

😕 Confused Happy

A Confused Happy customer may have filled out their survey incorrectly. They have indicated that the experience was very satisfying, yet would not recommend the builder. We recommend re-surveying the customer to confirm that they answered the survey correctly and didn't get confused. (Call AVID Ratings if you would like to attempt to re-survey a customer.) Another possibility is that this customer had a significantly negative experience with one or more individuals within the company, which has tainted the whole experience. This is rare, but possible. We recommend examining the survey carefully to see if the customer answered other questions low and try to address, or contact the AVID Ratings Client Service Manager for assistance.

😫 Potential Hostile

Potential Hostile customers are the most detrimental customers you can have. They are completely dissatisfied and unwilling to make any referrals. Also, this customer has a high probability of making negative referrals. They have extreme negative emotions toward you and may seek damages against your organization. A Builder SWAT Team is a must to deal with this customer.

SOURCE: AVID RATINGS, WWW.AVIDRATINGS.COM.

AVID Ratings clients are able to categorize their customers by their inclination to refer. Customers are broken into nine categories allowing employees to see which clients need immediate attention, and which clients will provide the highest return for the resources invested.

One of the main issues Eliant focuses on, as a key contributor to satisfaction and referrals, is home readiness. In its surveys, it asks specific questions related to readiness: *Was the home completed on time for move in? Was it clean on the inside? Was it clean on the outside? Was the construction site around the home clean, orderly, and neat?*

We need to remember that it's possible to complete a home, 100 percent. It's not easy, but it's possible, and should be probable. Read the documents and promises you provide your customers. No contract clause reads, "an almost complete home," or, "I will finish the home when I'm ready." If you break these promises, you've broken your contract. It's not like customers are expecting something unrealistic. The bottom line is it's either finished or it's not — there's no in-between. Yet, there are still many builders who think this is a totally unrealistic expectation.

READY OR NOT? YOU'D BETTER BE

Bob Mirman, Eliant CEO, says looking at data like this allows the builder to see how he performs in a changing market environment. How does a company adapt to the change from a seller's market to a buyer's market? How does a company continue to serve clients well, in consistent ways? Good builders don't see much of a change. However, things can quickly go bad, when there are management changes. A new manager who changes the tone of customer care or the incentive plans can have an extraordinary affect. Those are among some critical changes Eliant sees, the CEO adds. It's not long until bar graphs begin to head south. "The strongest catalyst for change is a change in management," Mirman says. And the loudest complaints of homebuyers are about frequent turnover in staff — what an important issue that is when we are making our way out of a down market.

The problem, Mirman observes, is that turnover causes you to lose institutional memory and buyers lose confidence. If a superintendent is replaced, it can create havoc. It's hard to win loyalty when trust declines. A new salesperson can be death, a deal killer, and it always creates anxiety. If you change or lose personnel, you'll see it reflected in the scores — with the potential for low scores and dramatic swings from month to month.

Whenever we ask people to do something, they are looking for what's in it for them. So how do you protect both your internal and external clients? You have to remember everyone involved has to benefit. Say you have a new salesperson and they need to pick up the pieces of a sale and take it forward. In

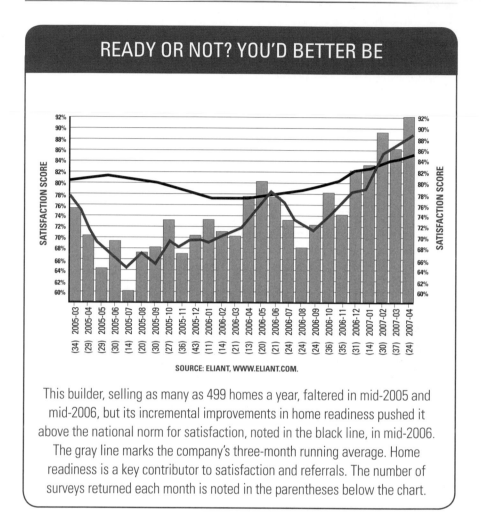

READY OR NOT? YOU'D BETTER BE

SOURCE: ELIANT, WWW.ELIANT.COM.

This builder, selling as many as 499 homes a year, faltered in mid-2005 and mid-2006, but its incremental improvements in home readiness pushed it above the national norm for satisfaction, noted in the black line, in mid-2006. The gray line marks the company's three-month running average. Home readiness is a key contributor to satisfaction and referrals. The number of surveys returned each month is noted in the parentheses below the chart.

many situations, they're not compensated, so they'll have to do this to enhance goodwill. If they're not yet part of the team, they'll see it as an added responsibility they're not paid for, and they already have a lot on their plate. If we develop ties and relationships, then it becomes personal — and it gets done.

In down markets, surveys will usually indicate improved delivery times, due to more sales of inventory homes. But the data will also reveal less-improved or weaker relationships with key personnel — since there was no chance to develop these relationships over the normal five to seven months of the building cycle.

How could you not want to anticipate those critical predictors of profit and performance?

WHO'S BETTER THAN JOHN?

Product delivery issues, market impact, and a customer's tendencies to refer aren't all you can learn from surveys. Ben Morey of Morey Construction, of Signal Hill, Calif., who uses GuildQuality of Atlanta to keep a pulse on his customers, likes the fact that he can use GuildQuality's tools to maintain his reputation, which he feels is priceless. "That's really what keeps people in business for a long time," he says. "Once you've lost your reputation, the ability to regain it from a cost standpoint is so much more than the immediate job you're working on."

One of his key questions to clients is: *Was your remodeling project easier than expected?* He can compare these answers to his peer group averages within GuildQuality's database. By working closely with their clients, giving them a schedule ahead of time, and lowering their fear factor, Morey Construction has improved this metric, at least within the most recent 12-month period.

SURVEY SAYS
Easier Than Expected

Overall Summary	Responded	Attempted	Recommendation %	Easier Than Expected %
All Of Your Customers	17	24	88.2%	52.9%
Most Recent 12 Months	6	9	100.0%	66.7%
Most Recent 30 Days	1	2	100.0%	0.0%
Your Peer Group	2981	3914	95.1%	70.8%
All Similar Guild Members	29918	45398	87.6%	70.1%

SOURCE: GUILD QUALITY, WWW.GUILDQUALITY.COM.

GuildQuality's overall summary of Morey Construction's survey results shows a solid recommendation rate compared to similar GuildQuality members. However, fewer customers thought the process was easier than expected, compared to peer companies, or all GuildQuality members.

Morey is able to monitor his recommendation rate, comparing it to the national recommendation rate among remodelers of about 65 percent, says Geoffrey Graham, GuildQuality CEO. GuildQuality remodelers, perhaps in recognition of the maxim that what gets measured gets improved, report an average recommendation rate of 95 percent, with the lowest performers in the upper 80th percentile. They know that with a 75 percent rate, their businesses will have trouble staying *in* business, Graham says. They know that unhappy clients tell more people about their experience than those who are delighted.

Morey, and others, benefit from business peer review groups. These include Remodelers Advantage of Laurel, Md., and NAHB's Builder 20 and Remodeler 20 clubs — great places to share business tools and best practices to improve client satisfaction.

Graham says the companies that obtain the most significant gains in satisfaction results are those that share their aggregate numbers with their employees. *I had no idea John was doing better than me*, is a common response, says Graham. The employees see that there's something more important than just completing the job, and that's making the customer happy. By measuring customer satisfaction, they see that the customer's happiness is the goal of the business.

Based on surveys of their builder and remodeler members, 78 percent of their members find that the most important use of the surveys is the real-time feedback (they receive an email notification when a customer replies via mail, email, or phone) and the ability to respond quickly to issues. About 75 percent find the succinct performance reports (online analytics showing how team members compare to peers) from their surveys to be most useful. And half of his clients appreciate the peer benchmarking and the marketing component of the reports — being able to use that information and leverage it during a sale.

Like the other market research CEOs, Graham reports that the surveys are both a management tool — getting people to see how they compare and can improve — and a marketing tool — *we are among the top builders in our market.*

The best companies use the real-time report to make every customer a raving fan. But let's not forget the detractors, either. Once you understand where the problem is coming from — sales, design, construction, or warranty — developing an action plan and *implementing* it can put the problem to bed. The difficulty isn't going from 65 to 85 percent in satisfaction scores. It's gaining that critical 7 percent that brings you to 92 percent satisfaction and guarantees more promoters than detractors. There's no easy route to higher scores, says Alex Saloutos, former marketing director of Veridian Homes' precursor Don

Simon Homes, who helped improve satisfaction levels on the way to making the then-$58 million-a-year builder the 2002 National Housing Quality Award winner (**See Love Mode, Page 158**).

Eliant's Mirman estimates that up to 15 percent of their clients do little with the information they get from their surveys. "They think the survey is enough, and they have more important things to do — they get back to building homes," he says. The Eliant CEO says that in most companies there are usually one or two managers who take them seriously, despite the corporate indifference.

The biggest challenge is to gain consistency. Creating consistency across divisions or departments is difficult, he says. Builders rarely do a consistently bad job, but because departments or divisions experience a range of scores, it's difficult to get them to participate in this process, he says. If 15 people are involved, 10 will do well, two will do exceptionally well, and three will do poorly. If they could generate a 50 to 75 percent compliance rate, responding with specific actions to their survey results, he says that for most builders it would be a significant improvement over the status quo.

GE Money has every employee follow up on surveys. At David Weekley Homes, there was a time when the founder followed up, in person, on any negative survey in Houston, Dallas, Austin, and San Antonio. Now, those follow-ups are done by project managers, division managers, and area presidents. *Remember, this is one of the largest 25 builders in the country.*

THE COST OF DISSATISFACTION

96%	Won't tell you why they're not satisfied
90%	Won't return for repeat business
100%	Will tell at least nine people they're not satisfied
13%	Will tell more than 20 people about their dissatisfaction

SOURCE: TECHNICAL ASSISTANCE RESEARCH PROGRAM, CONSUMER COMPLAINT HANDLING IN AMERICA: AN UPDATE STUDY, WHITE HOUSE OFFICE OF CONSUMER AFFAIRS, WASHINGTON, D.C.

While 70 percent of satisfied customers will come back to do business again, and they'll tell at least five people how well they were treated, the stakes are higher for dissatisfied customers.

The point is, your customer relationships are too valuable not to be taken seriously, and must be examined carefully, by everyone in the company, no matter what the company's size.

Examining the effect of survey results on a large company, Steve Petruska, Pulte's COO, says that for their Las Vegas division in the early 2000s, the repeat and referral business hovered in the mid 20 percent range. Then Pulte instituted a seven-step process that addressed customer treatment at key touchpoints by involving the entire team that had contact with the customer. Because they were building long-term relationships, their customer relations scores rose rapidly. One survey question they used was, *how many major or minor items were found at delivery?* The division, best in the company at the time, reported that 22 percent of respondents found major items. So a quarter of its customers were telling them there were major things wrong at the closing. At the time, that result led the company, and was good enough in 2000 to win a J.D. Power award for Las Vegas. Petruska was told by a construction vice president that single digits were impossible. But within 12 to 18 months, they reported single digits, and the numbers were dropping fast. "And it wasn't that in 18 months we were building fantastically better homes, it was that we were building fantastically better relationships," Petruska says. "We changed our focus

Guts To Love

Giving Away The House?
BY CAROL SMITH

One pattern that's clear in customer satisfaction surveys is that buyers of well-built and completely finished homes generate fewer noted items during the orientation and warranty period. Another pattern: When you treat people well, they're more likely to like you — *the quality of the experience matters along with the quality of the home.* Do you really need charts and graphs to see this?

Customer satisfaction does indeed lead to increased profits. First homeowners conclude that they've received a good product. Second, the warranty department has less work and it follows that less work is quicker to complete — further increasing satisfaction. Moreover, when your delivery and warranty staff work from a position of strength, they can more readily deflect a deluge of inappropriate requests while maintaining buyer goodwill. The resulting reduction in costs — combined with increased referrals — protects and builds profits.

When builders commit numerous sins during the new home process — losing a change order, leaving lunch trash and dirt all over the home and home site, failing to return phone calls promptly, delivering the home late and *still* incomplete, then top it off by failing to follow through on the items noted during the orientation — warranty personnel (consciously or subconsciously) give away more during the warranty period. This begins when buyers submit long lists. Who can blame them? They've internally at the cultural level of the organization to make it not just a construction thing."

Peter J. Keane, Pulte's senior vice president of operations, says Pulte found, roughly during the same period, that the offices around the country that got the best scores weren't focused on satisfaction, but on the cost of service, labor, materials, customer service, and profit. When he was division president in Chicago he inherited a 70 percent overall satisfaction score. His goal was 90 percent. When his team focused on delighting the customer and not so much on scores, or pestering clients for surveys, scores improved. Service and materials costs dropped.

The point is, surveys and scores are tools for the end game. You need to prioritize what you receive from these surveys and determine what to tackle first — issues change from company to company. How will you follow up on these findings? The plan has to be implemented in workable pieces. If it's too much to tackle, the team will reject it. You have to look at it incrementally, and what's appropriate to make it work.

I've barely given you a taste of what these tools can do, and how they can improve your customer care systems. What they do best is to provide a way for everyone in the company to see changes in customer care. If employees see this, they understand what it means to be rewarded for notching up customer care. But be careful — even that step presents pitfalls.

learned that they need to ask for 40 items in order to get 10 corrected. Plus, they're just plain angry.

Your warranty staff can try to follow normal standards, but the exceptions multiply and work grows in proportion to threats and accusations from frustrated homeowners. Guilt and defensiveness kick in along with sincere hopes of restoring some of the goodwill: Warranty personnel begin to fix things they shouldn't. As the workload grows, service becomes slower, leading to even more homeowner ire. The cycle feeds on itself and reversing it is a long, tough assignment. Word gets out in the marketplace. Salespeople begin to negotiate lower prices and concessions to meet their minimum sales goals.

On the other hand, when customers purchase with confidence, convinced by the builder's reputation and by what they see and hear that both the home and the experience will excel, they're often willing to pay higher prices. The peace of mind — and for some, the status — of buying a home from such a company is worth more. Many companies overlook the impact of these issues on personnel. Working in an environment filled with successful projects and happy customers results in less wear and tear on staff, consequently less (expensive) turnover. Attracting and retaining the best talent is another way companies profit from customer satisfaction. People want to be proud of where they work and want to work where showing up is a pleasure rather than an endurance test.

The benefits of getting things right, from the start and all along the way, feed a cycle — a positive and profitable one.

NO GAMES, PLEASE

More and more companies are rewarding employees based on how well their company, division, or department does on customer satisfaction surveys. But you must put safeguards in place to avoid "gaming," the deliberate influencing of customers in order to win good scores. Remember: Improving the survey score isn't the goal. The goal is improved customer loyalty.

In 2007, a major builder received media attention for allegedly paying customers $100 each for high marks on satisfaction surveys, surveys that influenced executive bonuses. Federal investigators were probing the issue. AVID Ratings, which was not involved in the scandal, collected the surveys and Paul Cardis, Avid Ratings' CEO, called the builder's mistake costly.

"It's a company that went bad," he says. "They made some serious mistakes. They misunderstood what customer delight was, and what the return was. It was about increasing their bonuses individually and they didn't care about building long-term loyalty with the buyer."

It was unfortunate, he says, that management didn't maintain a strict policy covering communications with buyers about the surveys. "They slipped into a bad place where even the division president was blatantly violating the system to increase his bonuses," Cardis says.

INSTANT SATISFACTION: PHONE HOME

LOVE STORY

David Weekley Homes swears by the immediacy of phone surveys. You can't beat the speed of the response, or the chance to connect with your customer.

For real-time feedback, to feel your client's pain, and to reach nearly all of your customers while strengthening relationships, two loyalty research experts suggest what some might call an "old school" method: Phone surveys.

David Weekley Homes, one of the nation's 25 largest builders, surveys by phone, through its Houston market research consultant, Creative Consumer Research, 10,000 clients each year. Marc Warren of Customer Follow Up, the Boalsburg, Pa. market research consultant who has since 1997 completed hundreds of phone surveys for clients, including home builders, affirms Weekley's experience.

The AVID CEO recommends that every company put in place definitions and guidelines on what to communicate to buyers regarding the survey and the assessment process. This bad actor was given AVID's policy, but chose not to implement it. (AVID ended the relationship before these issues came to light.)

AVID and Eliant have both built into their surveys questions asking whether the builder has campaigned for survey results or tried to influence the customer. When surveys indicate such behavior, builder clients are notified. Cardis says bonuses are appropriate and can be tied to customer satisfaction results, but there are pitfalls. He's in favor of well-thought-out programs, particularly those that are team-based. "They are powerful when done right," he says. "They can align the organization."

Eliant plans to add questions addressing undue influence to its

"Our method is the only one I know of where the customer feels that someone is tied into the process," Warren says. "If the survey is mail-in or done on a Web site, there's no one to feel their pain. This is the only way I'm aware of that will strengthen the relationship and the business."

Mike Humphrey, David Weekley's operations vice president, says near-immediate connections mitigate anything that breaks a relationship with clients. "We think that living in the 24/7 world, the quicker you get the survey back, the better it is," Humphrey says. Furthermore, he says because the company can reach as many as 95 percent of its customers by phone survey and receives near-instantaneous feedback, it can quickly resolve problems. It gives clients another chance to re-connect after these breaks, as they're asked during the survey: Would you like to be contacted by a David Weekley Homes representative? When clients answer yes, their project manager receives an email and is expected to respond to their request within 24 hours, and if possible, the same day.

Weekley has used some variation of phone surveys for 17 years. Humphrey says that when J.D. Power and Associates entered the homebuilding industry, his company contracted for a proprietary survey and overlaid their results on its own findings. The top three issues needing improvement matched the lowest scores on Weekley's own surveys.

Warren says surveys sometimes get so automated that you forget the person; you take them out of it. The phone survey allows venting.

surveys. "There's a growing importance and pressure placed on executives and managers at all levels in a building organization," Mirman says. "As the importance of the surveys are accepted throughout the industry, and as managers are evaluated on performance or given sizeable bonuses, the opportunity to game the survey becomes a significant consideration."

But he says if pay for performance is done correctly and managers gaming the system are uncovered and punished, there's a strong message: You can't game the system and make more money.

An alternative is to reward employees on other key measures, such as providing cash incentives, prizes, and recognition for zero-defect deliveries. One builder I know of tracks home closings, detailing items found on the initial inspection, orientation, and closing. When nothing is found, everyone working on the home receives a ticket entered into a lottery for cash prizes worth up to $10,000.

Many builders have shared stories of competitors' "influence" before surveys are distributed to determine J.D. Power scores. Some builders plant flowers for their clients. Others write letters, letting them know they "care." Maybe that's not so bad — some would say it's smart business — but direct influence is *out of the question*.

"If you're screwing up year round, you can't possibly, in one move, change everything that's happened to me as a homeowner over the past year,"

"Because the home is so personal and is a personal investment, generally speaking, we want to talk to them." If a customer is irate, Warren's firm issues a client alert. Usually, resolving the problem requires tweaking a process, not major overhauls, he says. The phone survey gets to the heart of the matter, discovering whether the problem is simply with an employee who got lazy executing a process, or something unexpected: *Your voicemail is so complex, I got frustrated and didn't leave a message. I called four months ago.* Or, *There's an emergency number on your Web site, but whenever we call, no one answers.*

That's like calling 911 and being put on hold. In my opinion, this is not just another whining customer. That's a valid complaint. Listen to them.

Warren's builder clients mail their customer contact information weekly and it helps that Customer Follow Up is independent. These builders tell their clients during the sales process and remind them throughout production that they will be called for a survey within 30 days of closing. This also helps overcome any Federal Trade Commission Do Not Call Registry restrictions since the builders continually ask, up front, for the client's OK to call as part of their customer satisfaction system. If clients choose not to be contacted, their request is honored.

Because Warren's firm lets client builders know of problems immediately, they're easier to resolve. "The longer it goes on, the harder it is to take care of," he says. While customers might feel an issue needs attention in 10

Mirman says. "You can't fool the public to that extent."

Keane says that years ago, Pulte Homes was only getting 40 percent of their mailed-in surveys returned because employees asked clients to return them. "Potentially, that leads to unintended behaviors, and in some cases it did," he says. Now, Pulte Homes has a Web-based survey, and a letter is sent from chairman Bill Pulte to the customer, giving them an online log-in number. Results are collected by Morpace, the market research firm. Employees have no idea when the letter gets sent. "We put much more effort into it in the past, convincing ourselves that we would get a higher return rate," says Keane. "But our current methodology proves that was a waste of effort."

We owe it to our industry and our customers to build integrity into this vital process.

DON'T DULL THE LOVE

How do you continue to obtain opinions and research without dulling the *Love?* The customer has to know what's in it for them. And you need to thank them for their comments. You can't tell them *the survey goes into the pool.* You can't say: *We get 150 of those a month.* You need to follow up and show your appreciation after you receive their survey, giving them the comfort that

minutes, often they can live with it for 10 days if the builder commits immediately to a plan to resolve it, and then follows through.

Warren believes phone surveys are more insightful because you can probe responses. If the customer says the builder could have been more proactive, the caller asks for an example. "Then you have something you can point to," he says. "Or they say, 'I would have liked it if they had a nicer selection.' 'What do you mean? Give me an example, please,' the surveyor might ask. You can drive to the heart of whether it was a sales or a selections issue." It's important, whatever the case, for the surveyor to remain neutral. You can't have a surveyor who wants to fix problems. They have to like people and want to help them, but they can't solve problems. Their job is to elicit responses and carefully draw clients out.

Warren feels Web-based or mail-in surveys cater to people who are better writers, and whose answers are definitive. But if they're asked on the phone if they'd recommend, and they hedge, the surveyor can explore that tentative yes and learn why they feel that way.

"It comes down to the integrity of the process," Warren says. "If you have the right people on the phone, they can see inconsistencies in the customer's answers. If you're going along well, and then you ask 'would you recommend?' and they say 'no,' or, 'perhaps,' that's inconsistent with an upbeat survey. So the caller can say, 'OK, maybe I missed something. In the first five questions you seemed happy. Now,

you're considering their comments. You need to tell them their comments matter, that this isn't just an exercise.

We need to appreciate the customer and value their opinion. It's hard for a customer to say no to a request for a testimonial if you've showered them over the past 12 months with appreciation. Asking for a testimonial should be a complimentary experience, not an obligatory one. You compliment the customer by asking their opinion. Don't be afraid of hearing what it is. After all, by then you've truly earned the right to ask for it.

And don't be like the guy who got a note on his pillow and doesn't know why his wife left. Meanwhile, she's thinking, *if you don't know*, I can't tell you. You should always be open to hearing the worst about yourself — and the best, too.

If you keep your survey easy, short, and help the person taking it under-

you're a moderately recommend — can you tell me why?'"

Warren admits some customers might be more honest when they're not talking to a person, and writing down their answers. They could add more detail. "It's not categorically the way to do it," he says of phone surveys. "It's like advertising — there's print, the Web and so on — no definitive way trumps the others. Some people would rather write than talk and others would much rather talk than write. But oftentimes, the human connection makes it work."

Customer Follow Up surveys of 25 to 35 questions take 15 minutes. Weekley's survey takes less than 15 minutes — "we shoot for 13," says Humphrey, unless clients want to stay on the phone for an hour — and it is the customers who are dissatisfied or are extremely delighted who are interested in talking the longest, he notes. David Weekley Homes also lets customers repeatedly know, early in the relationship, that they'll be called for phone surveys at three stages — mid-construction, 30 days after move-in, and 11 months after move in.

Weekley, always seeking the definitely would recommend on surveys, realizes that the only way it can train people to execute at least 90 percent of the time on the issues homebuyers feel are most important is to let them see when key measurements change. "Our job is to identify whether it's a system problem, a person problem, an attitude problem, or a leadership problem," Humphrey says.

stand they're making a contribution, you'll be ahead of the game. Let them know they're making the process better for the next person. Have a good tracking system — don't ask the same person the same questions two weeks later. Let them know that not only have you considered what they've said, they've made a difference.

Thank people for giving you their time. They need immediate appreciation. Personalize your thank-you notes. Form letters don't work. Make it a personally signed letter from the division president. Tell clients that based on their input and that of other customers that this — point X, Y and Z — is what you've done to improve the customer experience. Not long ago I wrote Larry Kellner, chairman and CEO of Continental Airlines, to compliment him on the service provided by three employees, one of whom you'll read about in the next chapter. Kellner has thousands of employees, but he personally responded to my note. If Kellner can do it, why can't a builder with 20 people on the payroll?

Never allow people to drop off your radar screen. No one is an ex-buyer. They are all, and will always be, your homeowner clients. Recognize, appreciate, celebrate, and use your surveys to build loyalty for life.

Once you do, you'll have made the leap toward success: You'll be an *Information-Experience* company.

Because the data is constantly changing, Weekley records it in Lotus Notes, and aggregate information is updated monthly. Any employee can review data by project, division, city, community, or total company. Project managers in Houston can compare themselves to their peers in Dallas. "We can look at what we do well, and use that for celebration, training, and to validate what we do in our training," Humphrey says.

Compared in price to the two leading mailed survey companies, costs are 30 percent to 50 percent less, Humphrey says. He works with Creative Consumer Research, of Houston and Phoenix.

Warren says that to interview as many as 500 homeowners a year, by phone, two or three times, provide the builder reports, and on-site and phone consulting, could cost a minimum of $50,000. For mail and email services, surveying buyers three times a year with a series of reminders and detailed online reporting, you could expect to pay $75 to $95 per surveyed customer.

I encourage you to talk to the great market research companies out there and assess which proposal is the best match for your company. Look beyond the price tag. Thoroughly understand the value you receive for your investment.

Some might consider phone surveys to be old school, but for Humphrey's company and Warren's clients, they're fast, affordable, and provide the most accurate interactive knowledge they can obtain, allowing them to build companies with clients for life.

CAN YOU HANDLE THE TRUTH?

GE Money uses a variation of a customer satisfaction system that builders have begun to explore. The survey asks a key question, but also targets performance and the competition.

It's easy to accept mediocrity: If you're not upsetting customers, you must be doing OK.

That's how Bruce L. Christensen of GE Money, GE's $2 billion-plus financing arm for 10,000 home improvement contractors, describes the old way of thinking about satisfaction surveys.

GE and GE Money have never been happy with the *status quo*, and the company knows that only with a firm respect for what it calls the *Voice of the Customer* will it understand the new way of thinking: Convincing clients through world-class service to promote its brand of home improvement lending for life.

GE Money's next focus will be to evaluate through NPS its product price elasticity. It seeks to better understand how close it can get to its margins, as its pricing is higher than its closest competitors.

GE Money was an early adopter of Fred Reichheld's Net Promoter Score system because it was pushed by GE CEO Jeffrey R. Immelt in 2005. They adapted the system to ask passive customers or detractors, scores from zero to 8: *What can we do to improve?* Customers who rate the company 9 or 10 are asked: *What do we do well?* If customers chose a competitor, they're asked who it is. And GE Money asks the same questions about the competitor on the 12 attributes it feels are most important to its home improvement clients.

Christensen, general manager of GE Money's Home Improvement Division, says the company has several layers of customers — the home improvement company, its salespeople, and then, consumers. Contractors "must be confident in our company and confident in our products to offer them to a consumer while they themselves are developing their relationship," he says.

GE Money builds trust through face-to-face contact, training, and handholding. The consumer becomes as much GE Money's customer as the contractor's, staying with them through the repayment of the loan. These customers provide confidential information, so their trust in how the company handles their account is critical.

LOVE MODE

"Our business is all about high touch and relationship," says the GE Money vice president.

Brad Smith, a GE market analyst and certified Six Sigma black belt, says the NPS surveys work because senior leadership believes in them and understands the value of loyalty and listening to customers. He says while GE has spent millions on NPS, the system can easily be done on a shoestring.

GE Money's overall NPS is 5.9, one of the highest within GE, but Smith says while the score is nice to know, changes in the score are even better to know. "What's really valuable is the feedback we're getting on those open-ended questions," he says. "And then what we're learning from conducting follow-up calls."

Everyone across the company makes follow-up calls to the initial phone surveys to better understand clients' concerns.

They analyze key drivers and attributes to see which most closely correlate to the NPS responses. GE Money determined that if it receives a low score on those 12 attributes, it's likely the customer will score it low on the NPS question: *How likely are you to recommend GE Money to a business associate or colleague?*

GE Money surveys clients four times a year, several hundred in each survey. Management receives summarized results and talks to the sales team to validate the summaries. Then they determine what needs to be fixed, how its marketing message should be tailored based on their strengths, and finally whether additional actions are required. Anyone in the company can read, on a Web portal, what customers say. "That's part of the value, that everyone is able to see the data," Smith says. Twice a year, the feedback is shared at an employee meeting. Employees are recognized for going above and beyond the call of duty.

One issue they've tackled as a result of their NPS market research is a re-examination of their business partner *onboarding*: the process to bring on a new home improvement contractor client. They learned that the process was less than optimal. Using GE's "wing-to-wing" problem resolution, Christensen put 20 percent of his sales team in a meeting room for a week to focus on and disembody the issue, from one end of the process to the other. The idea was to pinpoint problems and come up with solutions on the spot. Then, test the fixes to see if they'll work, and if not, try something else. This problem resolution is an ongoing process.

Christensen says they discovered that they'd done a good job of signing up clients, but the client enrollment process and papers were cumbersome. While enrollments were processed, there was little communication on the approval status. Sometimes it took two weeks for a decision; at other times, only a day. GE Money streamlined the process so that it tracked everything and made documentation easier. Part of the delay was caused by incomplete application packages. By simplifying the paperwork, it made it easier for the contractor and the customer to submit complete packages. Now, a contractor can determine approval status within 48 hours.

GE Money also learned that the client's excitement level while filling out the paperwork was high. "They're totally excited to use us, to partner with us, but if it takes 30 days to get approved, the excitement level just isn't there," says the GE Money vice president. "We found with a lot of customers, we would approve them, but they wouldn't actually do business with us." The increased speed of the turnaround allowed GE Money to maintain excitement, tap emotion, and keep clients on board.

GE Money's next focus will be to evaluate through NPS its product price elasticity. It seeks to better understand how close it can get to its margins, as its pricing is higher than its closest competitors. "That's the biggest place where our detractors come in, in the comments, what we could do better," Christensen says. "It's always, 'lower your price.'"

Which GE Money won't do.

By listening to customers, it can see how elastic these prices are, and how its premium pays for world-class service. Can it extract these prices from such high-level service? At what point does it lose business because price is too high?

Christensen says NPS isn't about averages, it's about finding what your detractors say, and how you can get better. "It's trying to move people who are apathetic to become supporters," he says. "That, to me, is what makes it more than just a survey. Because we are requiring ourselves to make sure we take action based on what comes back."

With that perspective, mediocrity is never an option.

LOVE ✓ CHECK

What's The Value Of Attitudes?
Caring attitudes can help lock-in satisfaction, then loyalty.

Satisfaction ratings and scores often reach back to attitudes a company establishes and nurtures in its people. The value of attitudes is immeasurable, and these values are often a direct link to loyalty. Think of how the smile and easy-going manner of the person who handled your last purchase framed your perspective of the company they represented. Was it because their leader set the tone starting with the hire?

✔ Dial In On DNA

Hire for attitude first, skill second. You can teach skills, not attitude. Look for people with the right disposition and the right thought process. Genuine caring is part of their DNA. People without a caring, loving, giving attitude can't be taught. Do they care about human beings, or processes and products? On first glance, what does their face tell you? If someone's body language tells you they're nervous at first, that's one thing. But if their actions make clear this is only a job and a paycheck, you can't work with that person. Some people approach life seeing dollar signs in their pupils. They give only as much as it takes to get the check. How do you pay someone to genuinely care? You can't. So look for the caring attitude.

✔ Lose Your Leos

Even negative attitudes get reinforced. Management must promote itself as a caring, giving company. Everything we do must accentuate and reward that behavior. Accept anything less, and you reinforce negatives. Consider Leo the Tile Setter. His work was exquisite, but he stunk as a human being. He was one of the most negative whining complainers I've ever been around. He darkened any room when he walked in. No other trade could stand to work around him, and the builder's secretary dreaded when Leo came to pick up his check. The bottom line: Nobody's that good. Leo's ability to lay tile was overshadowed by his personal posture and attitude. Because he was so good at his craft, people put up with him. The job always sacrificed for that. He got reinforcement because people kept working with him. Some people, especially builders, will accept mediocrity, because it's easier to deal with than change. But if you accept that, you've just set a standard. You can't lead a fun-loving workplace when you have a Leo on the team.

✔ Check Your Rearview

Attitudes have to be checked, constantly — by individuals and by management. Attitudes have to be a part of the performance appraisal or review process. And we need to look within as well. Now and then, I sit down and think, "Hey, you're being so darn negative — snap out of it!" When that happens to you, kick yourself in the tail, get an attitude adjustment and move on. Look in the mirror: Are you smiling as much as you used to, before your challenges? Do you need a smile on a stick? If you can't smile, you don't have the right attitude. As a manager, listen for language, watch for body signals. It's easy to spot an expression, and it's like a cloud that follows people. Bad attitudes are contagious. So watch the rearview mirror and latch onto a real good attitude.

✔ Watch What You Eat

The media feeds bad attitudes. If people always believe everything they see on CNN or read in the newspaper, what's reinforced? Their belief systems. If their systems contribute to their not loving themselves or what they do, they won't have the ability to care about someone else. You can't give something you don't have. If in turbulent times you don't think you're worth it, you can't convey you're worth it. In turbulent times, the market stinks, but don't wallow in that truth, and by all means, stop sharing it with customers. Stop waiting until the stars are aligned: Believe in what you do, and do it now. It's OK to feel scared. If you waited until conditions were perfect, you'd never do anything. Go with what you know. Make decisions, move on. Sometimes you just have to believe in your philosophy, because you can't make progress standing still. A certain well-known builder has the right attitude. In 2007, he smiled as he said: *You know, I liked it a whole lot better when my stock was worth $200 million instead of $100 million.* He knows life is a risk-reward experience; he doesn't wallow in the truth.

✔ Hold Your Tongue

Attitudes have to be disciplined. If your people come to sales meetings every week and pour their problems on the table, next time suggest, "If you give me a problem, give me a possible solution. This is a creativity session, not a gripe session." I'd estimate that 75 percent of company meetings, especially sales meetings, are gripe sessions. If people only come with problems, they're not the right team. Suggest that your company is about solutions, not problems. Set the tone: *If you're fortunate to be part of this organization, it's because you have great talent, skill, and attitude.* We put those three things to work in all we do. So when obstacles arise, recognize them. Work to fix them. Management shouldn't dictate solutions, it should look to its talent to help fix the problem. Meetings aren't dumping forums. They're forums for thinking and creating. So while I, as your manager, want to hear concerns, I expect and require possible solutions. Make customers part of your solutions, too!

✔ Work Toward We

Attitude is personal. It's individual. It starts with *me* first. The company attitude can only be as good as my attitude. The strength of a chain is only as strong as its weakest link. But don't take this *me* business too far. If a person infects the organization with deadly *me* attitudes, it'll destroy the group. Inoculate your team against those things. Set parameters. Work it into your mission: *We're solution oriented, not problem oriented.* It goes back to looking for people whose burning desire goes beyond the mandatory. People who like to make a mark without being singled out, monetarily. Who will contribute without keeping tabs on contributions. To make it personal, you need people with *philanthropic* attitudes. When people share how they did things and how those things made them feel, behind the scenes of winning an award, for instance, those people are *we* oriented. Me isn't high in their vocabulary. They credit teams, or their mentors. The me-focused person says, *yes, I worked hard. And someone finally noticed.* Ask in an interview: What's the main reason you're so successful? The we-folk detail contributing factors to their success; the me-folk credit their own hard work and uber-intelligence.

✔ Train For "A" Attitudes

Do you hire people and then throw them to the wolves? The average home building company offers little training and development. But if you want "A" attitudes, you've got to give your people A's first, and set them up for the possibility of success. Do you give constructive comments, or criticism? The more you train and move forward, the better equipped your people are to deal with a constantly changing environment. Some people don't know how to learn, or how to go out and seek information. Are your team meetings training or complaining oriented? Are they administrative or improvement driven? When was the last time your meetings contained a good, productive training module? Do you train only top management? Remember, "A" attitudes are most important with your front line people, the ones who work with customers the most. Give them an "A" and then help them earn it.

"Wait! Wait! Before you storm out, would you please fill out our customer service survey?"

CHAPTER SEVEN

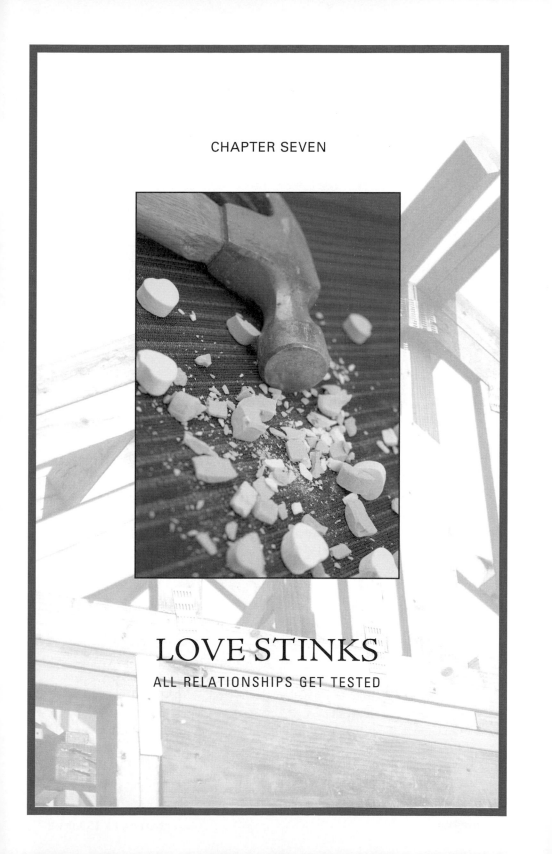

LOVE STINKS

ALL RELATIONSHIPS GET TESTED

THE EVER-SMILING BILLY WARREN, OF CONTINENTAL AIRLINES, 4.4 MILLION CUSTOMERS LATER. DOES HE LOOK ANY WORSE FOR WEAR?

You think we have it bad, with our tough customers? Think again. Just look at the airline industry. No, look at *one guy* who works for the airlines, an industry which has had it tougher than we've had it in housing.

Billy Warren started working the ramp on June 11, 1970 in the San Antonio International Airport. Now he's an airport sales agent for Continental Airlines. He's been through two, almost three, bankruptcies, and "lots of presidents and CEOs," most notably Gordon Bethune, whose remarkable turnaround of Continental is recounted in Bethune's 1998 book with Scott Huler, *From Worst to First*. After hitting the bottom of J.D. Power and Associates rankings, Continental has received stellar customer grades for five straight years. Those achievements are posted on the outside of each plane, to the right of the jet's cabin door, for passengers to read as they board the planes for their flights.

But, on to my key point: Over the eight years that Billy Warren has worked the gate in San Antonio for Continental, at least *4.4 million people* have passed by him during his 10-hour-a-day, four-day-a-week shift. That's 12,000 people a week, more than half a million a year. San Antonio is a critical feeder airport to Continental Airlines' hub in Houston, and it's one of its top 10 busiest stations in the world.

Even the largest builders, at the height of the market, saw fewer than 50,000 customers a year. Most saw less than 50. Are we smiling like Billy? Or are we complaining about *clients from hell?*

I tell Billy's story not just because he has ushered me onto many a flight, or welcomed me home with his million-dollar smile. Or, offered his cell phone number in case I needed assistance, no matter what airport I found myself in as I logged over 200,000 flight miles a year. I share Billy's story because he's the guy who has been through hell — through lost luggage, through missed flights, through intoxicated, belligerent passengers — you name it. Yet, he still *cares*. He still *loves* people. And he's one of the reasons why

HEART OF **THE MATTER**

What to take to heart from this chapter:

- Less than 1 percent of all clients are "unlovable."
- There are at least eight ways to spot the vigilante customer.
- You can avoid creating a vigilante through a vigilant desire for understanding.
- Expectations management, empathy, documentation, and honesty strengthen client relationships.
- Few vigilantes are born; most we make.

I love Continental. My link to Continental follows a direct thread through Billy Warren. And through Lorna May, Donna England, Beth Reininger, and Willard Lewis, four more of the company's smiling faces in its Presidents Club in San Antonio.

Understand Billy, and you'll understand why he doesn't really believe there are people we call vigilante customers, people you might say are from hell. It means understanding that Billy approaches people as a second-generation customer service expert. His dad, Joe, was a service manager for Pitney Bowes for 20 years, then worked with customers in his own postage meter and mailing equipment business for 30 years.

We have tough customers in housing, but *in one day* Billy Warren deals with more customers than an average builder faces *in a lifetime*. And Billy still manages a warm smile and welcoming word: *Hey, where're you off to today?*

THE BILLY WAY

Billy Warren has no control over weather, flight schedules, air traffic control, food service, or mechanical failures — any of it — but he deals with *all* of it. When a flight is delayed because of the weather, no one calls TSA or the control tower. They pounce on Billy. When he has to re-route someone, make a schedule work, or figure out how to seat a family of five together after a flight change, he gets no direct reward. His six weeks of vacation are just enough for him to wind down, go back to the gate, and do it all again.

Billy's name suits his easy-going manner — that's what his mother, Irene, called him (never gave him any options, he says), and he shares that easy-to-remember name with thousands of people. He's living the values his mom and dad have taught him since the day he was born 61 years ago. "My parents were a huge influence on me," Billy says.

Now you'd think that dealing with all those customers, Billy's perception of people, or his spirit of service, would dampen. No. He believes every relationship starts at the first meeting. "You'd be surprised at how little it takes to give a good impression," he says. "There's no reason not to give one right off."

How do you create a personal connection with half a million people, and never be fazed by, well, let's call it … the *chaff*? You can't. But with people constantly bombarding Billy with questions, whatever their mood, he still believes in the essential goodness of the humans he connects with; he never growls. "All people want is to be safe," he says, "to get there on time, to get their bags, receive decent service, and be treated like people, not cattle."

Just like your employees on the front lines — we can make or break a vigilante, from the moment we meet. Billy breaks the tension by making light of crushing weather, or gently teasing customers. If they face a missed flight, he gives them the best alternative — which might mean bending the rules and sending them on another airline. Continental gives employees the leeway to make decisions that are best for the passenger. But even when they can't be satisfied or are irrational, that doesn't faze Billy. "If they see you upset, it makes them madder," he says. "And if you're yelling at them that makes them madder, yet. We keep talking. Sooner or later, they realize it's them, most times."

Billy has had his share of unsavory clients — people who get into fights or who try to clobber him. "People swing at you," he says. "They throw staplers at you. They're mad, really mad. It gets to the point where you have to call the police. Just last night, as we let people off the plane, we had a guy hollering and screaming and they took him to jail."

Still, Billy manages to smile. "Unless they're throwing something at you, I don't have it in me to treat people badly," says the 6-foot, 2-inch former semi-pro baseball player, who, for nine months in 1981, during Continental's first bankruptcy, started building a home with a friend, until he was called back to work at the airline.

Yes, Billy could have been a builder. He would have been a *great* one. He always, always, keeps his perspective. He always keeps his cool. He always *loves*.

REFUSING — OR DEFUSING — TIME BOMBS

While Billy is dealing with people who fly to support their heart, their livelihood (which causes its own high emotion), he still isn't dealing in $250,000, or $500,000, or $5 million homes. How could he possibly love a client who takes off her shoe during a new-home walk-through and runs her foot around the baseboard to see if her pantyhose snags on any nails our finish carpenter failed to countersink in the molding? This actually happened to me when I was selling homes.

Oh, but you can love the Pantyhose Queens, if you keep them in perspective. If you look at people another way, a deeper way, a *Billy Way*. As Dawn Harshman, customer relations manager of FCB Homes in Stockton, Calif. says: "We've found that clients who nit-pick are actually the best customers in the end. Because it's easy to identify what makes them tick and know what their expectations are, so we can exceed them."

Harshman frets about clients of another sort. "It's the clients who won't give you the time of day and won't return calls or surveys that we worry about," Harshman says. "We think they're Time Bombs, waiting to explode."

That is the client I'd like to address here. Because I believe most vigilantes, customers who rip at the heart and take the law into their own hands, who are out to get you for no reason, are mostly made, not born. Whatever the case, there are ways to avoid the most dangerous varieties. (**See Love Checks, Page 209.**) There are ways to continue spreading love with clients who, deep down, want your friendship for life.

To mix metaphors, Time Bombs unravel over time. As I pointed out earlier in this book, a small percentage of the population is impossible to satisfy. Do you know that Sprint Nextel Corp., with 54 million subscribers, recently "fired" 1,000 of its customers? These folks had each made 40 to 50 calls a month to customer service, often with the same problem, when Sprint felt it had resolved the issue. Some of these customers repeatedly asked for information from other customer's accounts. A Sprint spokesman told the Associated Press that the average person calls less than once per month and these customers were calling 40 or 50 times which affected overall customer service. So does that mean Sprint needs to improve their service, or is it that they've discovered the 1 percent of the population that can't be satisfied?

Attorney-Remodeler Dan Bawden of Houston says people who have a history of being controlling tend to be controlling in every aspect of their lives. They are the people psychologists will tell you are the most insecure, who overcompensate by becoming controlling and angry at the same time. "What flows from that are unrealistic expectations," Bawden says. "It's never good enough. They get that from their parents."

These are angry people. To use another metaphor, angry customers are like tidal waves. You have options: You can tense as they approach, or you can duck and take cover and wait until the wave has passed over. You can diffuse the anger by becoming an active listener, by stopping everything, and listening with more than just your ears — using your heart. Watch your body language and soften your stance. *Remember: When it comes to a builder's credibility every negative is believed, every positive must be proved.*

So rebuild that essential trust. Do it now. Keep them in the loop. Apologize for any inconvenience, not the problem; and ask for additional comments or suggestions. In dealing with angry customers, here's what I suggest to clients:

- **Keep *you* in control.**
- **Don't take it personally.**
- **Engage in positive self-talk.** (*When you meet someone, everything you say to yourself affects the interaction's outcome. If you're thinking "this guy's a jerk" the subliminal will be out of sync with the actual. Align them.*)
- **Realize you can't talk to an angry person.**
- **Pause, then respond.**

BLOGGING OUT THE ANGER

These days, angry people who go unsatisfied have an effective weapon to spew their venom — the Internet. Just visit the Web to see how many homeowners, how many *super detractors* you might call them, capture the power of the written word and magnify it through gripe sites, tearing apart the reputations of small, medium, and large companies alike. These fear-inducing scare sites *detract* from your reputation to the highest degree. Builders aren't completely off the hook here. But an intensive Web search couldn't find any data to support the claim made by one site that a nationwide Federal Trade Commission investigation showed that 76 percent of all new homes built in the

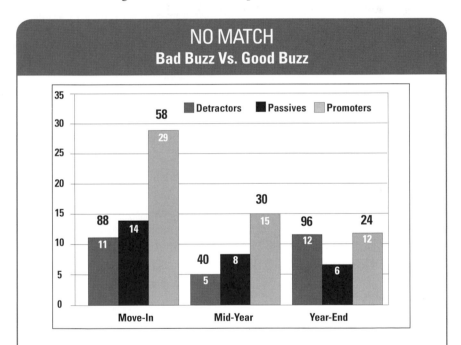

NO MATCH
Bad Buzz Vs. Good Buzz

SOURCE: ELIANT, WWW.ELIANT.COM.

Eliant shows clients that the effects of an equal number of promoting customers never offsets the effects of those who spread venom. Dissatisfied people tell eight to 16 others about their experiences, while satisfied clients tell one or two.
Each number of responses (within the bars) is based on the key survey statement: *I would recommend my builder to a friend or family member.* Using the surveys from one builder's division over an eight-month period, Eliant shows (the number above the bars) how many people detractors pollute (88 at move-in; 96 at year-end) compared to the positive recommendations (58 at move-in; 24 people at year-end). So at year-end, only 24 people have heard something positive about the company, but 96 are literally digging its business grave.

U.S. have serious construction defects. Clearly, we've evolved further than that, no? I'd say construction quality is at its highest ever. But, this dubious claim shows we are not immune to baseless attacks. Again, do your own Google search. You'd be amazed how many sites are out there, and how many times your name is on a site and you don't even know it.

While their intentions might seem noble to some, the organizers of these gripe sites aren't working with builders to resolve ongoing issues like water intrusion, mold, shoddy construction, structural defects, or soil erosion — the popular jumping off points for builder bashing. But then again, how many of these sites, or how many of the people who run them, did we create by our failure to align expectations, our uneven definitions of quality, lack of personal attention, or our failure to build trust throughout the process? I agree that 1 percent of clients just can't be satisfied because they're unhappy, never-will-be-happy people, but how many cases could we *avoid?*

Binding arbitration clauses in most new home contracts prevent court hearings on these divisive issues, but builders need to be careful because consumers are grabbing a louder voice in the court of the Worldwide Web. Let's not join the ranks of Fortune 500 senior executives who report that 20 percent of their time is spent in litigation-related activities. Let's really listen to what homeowners are saying.

Guts To Love

The Seven Service Sins
BY CAROL SMITH

Think you can't create a client from hell? Think again ...

Poor communications, bad expectations management, and a lack of empathy for customers are among the seven service sins that can contribute to the creation of a client from hell. If you guard against these sins, however, you can avoid a perilous trip to the netherworld.

What to avoid:

- **Communication Chaos.** Lacking specific information from their builder regarding routine communications, homebuyers rely on their own expectations. Meanwhile, builder personnel each respond differently — resulting in homebuyers enjoying prompt responses from one staff member or department and slow responses from another. How do you prevent this sin? By establishing consistent communication performance standards for all personnel and sharing (slightly padded) targeted timeframes with homebuyers.

- **Poor Expectation Alignment.** Informing customers about products, processes, and services is a process rather than a single event. Builders need to designate the personnel who will introduce and reinforce key points to customers, when these efforts will take place, and how these details will be covered (demonstration, conversation, document, and so

Let's not follow the path of Pacesetter Corp., a 40-year-old, $122 million-a-year remodeling firm, whose downfall, it could be argued, was aided by an angry homeowner's Web site that, over time, drew more than 300,000 visitors. As the company fell into Chapter 7 bankruptcy, even bitter ex-employees visited the site, according to Jim Cory, editor of *Replacement Contractor* magazine. The company experienced an unknown number of sales cancellations because the revenge site was the first to pop up on a Web site search for Pacesetter.

Cory, writer of the article *Pacesetter's Perfect Storm*, chronicled the company's demise **(See www.replacementcontractoronline.com)**. "What started as a revenge blog by a pair of disgruntled customers turned into an online hornet's nest of gossip, insult, and innuendo," the editor says. "As one source observed, there's lots of business out there, but it's business that's easier to win than to keep. If you want to keep it, you have to realize that you have to always serve the customer."

Cory says that these days anyone mad enough can strike back. Anyone can come after you, and all they need are computer skills, and maybe not even that. One company was savaged on a township blog. Cory recounts the story of a woman angered by a window company's policy to visit homeowners only when both the husband and wife were home. Now, her venom comes up first when you Google the company's

on). Repetition is essential in this process. Builders must be subtle or they risk giving the impression of harping.

- **Sloppy Documentation.** Unless commitments and agreements are documented, follow through is at risk. Memories often generate conflicting interpretations. From change requests to orientation and warranty items, every issue should be documented, either electronically or on paper. This will benefit everyone. Field personnel need simple, quick, and convenient methods to record the details of every customer contact.

- **Failure To Resolve Issues.** Reliability is essential to customer satisfaction. When details are forgotten or take too long, dissatisfaction grows. What, to a staff member, may be just a minor detail can be vitally important to a homebuyer. Whether the buyer believes the wrong exterior trim paint was applied or a dining room screen has a hole in it, these details need to be corrected within the promised timeframe.

- **Lack Of Empathy.** Cavalier attitudes have no place in customer satisfaction efforts. The field staff may find a buyer's seemingly endless hand-wringing annoying. *Why can't they just leave us to do our jobs instead of telling us about every little thing?* The reality is that the buyers are paying for this home. They're going to live in it. A buyer's attachment to a new home — even while it is being built — is unlike any attachment that company personnel can have. Minimizing customer concerns, name. Imagine how many people turn away at that point in their search, based solely on what one *almost*-client wrote?

"The lesson for companies is they have to understand customers' expectations," the editor says. "They have to find out what they are and then strategically go after each customer. How do we exceed the expectations? When do we do that? How do we put ourselves in a position to get a referral? Anyone who thinks customers are expendable these days is crazy."

The only way to avoid scenarios completely lacking in love is to stay focused on clients from the start, and avoid doing business with the 1 percent who can't be satisfied. Because you can't love someone who has no concept of love, or even *like*. Contrast that perspective with my airport hero, Billy. If he can love 4 million people, you certainly can find a way to love one tough customer, no?

GHOSTS FROM THE PAST

As Dan Bawden observes, the primary cause of most conflicts are past experiences. We all have them. They're either ghosts that move in and move on, or ghosts that haunt us our whole lives. They change us for better or worse. That's why those who probe deeply into understanding customers, like consultant and trainer Gust Nicholson Sr., formerly of Engle Homes Orlando/

slow or condescending responses to questions, and, worst of all, telling buyers to stay away, all send the wrong message.

- **Delivering Incomplete Homes.** After ordering, scheduling, and overseeing the assembly of thousands of parts, it's understandable that the last few details may seem somewhat trivial

> **Detailing for the delivery is critical to building buyer confidence.**

to construction personnel — "nothing urgent, we'll get around to it." To the buyers, a different standard applies. The impression the home makes at the orientation creates an indelible memory. Detailing for the delivery is critical to building buyer confidence. This means demonstrating an absolutely sparkling clean home; the emphasis at the demonstration must be on education, not inspection. Success is possible only with a complete home.

- **Reluctant Warranty Service.** Here's a real referral killer: cumbersome request procedures and generally being unenthusiastic about after-move-in service. The goal shouldn't be to have no further dealings with customers once they close; it's to maintain a positive long-term relationship. Proactive warranty procedures include setting the first appointment before settlement takes place and inspecting the home on behalf of the customer, actually looking for items that need attention. To earn a good reputation for service, *you must serve.*

Technical Olympic USA and Pulte Homes, say we need to re-shape customer experiences, from the start. I'm sure Nicholson would agree with me that there's no single "right" way. There are simply unlimited possibilities.

He tells the story of an incredible experience he had with a client that reshaped forever how he makes assumptions about people's preferences, or "demands." As former director of customer relations at Engle in Orlando, Fla., the most extreme client conflicts arrived in folders on his desk only when they had reached their worst.

One complaint made its way to his office because the customer refused to take the final walk-through on his new home. Nicholson called the customer, who was from Asia. Nicholson and the client discussed traditions. He asked: "Can you tell me why you won't walk through the house? He said, 'In my religion, you need to move the oak tree in the yard or I can't walk in the front door. It's lined up with the front door.' For him, to cross over the threshold was bad luck, a bad omen."

Nicholson told the client he could put the tree wherever the client wanted. "We moved the tree, and he bought the house. And he bought two houses after that from us for investment. We created the situation. We were calling the customer goofy, crazy, nuts. When I asked warranty service to move the tree away from the door, they said the builder told them he wanted the trees on the block to look uniform. But code enforcement didn't care where they were, as long as there were three of them. So I ask the question: Was that a *customer from hell?*"

Nicholson later followed up and found that the man hardly ever called for anything other than normal warranty items. "Ever since, I realized I had pre-judged this man. I was as guilty as everyone else." Since then, he has enjoyed digging into the souls of "tough" customers, always asking himself, "Did we do this? Or did they just have a bad childhood?"

This customer service guru believes there are people who are medically and physically challenged in life, who aren't anything like the rest of the general

population. The problem is usually not with the home, but that person's perception of the home. It only means that it will take longer to make the customer happy. It's possible. "They're special, and they deserve the same experience as any other person," he says.

They just require accommodations. "I can't say I'm an expert on these things, but I know enough to be dangerous," Nicholson says. "People with attention deficit disorder change the page every two seconds. *What about this? That? Now talk to me about this.* How you should deal with that is to turn the pages faster, because they're able to follow at a faster pace. The dyslexic person sees things that aren't there.

They see shadows — *see over there?* — and they'll point it out to me. There are no shadows there. But I say, *what if we re-paint the wall from this corner to this corner?* Nothing is wrong with the wall but painting it doesn't cost much and makes the customer happy. So why not do it?"

Nicholson shares another story describing how he once sat in a builder association meeting with eight CEOs, and heard one say, "The *customer from hell* called today." Nicholson jumped in: "I don't believe he's from hell, and if he's from hell, we created it. We created the hellish situation he's in. What is he complaining about? A window leak? Who put the window in and created that problem? To say that about your customer is the saddest thing an executive can say," he says. "You created the environment they're living in."

If you find yourself in this situation, have you evaluated why the customer is in the condition they're in? Are they really a *customer from hell* or have you been to the house eight times and still haven't fixed the problem? If you created the problem, who created the hell? *We did*, says Nicholson. If the customer is unreasonable and not dealing with the real world, or had a hard time coping with the fact that this is the best it gets, you need to look at the problem more closely. It's a fine line, so check the line.

Bob Birner, vice president of Amazing Siding Corp. & Renewal by Andersen Window and Patio Door Replacement of Houston, says if a customer is unhappy with the quality of work, oftentimes it's to get attention, to see if someone is listening. "Everything is fine when you go out there, but you need to treat it as a legitimate emergency," he says. "I always try to find something they didn't find. It's important for the client to know I'm on their side, not my side."

By saying that the window caulking needs to be applied more neatly, or some other small improvement, it allows Birner to show he's there to help *them*.

Nicholson says his research shows that as many as 10 percent of customers could have a psychological condition. "Before you write off a customer as unreasonable," he says, "it's a good point to stop and look at what caused the problem in the first place. If we fixed it, he will turn. And if we fixed it and that's as good as it gets, the customer has a problem."

YOUR FAVORITE COLOR?

Maybe that's deeper than you'd like to go with customers, but understanding that you can dive that deep might help you understand all the more. I've said it before and I'll say it again: *The more you get customers to understand the emotional components of remodeling or building, the more you can modulate their emotions and get those highs and lows to work in everyone's favor.*

Nicholson says we have to be conscious of our words — we can make people literally sick with our conversations. Speaker and author David McNally, author of *Even Eagles Need A Push* and *Be Your Own Brand*, reminds us that *"language is the software of the mind,"* not just for our clients, but for the thought track we constantly let run through our heads.

"My language can take your hope and faith out of you for the day," Nicholson says. "You want to build hope in the customer, and faith in the system, and if I do that, I've already won you over."

So *demanding* doesn't work. As my friend and colleague Carol Smith says, instead of *demanding*, try *proposing, suggesting,* or *recommending*. Don't use phrases that tell customers what *they have to do*, or use phrases that contain words like *that's company policy* or that blame and make assumptions. Don't use words that build walls — *no, can't, impossible, why, what,* or *listen, wait, wrong,* and *should've.*

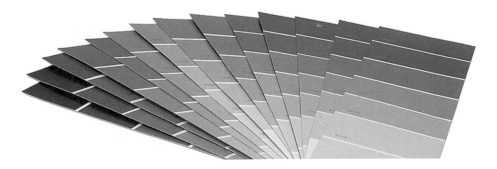

My friend Roxanne Musselman would say highly competent companies have fewer customers that are impossible to please than less competent companies. She suggests not using the word *quality*. "When a company's mantra is *quality*, they set themselves up for trouble," she says.

One way to handle *emotional quality* is to clue clients in to the fact that they are about to experience their emotions to a heightened degree, perhaps greater than they ever have before. After all, it's their *home*, it's their *heart*, we're talking about.

Bawden, owner of Legal Eagle Contractors Co., using a model drawn from David Lupberger and Bill Still's 2000 book, *Managing the Emotional Homeowner:*

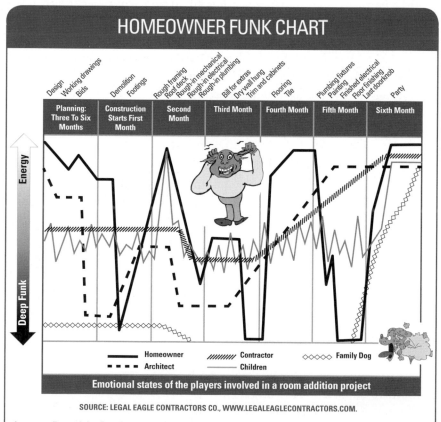

SOURCE: LEGAL EAGLE CONTRACTORS CO., WWW.LEGALEAGLECONTRACTORS.COM.

Attorney-Remodeler Dan Bawden of Legal Eagle Contractors of Houston, using a model introduced in David Lupberger and Bill Still's *Managing the Emotional Homeowner: The Remodeler's Guide to Happy Customers*, developed a "funk chart." He shares it with clients at pre-construction meetings to show how energy and funk plummet or skyrocket throughout a project — for *everyone* involved. By presenting, early on, potential jagged emotional states, he sets expectations. When homeowners hit a low, he points out: *Remember when I showed you the funk chart?*

The Remodeler's Guide to Happy Customers, developed a "funk chart." He shares it with clients (**See Homeowner Funk Chart, Page 200**). It shows how their energy and funk will ebb, flow, plummet and skyrocket, from the architect and the contractor, to the homeowners and their children, and even the family dog.

Bawden says that by reviewing the chart with homeowners, as part of his pre-construction checklist, and making known upfront that there will be not only dust and fumes, and policies for additional work requests, but also a whole series of emotions they'll experience, he can head off trouble. He can set expectations. Long before that point, Bawden will have used a 10-question personality test on his Web site to help him assess whether a client is a good candidate for remodeling. Using answers to questions such as: *Which of the following colors do you like the most?* and *When do you feel your best?* he gets a quick check on how this potential client thinks, and even, sleeps. "It will all but rule out someone on the extreme end, unless they convince me otherwise during the next phone call," he says.

Now would this work if you're a production builder in a mediocre market, scratching for every sale? Maybe not. But for high-end and custom builders, assessing the personality and emotional state of homeowners has to be a consideration. Remember smart builders ask essential questions and

LOVE mode
Courting Horror

Builder Todd Booth shares what he learned from a client whose expectations seemed different from the start.

When you're in business for 40 or 50 years, you figure you've seen the best and worst of everything. So when Todd Booth of Prestige Homes heard from his friends that he'd never make his newest prospect happy, he thought, *I'm a nice guy and an honest guy. I'll treat her straight and I'll be able to make her happy.*

If only the San Antonio builder, now in business for 49 years, had listened to his friends and remembered the adage that oftentimes, nice guys finish last.

The first red flag was that the client wanted to make the move-in date the most important part of getting into the home. But then, after the contract was signed (in the mid-1990s), she started making changes, without allowing any changes to the closing date. Soon after, she had her own construction materials delivered — which she wanted installed in the home. One was the front door from listen carefully before proceeding. They align expectations early. Clarity on the front end minimizes conflict. They never get into an either/or mindset — in other words, *you get yours* and *I get mine*. Like Nicholson, they refuse to see the other person as the enemy.

Consultant and speaker Tom Stephani, of Custom Construction Concepts, of Crystal Lake, Ill., says builders would do well to look for compatible people, who share their values, their interests, and traits. People from some cultures and professions will always be tough to work with, he says. With certain cultures, the negotiations never stop. "That's not necessarily bad, but is that how you want to do business?" he asks. "Engineers are always tough to build for." But if you are comfortable with their endless questions and the nitpicking of process, procedure and product, they may be right for you. "Some lawyers are great to work for, but some are litigators, trained to fight. And they like to fight. There's no win-win in court. I have to win and you lose."

The one thing Stephani tells clients to rely on is a gut feel: Do you feel comfortable with this person? There is medical evidence that the queasy feeling you get in your stomach when you don't feel right about something has its basis in science, he says. Your body is telling you something your mind hasn't yet picked up.

But even the best gut check and client protection or vigilante detection

her current home, that Booth later learned had borne a sticker that gave notice for her foreclosure eviction.

Despite all the red flags, he and the client closed on the new home, and it was funded by her mortgage lender just days prior to the foreclosure on her previous dwelling.

> **Everything was fine for two months. Then, daily, or every other day, the demand letters came for some minor objection.**

"Everything was fine for two months," Booth says. "Then, daily or every other day, the demand letters came for some minor objection. And each one was a huge event."

Like any good builder, he tried to fix everything. But the demands only worsened. The client began accusing the builder through the local media, signs in her yard and on her car, despite warnings from Booth's attorney to the media that her comments were historically inaccurate and overblown. The attacks grew venomous. "We worked on the home for months and months to make her happy," he says. "We got to three or four items, and she would not accept any repair." None of the items included significant failures or discrepancies, and on the minor items, the homeowner repeatedly denied the builder access to the home to fix them.

In Booth's contract is a binding arbitration clause, and finally, he fell back on it, and compelled the homeowner to go to binding systems aren't always enough. The best in the business still get waylaid. (**See Love Mode, Page 201.**)

182 CHANCES FOR LOVE

Bawden, in the business for 30 years, who has written and spoken extensively on prospects' red flags, was battling a difficult client when we talked for this book. "I committed a classic error," he says. He fell in love with the opportunity to do a spectacular three-story contemporary style project, larger than his normal contracts. Projects of the $1.8 million variety aren't usual for the 55-job, $1.4 million-a-year remodeler. And he quickly learned about the most dangerous person to work for: The client who can't be pleased.

"I got all excited about how the 'after' pictures would look on my Web site and in my brochure and I chose not to heed the red flags," Bawden says.

First tip: The client refused to take his personality test. Then, he didn't meet with Bawden until after the contract signing (a first for Bawden). Paperwork was completed via FedEx and DHL. The client was wealthy, flying around the world, while the project was managed by one of his designees in the company he ran. He started substituting contracted materials with his own that he had shipped from overseas. When he visited the house, he would highlight hundreds of spots

arbitration. But even after a $10,000 judgment was awarded to Prestige Homes, she continued with the media attacks and signs. To this day she hasn't paid the judgment. In December 2007, Booth filed the paperwork that renewed the lien on her home so that if it is ever sold, he will be paid the $10,000 he's owed, which is less than a third of the $35,000 he paid in legal fees.

Booth says these are a few lessons he learned through the experience:

- **Listen to the advice you're given.** If Booth had listened straight off, and not been prideful, thinking he could satisfy any client, he'd have saved himself years of aggravation.

- **Clearly write change requests.** Booth no longer allows owner-supplied materials, since that's where most of the problems arose.

- **Document your files.** Keep excellent records of conversations with homeowners. Many different types of builder software allow tracking of pieces of conversation over long periods of time.

Don't think you can fix the world, Booth says. Give the money back or double the money back, and you'll be ahead in the long run. While many builders don't make it a practice, they have bought back, or offered to buy back homes from problem homeowners.

And in hindsight, Booth says he's not sure he wants the judgment paid anyway: "If I collect, she might set her sights on me and come attack me again."

Already, news reports indicate that she's moved on … to another builder.

in the drywall with orange spray paint that weren't within his standards for a smooth surface of skim-coated plaster. Bawden's crews refloated and re-primed the Sheetrock at least three times.

"It can happen no matter how long you've been in business, or how many college degrees you have, or how good you think you are," says the veteran contractor. "If they're better at tearing people apart than you are, they're going to have their way with you."

It's not uncommon for builders to report drastically lower margins on these jobs. But if you're just being abused, control the thing you can control — you.

Bawden believes he was picked from the three contractors who bid on the job because he was the most malleable, would take the most *chaff*, and was a pleaser personality as opposed to someone who would react negatively to

unreasonable behavior. Delays and indecision have drawn out a project that should have taken less than a year into two years. The client left bills unpaid for at least four months, and Bawden was trying to exit the job, which may end up in arbitration.

He says he should have followed his instincts and listened to his wife, Konne. Based on the limited information he shared, she wondered: *Why are you doing this project?* It's a question we should always ask ourselves. Bawden says the 130-plus change orders, or change requests, as I call them, should have clued him in to his client's vagaries of mind.

Change requests can be very emotional for clients — they involve change, money, decisions, and time — a lethal combination. John Barrows of J. Barrows Inc., who builds million-dollar custom homes on Long Island, N.Y. has found it isn't unusual to have a couple of hundred change requests on his jobs. "I try to be as upfront and transparent as possible," he says. "I tell the client, you're going to have changes, not because I want to make more money, but because you'll see things differently as this project evolves, and you should have flexibility to go with what you want. It's your custom home. But that doesn't mean I will *give* it to you."

He recalls one client who said he wouldn't make changes — and then at change request 133 "was going bonkers," as Barrows says. The changes added six months to the job. Clients have to know early on that they will pay for changes, and it nearly always affects the schedule. They have to acknowledge their dreams have an impact on the budget. Again, it means setting expectations and communicating all the way through the job.

Dennis Dixon, of Dixon Ventures in Flagstaff, Ariz., is accustomed to similar challenges to clients' emotional health — he recalls a job with 182 change requests. But the way he positions it is that it's all record-keeping. "If I told them they wrote 182 separate checks for all modifications and changes, they would never believe me," he says. "They'd say, 'Oh, Dennis, we wrote maybe 10 or 12.'"

He builds multi-million dollar custom homes, and when we spoke, he was planning a 2,800-square-foot second-home retreat budgeted at $1,000 per square foot. It was for a doctor, in an extinct volcano, a *volcanic caldera*, with a lake.

What Dixon has become expert at building is *expectations*. He tells clients he is doing what he does because it's what he loves, not what he needs to do to support himself. While he caters to client's schedules, even he has limits. He identifies their needs and asks questions about expectations. Through this, he maintains control of the project — not the client. And when he makes mistakes — and he has made them — he is brutally honest. He thrives on referrals, and clients aren't adverse to telling him which prospects cheat at golf (a red flag).

Dixon comes by his honesty like Billy Warren — from his father. At his college graduation dinner, his dad gave him the best advice of his life: *When you are out there in the world and things get convoluted, fall back on the truth. Sometimes things can get so mixed up, you tell the truth and that's all you can do.*

His honesty is evident in a story he tells that, ironically, didn't involve a client but could have created its own hell. It happened when he was far less experienced, and when, like other builders at the time, he rarely hired surveyors to mark property corners, setbacks, easements, or the home's footprint in an established subdivision. It was considered a waste of money. Yet, it was only a $500 line item. He told his surveyor he didn't want the full package, just the location of the lot corners. The surveyor marked the corners. He found the lot based on Dixon's job sign. No other homes were built on the street. This home would set the tone for the neighborhood. The house footprint was adjusted to minimize tree removal and to maximize the view.

The footing, stem wall, floor fill, and concrete slab floors were completed on a Wednesday. The framing package was set for delivery the following Tuesday. But when the excavation contractor showed up to dig and install the utility connections, he told Dixon he couldn't locate the city sewer and water taps at the street, just inside the curb. He asked Dixon to get a city official to locate the taps. The head building inspector pointed out that the sewer manhole cover in the street was skewed from where it was marked on the subdivision plot plan, then he exclaimed: *You're building on the wrong lot!*

Dixon says his heart stopped. He halted construction. He called the surveyor. Forty-five long minutes later, the surveyor reached the same conclusion. It turned out the lot dimensions on the adjacent lots were nearly identical.

Dixon located the name and address of the property owner, a dentist. After Dixon laid out his heart's lament, the dentist's first comment was extraordinary: *My God! There's another honest man in the world!* After extended discussion, the dentist asked the builder: *How about if we just swap lots? Your lot's a little bigger and has a better view.*

Six weeks later, the transaction closed, for $12,600 in fees and expenses, a bit more than the initial $500 survey would have cost. Dixon has had 400 clients since then, and he still tells the truth.

GUT CHECK: HANDSHAKE & A SMILE?

Ralph Cataldo, president of Cataldo Custom Builders, of East Falmouth, Mass., believes even the toughest customers will respect hard work and honesty. If you meet Ralph, you'll find he's one of the kindest, most sincere people ever;

one of the most genuine I've ever met. He typically builds four or five $2 million dollar homes a year, in or near Cape Cod. His clients' typical net worth ranges from $5 to $100 million, and he's constantly working to build trust. He has two referral bases to please — clients (50 percent of referrals) and architects (45 percent) — with only 5 percent of his work coming from advertising.

Until recently, and for 20 years, he had avoided clients from hell. "Statistically, you'll eventually end up with a very time-consuming, misinformed, extremely busy, or angry person," he says. If you find yourself in their death grip, here's his advice:

- **Communicate.** Make it more frequent to show you care and how hard you're working. Sometimes you can work with one of the spouses to help you through the nightmare.
- **Be Patient.** Never raise your voice, regardless of fault — and most times it will be your client's. Don't give them an excuse to say a bad thing. One bad word will cost you.
- **Work To Completion.** Take your lumps and losses and move on to happier, more profitable projects. It's not a good atmosphere for you, your staff, or your trades.
- **Share The Schedule.** Set it so you can beat it, even though they might not appreciate your diligence. How many builders beat their schedules? Word gets around.
- **Invoice Frequently.** So you don't get behind on your receivables, which affects cash flow.
- **Set Deposits High.** Work out a payment schedule in your favor where the deposit is gradually credited until you begin accumulating your budgeted profit.
- **Thank Them — From The Heart.** Give them a gift to remember, one they can't buy in the store or online. You need to leave a lasting impression — *always think long term.*

Cataldo's experience with his worst client drives home a critical point of my philosophy — *business is emotional, personal, and always reflected in human touch.* Cataldo was building for the owner of a multi-million dollar business, who could have just about anything he wanted. The architect gave the builder a set of hand-sketched plans on three, 8 ½ by 11-inch pieces of paper, and asked for a budget. Cataldo gave him a price, and then the architect provided 30 pages of detailed prints.

"We were really happy, because the price went up just 8 percent," Cataldo says. The contract was signed with just the wife of the couple attending. The foundation was poured. The husband flew in one weekend and walked up the driveway. Cataldo extended his hand to shake his client's. The man kept both his hands in his pockets, saying: *I thought we had a deal.* I'm confused, Cataldo said, what do you mean? *You had a fixed price of $1 million.* From those four pages of handwritten notes? Basically, a plan on a napkin? That's impossible. To tell you the truth, I'm pretty happy with what we came out with.

The client finally shook his hand, but repeated: *I thought we had a deal.* The builder said: You stay here, I'll go back to my office and be back in 20 minutes with a check for $10,000 — for your aggravation. My reputation is worth more than anything in my in life. Whatever you owe me, you can keep. I'll give you $10,000 for any aggravation we may have caused

RALPH CATALDO, LUXURY HOMEBUILDER.

you and you can have everything you've paid for to date — the cleared lot, the foundation, the permits, you can have it all. My reputation is much too valuable to have it tarnished.

The client took a hand out of his pocket, offering it, and said, *that's the exact answer I wanted to hear. I can't wait to work with you.*

"He just wanted it done at that point," Cataldo says. "I should have walked away."

The job was miserable throughout, and for everyone involved. The client changed everything, double-checked every price, brought in his own interior designer, his own trades, and Cataldo all the while was accommodating. But time was lost. Overtime hours skyrocketed. Cataldo was paid every penny he was owed, but it was the most difficult job he has encountered.

And it all started with a handshake — *or the absence of one.*

Never underestimate yourself and your innate senses. If at the end of the day you can say you had a *Billy Day*, and you're making your customer's new home or remodel an experience, an adventure, not a living *hell*, then you're in the right place. Keep smiling, and ask your customers, with a smile: *Hey, where're you off to today?*

How To Spot The Vigilante Customer

Your love for your customer will constantly be tested. But before you're thrashing your way through hell, and calling your client unmentionables, understand that 1 percent or less of the population isn't going to be happy, ever. Why? They're just not happy people. If you come across them and don't recognize the warning signs, you're in for a battle. In the end, you'll lose. You must polish your interview skills with perspective clients so that you not only recognize the signals, you take heed. And, never, ever — even in tough times or slow markets — allow your brain to override your gut. Your gut is based on feelings, and feelings are rarely wrong.

✔ **Tough From The Start?**

Do they procrastinate when making decisions? Do they balk at the terms and conditions of your contract? Do they want to re-write your contract? People have to make decisions throughout the construction process. Do they want you to re-write your business model for their benefit? Linda Gridley of Gridley Co. in Campbell, Calif. says two of her clients from hell were entrepreneurs who thought her business should run like theirs. Do clients want to tell you how to go about your business? Are they skeptical going into the process? Are they looking for you to prove yourself before you begin? If there's no trust going in, there will be no trust coming out. Make it a personal process, because if there's no personal relationship, they're already thinking it's not going to be a good experience. And should they become a vigilante customer, it rarely has to do with you personally. It has to do with their perception of the process — for example, *builders are out to get buyers*. Don't let them feed wrong perceptions.

✔ Duking It Out?

Are the buyers, typically couples, discourteous to each other? If they don't respect each other, they won't respect you. The dynamics of human behavior have to be a huge consideration as you select clients. If they're calling each other derogatory names, how will it be different for you, your team, or your trades? Michael Strong of Brothers Strong of Houston tells of a top woman executive who treated his people miserably. He finally deciphered that it was him, as owner of the company and as her perceived executive equal that she wanted to deal with. As the owner, he became a project manager of sorts for all communication, and finished the job; but it wasn't an ideal situation, particularly for his project manager. You need to let clients know that their behavior isn't acceptable in your organization. If the husband says, *Don't listen to her — I'm the one paying the bills and she doesn't know anything about handling money,* what does that tell you? These people can be "mudslingers" — Dan Bawden's word. Besides slinging mud, their cup is half empty all the time. They talk negatively about anything and everyone. Avoid them! Or it will cost, in many ways.

✔ Starting Fires?

If they balk at the terms and conditions or if they're already nitpicking the paperwork, they'll nit-pick everything. Most contracts are written by legal counsel and they're in place to protect both parties. If the buyer wants the contract to protect them more than the builder, that's not a good sign. They don't understand the nuances of the business like you do. Furthermore, if you change your contract without telling your team, you create a problem. You don't want to change the rules of the game, but if you do, make sure everyone knows this is an exception. What if they want to hire their own inspector, or they want to change terms and conditions, or the payment schedule, or they want to put money into escrow after the closing? I call these *fire starters*. All are warning signs.

✔ Memory Impaired?

Bawden calls the eminently forgetful *space cadets*. They don't remember anything. You can review it 25 times and they won't remember. If you meet with them two or three times before you sign a remodeling contract or a purchase agreement and every time you review the same material and they lead you to believe it's the first time that they heard it, a flag should go up. These people sign things without reading them, or if they did read the paperwork they don't understand it and don't care. You have to be careful about accentuating and over-documenting, sometimes requiring a signature on a signature.

✔ Unethical And Illegal?

Do they ask you to do things that are unethical, like hide information? Sometimes they can tread the line of illegal acts, although unethical people know how to walk that fine line. These people are always looking for a way to abuse the system — and they blatantly make suggestions. *How can I not pay taxes on this item? How can I get around an inspection fee? Is there a way we can avoid using the title company?* They're always looking for a "better" way, a way for you that's best avoided.

✔ Power Or Control Freaks?

They're hiring you to do a job, to manage a job, and at some point, they have to relinquish control. If they can't do that, or if they micro-manage you, you can't get things finished. These people will tell you to do something and when you do, they'll call other people to make sure you did it, even though you've shown them it's done. They want to negotiate everything and they're always trying to get something from someone. It's power and control they crave, and your best bet is to let them have control — of someone else. Bawden says these people also may be *psychic vampires*: clients who suck lifeblood out of you throughout the process and who innately sense how to manipulate you. They don't put any *fun* in *dysfunctional*.

✔ Sue Happy?

Are they proud of their efforts to file lawsuits? Were you the only one of two or three builders to call them back? — they will tell you. They're abrasive. They try to make you feel you need them more than they need you. The true vigilantes have a reason why they've not selected a builder yet — no one wants to work with them. If they've sued three builders before, what makes you think you're special, that they'll not sue you? As with employees, or the people you're about to hire, it all boils down to attitude. Buyers' attitudes are as important. If they're coming in angry, you're in for a battle. Life is too short to spend time in court. And even if you win, it will take so much out of you, it's not worth it. Live happy. Live the *Billy Way*.

© 2000 Ted Goff

"Yes, I know you just slammed the phone down on me. This is a courtesy follow up call."

LOVE LASTS

PICTURE AN 88-YEAR KISS

Aunt Mary Alice and Uncle Joe share their love.

Don't *ever* stop loving your customers.

What you have with them is something special, something mutually beneficial.

My Aunt Mary Alice and Uncle Joe, married for 60 years, fall in love again every day. *She was the most beautiful woman I've ever seen,* says Uncle Joe. *And she still is.* She still surprises him — do you see it in his eyes? When I think of my uncle, I hear Hal Ketchum's song *The Richest Man in Texas* rollicking through in my head. Ketchum sings that he may not have a nickel to his name, nor ever get his share of fortune or fame, but he still feels like the richest man in Texas. In his safe and happy home, waiting there is the woman he loves, with eyes that shine like diamonds and a heart as good as gold. She's worth more than all the stars above.

Any more in business, it's not about how much money you have. It's about how people feel about you. The poetry you create with lasting relationships, lodged in a happy home, is much more valuable than anything you can *do* for your customers. At some point, you stop counting dollars; you start counting relationships.

We need to nurture those relationships and surprise our clients in the same way my aunt and uncle surprise each other every day. I don't mean laying a kiss on your clients, like Aunt Mary Alice did in the picture above. I mean keeping the connection new and exciting, *every day.*

Why do I suggest that a client for life is in an 88-year relationship? Because the number 8 is mystical. On its side, it's the infinity symbol, and if you have double infinity, let me tell you, you have a client for life.

How do you get your team to see business in that way? With new vision and inspiration. How do you stay in love with your customers in troubling times?

We can stay focused in tumultuous times by treating every person who walks through our door as our favorite guest for the day, as they do at The Ritz-Carlton. Ritz-Carlton employees re-create themselves

HEART OF THE MATTER

What to take to heart from this chapter:

- Keep the courtship alive. Make every interaction real.
- Improve your company by recruiting future hires. Who are they?
- It starts with you. Do *you* have the passion?
- Make a mistake. Give customers a chance to love you.
- Who says you can't dance?

every day. How do musicals like *Cats*, which ran on Broadway in New York

City for more than 7,000 performances, and *Phantom of the Opera*, now the longest running Broadway show in history, last for 20 years? And perform four, five, or more nights per week, winning standing ovations? Because each and every one of the actors realizes they touch the essence of people's lives, just as we do. If those performers can stay that jazzed for that long, why can't you?

Think about your processes. Is there any arrogance in the way you look at and price your "options and upgrades?" Are you still using those words, instead of *custom options*

and *customized amenities?* The market research and satisfaction survey companies say the feedback they receive on this issue adds up to thousands of stories — why do "options and upgrades" cost three to four times what a customer might pay in a retail store? This huge disconnect *eats* at loyalty. This is what Bob Mirman of Eliant calls *bad profits.*

Are you chasing bad profits? If your prices increased 30 to 60 percent a year before the market crunch, is that part of the arrogance? Are you getting a dose of humility, now? We're suddenly looking at everything from a customer perspective, when we should have been doing that long ago. Suddenly, the customer is absolutely central to our business.

Keep them at the heart of what you do.

YOU JUST CAN'T DANCE

I see customer relations and the creation of loyalty as a dance. There aren't many things you can do in public that are closer than dancing with another person.

I've always loved to dance; I just wasn't very good at it. One night, more than 10 years ago, at an industry networking function, one of my builder friends asked me to dance. Halfway through the first song, he said: I don't think you're going to get this. You look good, *but you just can't dance.* At that moment, I decided I'd take lessons. That criticism, eased with flattery, never stopped me. In fact, it only made me want, with a burning desire, to get better. About four years later, I was at the Harvey Hotel, in Dallas, in my first dance competition. I was just happy I didn't fall down. (Many dancers do.)

It took another four years to qualify for my first major competition. Let me tell you, it was something when I stepped onto the dance floor at the Gaylord Opryland Hotel, in Nashville, Tenn. The competition covered eight styles of dance, including the two-step, waltz, polka, cha-cha, and East Coast swing. To compete in eight dance styles is rare. It certainly was something I'd never imagined doing.

COMPETING IN THE TWO-STEP WITH MY FORMER DANCE PARTNER, ROGER SHARP.

That week in Nashville, my partner and I qualified for the United Country Western Dance Council world finals. We were headed for Canada, and then, to the Netherlands. From there, back to Nashville. What a trip! My persistence in the face of *you just can't dance* paid off. At one competition, we placed in the top 10; in another, the top five. *Yee-Haw!*

AND THIS IS US WALTZING.

It showed me just what I could do when someone told me *it can't be done*. After all, I'm a Texan. The only way I got to the world finals was by practicing the basics over and over and over again. As I got more comfortable with the basics, the movements became second nature.

It *can* be done. And that goes for all the ideas I've discussed in these pages, you can do it, too. *Customer care can become second nature to you.*

Oh, you'll have setbacks. Even in dance, when two people work toward a common goal, there are problems. You get competitive. You blame the other person when you're penalized. You get irritated by every simple thing. Sound familiar? But while you're on the dance floor, to convey the passion of the dance, you need to pretend you're *in love*. And handsome though they were, my partners and I were never in love. My lack of grace and coordination, in the beginning, meant that I bloodied their noses with my swinging arms so many times it wasn't funny. But there were times, like in the world finals, that my partner and I really connected. We *danced*.

And although we danced over and over, the dance could never become routine. Even though it was structured, planned, and refined, we always kept the dance fresh and alive. We were all about routines. We memorized routines. We practiced and practiced. I spent so much money on lessons, it was scary. I was practicing five days a week. But I had fallen in love with the dance.

I discovered the quality of my dance depended on my ability to go with the flow, or to follow a good lead. I had to learn about my partner. I had to feel a connection. In dancing, all the signals come shoulder-to-hand, and you lead from the waist up. If there are mixed signals, there are mixed results.

It's the same with our customer service systems. They can't be routine. They constantly require modifications. They require going with the flow. They often involve mixed signals. And, they mean adopting the right body language to show we love what we do. In dance, my partner's body language made a big difference in my ability to dance well. If he had a bad day, I had a bad day, and we had a bad dance. The same holds true with customers. So smile. Be confident. Don't just greet them, sweep them off their feet. Let them feel your energy and excitement. *Every time is the first time.*

When my partner and I connected during a waltz, it felt as if we were floating. It's a feeling you just can't match. Today, I love the dance for another reason. It's not to be judged. It's to enjoy the dance with my dear friend and first dance partner, John Sippel. He's the consummate lead, the one who always makes me look good. I get to play, and be swept away. It's love in motion.

Your dance with the customer should also look, and feel, like a beautiful waltz. Who couldn't love the waltz, even when they simply watch it? It's graceful; it's beautiful; it's natural.

And when your customers bloody your nose or step on your toes, smile, and say, *no problem, what can we learn here?* Move on. You've got another routine ahead and you'd better be *on.* Plus, *they're going to tell all their friends how well you led the dance.*

I recall when a late friend of mine was competing with his dance instructor as his partner. The music started and he went into a two-step, and the instructor, after hearing the music a second longer, nudged him and said: *Polka!* He'd been dancing the two-step to the polka. Anyone who dances knows that doesn't work. Sometimes that's where we are with our customers — the music we hear is a

Guts To Love
The Life Cycle Of Care
BY CAROL SMITH

Once clients are accustomed to new levels of service, you'd better deliver the next best thing.

Customer satisfaction is an intangible: difficult to measure, sometimes hard to define, and always challenging to achieve.

The effort you put into reaching satisfaction goals must continue even after you've met them. As customers become accustomed to improved services, those services become expected. They cease to be improved — they become ordinary. Competitors take note of service leaders' methods and imitate those methods, further diluting the effectiveness of these once exciting techniques. New issues arise and must be addressed. Many recall the days when mold, radon, and low-flush toilets weren't part of homebuyer conversations. As new concerns appear, they must become part our dialogue with customers.

Accounting practices, once they're in place, are fairly stable. An effective scheduling system can operate a long time without major changes. Part of the charm of company traditions is their long-standing repetition. Think, perhaps, of the company trade contractor picnic, the one everyone has looked forward to for 28 summers.

Customer service is different. Like floor plans and elevations, service evolves continuously. How can two-step, but to them, it's a polka. That'll never work. Ask them if they waltz.

My point in all this is that your love for your customer can never be transactional. Like a marriage, it's a contractual obligation, yes, but it's not about the contract. You don't stay in love for 60 years because you have a contract. You're in love with a person because you're in love with them. *You've danced with them: closely, carefully, and passionately.* You have a long history of day-to-day interactions, and have shared deep-rooted feelings. You take all the right steps, even a few wrong ones.

Sometimes, a customer just wants to be sure — *they just want to know you're there.*

DON'T BE AN ISLAND — LIVE ON ONE

By now, I hope you know what it takes to develop that kind of feeling and then nurture it for years, seeing the beauty in a person, in a customer, every day. I know it's hard when you go to your office and you're bombarded with 100 emails, 20 urgent phone calls (including five from irate customers), and 10 trade contractors haven't shown up at your jobs. To top it all, Wall Street is running amuck. It's just wild, I know.

But as long as you remember our unique link to people's lives and their

a homebuilder make this endless evolution seem to be part of a predictable routine, rather than self-imposed chaos? By planning for regular reviews and updates to customer materials, policies, and procedures.

Begin by identifying the components. Include the homeowner guide, meeting agendas, methods for routine updates, systems for managing customer-initiated communications, and standard form letters. Add controversial topics and memory points and you have an excellent list from which to work.

Next, ask all of your company personnel to set up a file — paper or electronic — where they store notes about changes or additions they believe would improve service. These notes could include items such as typos found in a form, a cabinet cleaning suggestion for the homeowner guide, or a new step to add to the delivery process to make it run more smoothly for buyers. Employees might comment about the friction between design and construction or the delay in getting change orders priced and out to the customer. Service practices that impressed employees when they were customers may apply to your program.

homes, you'll thrive. As an example, visit The McCaffrey Group's Web site (www.mccaffreygroup.com), to learn of a man who proposed to his fiancée on one of McCaffrey's empty homesites. He and his wife-to-be already considered it hallowed ground, a place where they planned the home of their dreams.

We fulfill dreams for people.

We have to be more like Dick Bryan in action — how did he elevate the level of customer service during all those years when he was with John Laing Homes? Was it the 300 suits and 450 ties in his closet? Did he use them to get excited about his day, about the people he'd meet? I mean, imagine his closet — its size alone had to make him smile. Bryan isn't a young man, but he loves what he does. He couldn't fake it on the job. Neither can you.

Bryan got so excited about what he did that men almost half his age had a hard time keeping up with him, even when visiting homeowners in the 125-degree heat of a Las Vegas summer. Bryan loves this business, he loves this industry, and when he hears anything that varies from a proper customer response, it physically upsets him. It hurts him to his core.

But if Dick Bryan can make the customer central to John Laing Homes, a huge home building company, you can do it, too. It simply requires taking these concepts and making them work. I think back to the wonderful story I heard about Laing CEO Larry Webb when he thought Bryan was bonkers

At least once a year, gather these notes. Ask a task force made up of representatives from each department to review them. A comprehensive review of all customer procedures and materials — don't forget the company Web site — within the space of a few weeks increases the likelihood that you'll find contradictions and omissions. You are working toward replacing stale practices with fresh methods. Your customer feedback data will be part of this. To stimulate original thinking and to generate excitement about this review, kick it off with a focus group. Invite eight to 10 homeowners. Have your task force serve as the audience. Hearing from actual customers is a powerful motivator, and nearly always results in new insights.

In the end, the task force makes recommendations. Management reviews and approves the recommendations. Follow the implementation with training or re-training, if necessary. Follow up with a comprehensive review 60 days later to confirm that everything has been addressed. Then plan for the next annual review. Continue this cycle for as long as you want repeat and referral buyers. Once the system is in place, rest assured that what seemed like chaos will become the normal pattern of operating a highly successful business.

for proposing a 15-minute customer response time. I can hear Webb yelling, "We can't do this!" And I can hear Bryan slamming his fist down on the desk, insisting, "Yes, we can — we're going to do it!" You'll hear the same resistance in your own company. Nothing in this book is easy. There's no magic pill. But it's a prescription that — over time — is going to give you the long-term business health you crave.

I love this stuff. It's the essence of what I do. Customer care is such a part of my belief system, that I can't describe myself without talking about it. Can you do the same? Let me tell you, the reason I wanted to write this book wasn't because I dreamed of a bestseller, although that would be sweet. I wrote it because I had to tell both my story and the story of customer care. They're intertwined. I had to be like Bryan, who has an identical passion in his blood. I had to slam my fist down on your desk, look you in the eye, and say: *Yes, you can do this. To thrive, not simply survive, you must do it!*

I know of a builder who has a coveted homesite on an exclusive island. He purchased the property through a lifetime relationship he had with an accomplished individual who so valued his friendship with the builder that he wanted him to have the property. Imagine that! He could have sold it for millions, but he chose this builder and gave him an unbelievable deal *because of this personal relationship.*

The builder is an incredibly bright guy who could do anything, but chooses to build homes. Dick Bryan chooses to do what he does and Bill Pulte is the same way. In Pulte's nearly 60-year love affair with this business, he has been raked over the coals, fed to the wolves, and flipped over the cliff. The bottom line is, we will come out of what we're in and be fine. The trick is to learn from heroes like these, who, through chaos, thrive and project an incredible attitude.

My builder friend, and many others like him, doesn't look at building homes as just a job, it's a part of who they are. It's builder DNA. I can't imagine describing Dick Bryan or Bill Pulte without putting the word *Builder* in the description. All the people we know and all the people in this book, to a greater or lesser degree, share the same DNA. To some degree, I do, too. I could earn more working for a builder, selling homes. But training and consulting in the housing industry, that's my passion. The housing industry is my passion. I want *so much* to make it better than it already is. We can do it, but we need to start loving and liking our customers through our teams.

It sounds obvious, but from a customer standpoint, loving and liking are two different things. With customers, you have to really *like* them. I've learned this in my relationships with the people closest to me. Some, I love, but we don't *like* each other very well. That's the bottom line with a relationship. Sometimes liking someone is more important than loving them, especially when you're talking about customers. You have to like what you're doing. Do you know that children abused by their parents still love them? It's amazing — they still *love* them. But I don't think they *like* them. Love is something you don't have much control over. Liking, you control. Loving is deeper.

So perhaps the title of my book should be *Like First, Love Later: Loyalty Comes Last.*

BE REAL: WIN CLIENTS FOR LIFE

If you like customers, you understand the buyer's attachment to their new home — even while it's being built. You understand that their attachment is unlike any attachment your company personnel could have with that same home. And from this attachment springs all of your future business. Think I'm kidding? "Listen" to the stories from a customer of Brothers Strong, the Houston remodeling firm, and two of David Weekley Homes' buyers. Listen to what these clients say. Notice how they talk about price, but focus on *value*. Notice not only how they mention problems, but also how they overcame them through *trust*. Notice how quality got them in the door, but everything that followed made them stay.

Michael Strong's client was in the midst of a $175,000 kitchen remodel when we talked, and in the prior year had hired him for a $75,000 master bath renovation. About three years previously, she had contracted him to build a

$200,000 media room addition. Recently, she referred Strong for a $350,000 remodel. "That's all caps when it comes to REFERRAL," he says. "It was the client's friend who was out of the country, and the client said, 'let's go' and we walked through and she read me the scope of the work." *Talk about a client for life!*

Clearly this busy woman executive, whose name I'm withholding to protect her privacy, is a legacy client for Brothers Strong. She learned of the company through her friends and then checked with her local builders' association. She settled on 10 contractors, and with phone interviews, narrowed her choices to five and met with each of them. "I felt very comfortable with their work and they were very honest," she says of Brothers Strong. "They were the only contractor who told me not every project is perfect. But that they would address the problem and that I should know that every problem gets taken care of."

Michael Strong even gave her the name and phone number of a client who experienced serious problems on a Brothers Strong job. "That person was very open," the client says. "And she told me everything that happened and assured me Michael made everything right." What sealed her choice was that she sits on the board of a children's charity and Strong's similar charitable interests convinced her to choose him.

She says trust was a critical factor in the ongoing relationship because she travels a lot and has valuable belongings in her home. Despite the glitch in her project, she says she'd still trust Brothers Strong "with my life."

The glitch involved a new electrician who worked for Strong's electrical trade contractor. He gave the lockbox code to an art lighting company that was installing projection lighting. She was livid when she found out. But *within*

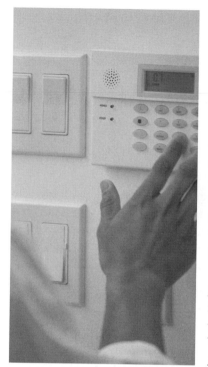

the hour, the code had been changed, the electrical contractor was called, and Brothers Strong had gathered the employees into a company meeting, so everyone could better understand the importance of client security.

Problem solving is one reason she'll continue giving Brothers Strong work, she says — and referring them to others. "I refer constantly," she says. While work quality is very important, both trust and communication are crucial to their relationship. While she travels, Brothers Strong keeps her informed with emails every other day.

Resolving inevitable glitches and good communication are important for David Weekley Homes' clients, too, and it starts right at the company's Web site — visitors can call its "Internet Advisors" via an 800 number, even after hours, getting a callback within 12 hours or less. The advisor refers them to the right person, so they're able to discuss David Weekley homes in their price range.

Weekley has customers who are as loyal as Brother Strong's. Some large extended families have bought David Weekley homes for three or more family members, often in the same neighborhood, while other customers refer them over and over again.

I noticed how little these clients talked about home quality, and how much they appreciated being treated fairly, honestly, and openly, particularly when the inevitable problems arose.

When the day before her closing Jeanette Dunn and her husband Donnie discovered that someone had stolen one of their bathroom's glass shower enclosures, it was replaced by David Weekley Homes the next day. Even that event didn't break the trust Dunn had built over time with her lead sales consultant, Marianne Ebeade. "Marianne not only became my friend, she's like family to me. She's like a sister." And for Dunn, that's saying a lot — she already has six sisters. It seemed to her that Ebeade helped her 24 hours a day, or at least not just during working hours, to get her home built, Dunn says. "Even on her days off, if I needed something, she was available." After move-in, Ebeade provided her with information on grocery stores, hospitals, and other key contacts. Not long after Dunn purchased her home, she convinced her sister to buy one — across the street! — and now she's trying to convince another sister and a niece. (Can you see the value of promoters?)

Dunn bought a 2,200-square-foot single-story home in Lakewood Crossing, a 34-home community on the north side of Houston. She and her husband purchased $30,000 worth of options, bringing the total cost of the home for the first-time buyers to nearly $200,000. "David Weekley is expensive," she says, "but it's the house I always wanted and I love the homes they build. It's a costly home, but it will hold its value forever."

Mary Shafer, who purchased a David Weekley home in the Homestead at Big Stone Gap, in Duncanville, Texas, says, "from day one, whatever our concerns were, whatever we wanted, whatever our needs, they took care of it. When we were building the home, it was like doing the whole thing with a part of my family."

HOMEOWNER JEANETTE DUNN, SEATED, SHARES SOME TEA WITH MARIANNE EBEADE OF DAVID WEEKLEY HOMES. DUNN SAYS OF HER SALES CONSULTANT: "SHE'S LIKE FAMILY TO ME."

Shafer says from the first day, she and her husband Richard were made to feel at home, and when they visited the community, their names were never forgotten. Prior to the Weekley purchase they had put a $500 deposit on another home, built by another nationally known builder, with the promise they could get the deposit refunded if they couldn't sell their existing home. When that sale took longer than they thought and they told the builder they wanted their deposit back, they only received $250. "We were lied to," Shafer says. "Thank God we didn't go into that community."

LISTEN TO — NO, BE — A CUSTOMER

So while we're making strides as builders, some of us are still psychologically abusing our customers. What that builder gained for $250 from Mary Shafer was lost in goodwill a thousand times over.

Strong, of Brothers Strong, tells me every builder should remodel or build their own home just to understand the experience. You think you're doing a good job keeping the home clean? Well, when you come home to live in it, it's not as clean as you think. "When there are gaps in production — *only* a day or two — when you're sitting watching the hands of the clock tick by without any work being done, it's a lot more painful than it appears from the comfort of your office," he says. Inconsequential things become exaggerated. Strong has put himself through it at least six times. "Moth to flame," he explains with a laugh. I agree with him. Buy from yourself. If you've never walked in the customer's shoes, you'll never understand what they go through.

Creating a client for life doesn't mean doing it the exact same way as all the builders and remodelers you've read about here. So much of what's written in business books can't be taken literally. In other words, do you need to change the lightbulbs in a customer's home when they stop working to win a client for life? Strong's companies have struggled with that question, and have concluded that while they may not be the one who changes the lightbulbs, they'll find someone who can or have a service provider call the client within 24 hours. "We become the go-to company," he says. "We want to be the one that's watching things go past, and decide what we want and don't want. If there's a bathroom remodel, we want to grab that. We want top-of-mind awareness so they do call us and don't forget us."

How far you go is entirely up to you. Peter Shands, the Australian remodeler I introduced in Chapter 1, tells me that because of the incredibly clean air Down Under, customers routinely hang their freshly washed laundry on a clothesline to dry. As his company becomes more relationship-based, his employees have been known to take in the wash for customers if it starts to rain. What a nice thing that is. And what does this tell you about the relationships you must have — laundry can be pretty personal, no?

One of the most important things we can do, both for the long-term good of our business and to truly support clients during their experience, says Shands, is to show genuine empathy with their circumstances. "We encourage this by constantly asking our team to imagine what they would like if they were the customer," he says. "Families in the throes of remodeling as a general rule have had their routines fractured sufficiently by the work alone. When you consider routine tasks such as washing, ironing, cooking, vacuuming, bathing, dressing, and eating are frequently disrupted, the last thing they need is to come home and find a line of wet washing that needs to be left out for yet another day. After all, remodeling generally equals dust, and dust adheres quite nicely to wet laundry."

Sure, he says, there might be circumstances where privacy is an issue. But as his team develops a friendly, professional relationship with their clients, trust also blooms. Clients view something as simple as bringing in the wash as a considerate act.

"I think we should reserve this kindness for situations where it rains," he says. "I don't know how it would be viewed if we were to do this every time washing was out. There are any number of considerate things we can do if we empathize. It might be as simple as topping off a pet's water bowl or bringing the morning paper to the front door when we start work each day."

Strong's client remembered his employees' kindness to her dog, patting the retriever's head and always making certain it was safe during construction.

We can't deny the human, emotional connection we have with our clients, can we?

WHEN YOU ARRIVE

Trust, not technology, is the issue of the decade, Tom Peters says. What I'm writing about here is all about trust. It's not what you tell your clients, it's how you make them *feel. Aim for the heart because they don't care how much you know … until they know how much you care,* says Mac Anderson, author of *The Essence of Leadership.*

It's my belief that the economic changes over the past two years will be a positive influence on customer experience and a factor in building business and increasing loyalty. Why? Builders were grasping at straws for answers. This one — love, and trust — is nearly obvious. Unless you're blind and can't see the gorilla in the room, you can track the results of increased care. You can see what works. You can see what makes you the best in your market.

The economy is forcing us to do what we should have been doing anyway. Every downturn has a reciprocal positive, one that's not always comfortable. To say it nicely, a flushing of the system, while incredibly painful for those left without jobs, is good for the industry. "I don't believe your customers should pay for your inefficiencies," says Roxanne Musselman. "Part of the reason pricing is so skewed is that we've created false value, and it's one of greed. Builders aren't disciplined enough to hold their price down and every time they raise their price, they actually put their company in jeopardy."

Many homebuilders are inefficient in the operation of their businesses, and they pass these inefficiencies along to the consumer. When the market is tight, they start doing all the things they should have being doing in the first place. Their lack of discipline starts by not addressing issues raised by customers. Change needs to occur in markets good and bad, and it will be what helps builders survive the downswings.

Now, people aren't saying we don't want to buy from you, they're saying we don't want to buy your way. *We can buy our own way, and without us, you don't have a business.* While prices get slashed nationwide in order to win customers, let me say this again: *It's not about the price.* Recall what Jeanette Dunn said of her David Weekley home.

One of my clients, who used to run a major auto dealership, told me the dealership conducted studies that showed buyers who paid full price were consistently more satisfied with their purchase decision five years later than those who haggled. So when you're absolutely sure you're providing the best value, you need to be confident in your offerings. Your inclination to give things away and haggle are going to affect consumer confidence. This is the case in the auto industry, but it's also relevant, and appropriate, in housing. Research with GuildQuality (**See Love Mode, Page 53**) would seem to support the fact that happier clients mean higher profits; unhappy clients push margins down.

To build value, you need to constantly look to your employees, and those you plan to hire. You have to discover what's going to get your people jazzed. Maybe it's a movie that does it. The underlying lessons in movies touch the emotions in all of us. While the language in *Glengarry Glen Ross* is atrocious, the film, starring Al Pacino, Jack Lemmon, Ed Harris, Alan Arkin, Kevin Spacey, and Alec Baldwin, depicts two crazy days in the lives of four real estate agents. It shows how they become desperate when the corporate office sends a representative to "motivate" them by announcing that, in a week, all but the top two salesmen will be fired. The company is a fly-by-night outfit, and the land they're selling is in the middle of nowhere. Alec Baldwin, as the out-of-town sales VP, pumps them up. He talks about the first prize — a new Cadillac — and the second prize — a set of steak knives.

But it's what you and your team would get to talking about afterward that would be the real prize from watching a movie like this, or *The Big Kahuna*, in which Kevin Spacey and Danny DeVito play lubricant salesmen. At a convention, they try to get in front of a buyer for a huge company, and the new sales guy, Bob, played by Peter Facinelli, gets in front of the buyer, but starts witnessing for Christ, instead of talking about lubricants. Beyond the humor, the sales and customer service lessons are priceless.

DeVito's character, *Phil Cooper*, says: "It doesn't matter whether you're selling Jesus or Buddha or civil rights or 'How to Make Money in Real Estate With No Money Down.' That doesn't make you a human being; it makes you a marketing rep. If you want to talk to somebody honestly, as a human being, ask him about his kids. Find out what his dreams are — just to find out, for no other reason. Because as soon as you lay your hands on a conversation to steer it, it's not a conversation anymore; it's a pitch. And you're not a human being; you're a marketing rep."

You can look for lessons in customer service everywhere.

I know, the time's not right. You're busy. There's all those emails and calls. Wait — *I've got a plateful now* — let me wait until later. Our market is proving *there may not be a later.* Companies we've all heard of are leaving the market, or filing for Chapter 11. If that's not a wake-up call, what is? You're not bullet-proof — no one is.

Human emotion: You can no longer guard against it or try to pretend it doesn't exist because it does. It was human emotion that pulled our country together after 9/11. What was it in a 24-hour period that caused people to be patriotic? It wasn't logic. I don't mean to insinuate that where we are now is similar to that part of American history. But we're at a pivotal point in our industry. We've had it too good. We've been lax in how we treat customers. Why? Because we could, and they still bought from us. Sometimes it takes something devastating or dramatic to make us aware of how important our customers really are.

You can't wait until the next cycle because you may not be here. Then, it won't matter.

When you're dealing with human emotion and human behavior, it's immediate. The power of emotion rules everything we do, *especially* now.

What I've suggested on these pages doesn't require a major financial commitment during times when finances are tighter than they've ever been. What it requires is a *mental shift*, a change in focus, getting in touch with the *human* side of business. *That's* what's required.

And even though we've beaten up our customers over the years, they still embrace us. Regardless of what happens in the market, no matter how much we abuse ourselves, our customers, and our teams, the home is still the coveted American dream. *That's pretty darn special.* You're never going to replace that. So embrace it. *Love* it. And build on it to win loyalty for life.

We've abused our customer for so long, it's crazy. *Isn't it time we change?*

LOVE ✓ CHECK

8 Ways To Make Love Last

Love's not a one-time thing, it's an all-time thing. Make it last forever and your business will, too.

To nurture enduring relationships, those that generate loyalty, you need to constantly be courting others, yourself, your team, and prospective employees. Together, you must create a business that leaves a legacy, a legacy of *Love*.

✔ Never End The Courtship

Take it from my aunt and uncle: The courtship never ends. But as Carol Smith notes, it's not cookies and balloons. Or even, Happy Nothing days. It's looking at every step of your process and identifying ways to connect. Instead of giving every customer a move-in gift, what if you called customers at year-end and asked, sincerely: *Are you OK? What do we need to do for you?* In between move-in and year-end there are 363 days. Every one gives you an opportunity to create one more memorable experience. Getting flowers on your anniversary isn't a surprise. Even getting a Christmas card any more isn't a surprise. People receive so many, I doubt they read them. Getting flowers on any Tuesday morning — *that's* a surprise. It's most likely not a day for celebration. It's a simple act of kindness or appreciation. It's like the Hogan Homes superintendent who stops in his tracks in a community to say hello to a homeowner. He makes the courtship last.

✔ Court Thyself

Always look at ways of self-improvement, ways to improve your business through the driver of your business, your people. How can you, and they, improve personally? Are you and your team reading the right books? Are you taking care of your mind, body, soul? Are you attending to you? Are you getting better or just older? Look for ways, through books, movies, seminars, conferences, other companies, and people, to be the best you can be.

✔ Court Your Team

You have to be constantly recruiting, always looking for that one person who's going to improve your team. When you see someone who's a perfect fit, even if you can't hire them then, you need to develop a mechanism for staying in touch. I know sports teams often develop short lists of players they'd like to recruit to improve the team's performance. Remember, your courtship lasts a lifetime, and you need a team that can grow and learn to follow through on that feeling.

✔ Compel Events

Do you think strategically, or are you so wrapped up in the moment, you forget about the future? Industry guru and dear friend Lee Evans, 91, *still* says: *Compel events to conform to plan.* In other words, *Do the things that make your strategic plan work.* If your plan is to improve profitability 5 percent in the next 12 months, what do you do? What do you do *every day* to make sure that happens? If you want referral rates so that one out of every two customers refers business to you, what do you do to give them a reason to refer? Are you going to call people after a month, six months, 12 months? Or will you just know it needs to be done and hope it happens? Hope isn't a strategy. Action toward a compelling goal is.

✔ Embrace Change

Change will always happen. Change is part of life. It either propels you or destroys you. You've got to embrace it. People tend to wait to see it. As I've said, our market is proving there is no "later." When companies we've all heard about are leaving the market, or filing Chapter 11, that's a wake-up call for change beyond what you initially suspected. So embrace change — *now*.

✔ Puff Up With Pride

I'm talking about the good stuff. As a builder, remodeler, craftsman, or supplier, never apologize for being what you are and doing what you do. Smash all the stereotypes of our profession. Be professional. Some people don't think building is a reputable profession. It is. You should be proud of what you do. If you can't take pride in that, how can you possibly extend your feelings when it comes to this type of customer care? With genuine caring, you can't fake it. You can fake a lot of stuff, but you can't fake sincerity.

✔ Believe In The Unseen

You have to believe there's magic out there, in the connections between people. There's energy between everyone. If you don't believe in love, if you don't believe in passion, if you don't like giving roses, or sharing a smile, you're never going to get it. You have to believe in the invisible. Remember Billy Warren, who first learned the power of caring from his mom and dad, and how, after 30 years on the airport's front lines, he still loves people? Is he nuts? No, it's in his DNA. Make it a part of who you are, too.

✔ Imagine Your Legacy

What will it be? Do you have one? If you want your legacy to live on perpetually, you have to plan, now. What do you plan to leave behind? What do you want people to say about you? What do you want them to remember? That you built more homes than anyone else? That you were builder of the year? Or, that you made a difference in the lives of every person for whom you prepared a home? Start with the end in mind. Then, prepare for it. What are you waiting for? *Get going!*

AFTERWORD

You know, I almost forgot this, and it may make you chuckle.

Back when I was 14 — and I kid you not — I worked as a waitress in *Love's in* Troy, Texas. OK, go ahead and smile. That was the name. Believe me, there wasn't much love in that roadside restaurant. From my humble beginnings, I began to understand serving customers.

My final challenge to you is this: Dig deep into your well of experience to become a genius in customer care. Don't think complicated. Think simple. There's genius in simplicity, isn't there? It starts with a person who wants to be where they are — you — and then, your team. Maybe this desire grew out of where you've been. You and your team want to make your customer's experience as great as it can be, because it's about pride, and about almost everything except the money.

In my opinion, we still work in one of the best businesses in the world. What else could I do that so closely touches the way people live? We're working with the essence of life — think of all the memories that get built into a home. With a bit more focus on human dynamics, we can change. We can transition from being producers of products to *enhancers of life*.

That's how I feel about it, and as I said at the very beginning, it all comes from where I started. As Gust Nicholson Sr. says, if it sounds touchy-feely, to be honest, it is. What's more touchy-feely than talking about how you live? If that's difficult for you, remember, when you get that personal with people, they'll never forget you.

Building homes is your opportunity to put your signature on everything you do. Where else do you get a chance to do that? How often does your framer get to do that? Your electrician? How often does your mason get to make a difference in a person's life? Are they thinking like that Disney guy who's picking up trash but understands his role in the bigger picture? We must look for caring opportunities, and teach our teams to do the same. We must watch for examples of this way of thinking, this new order.

Recently, on an evening flight from Ontario, Calif. that had stopped in Phoenix on the way to San Antonio, I sat on the plane with about 10 other continuing passengers. The Phoenix passengers had disembarked and there was that brief lull before new passengers boarded. A flight attendant, knowing that the 10 of us would probably sit on the airplane for nearly five hours without eating more than a handful of peanuts, came down the aisle with a smile and two bags of hamburgers from Wendy's.

I marveled at this one particular flight attendant and his company. For less than $30 of his own money, he had intuitively cared for us, his treasured cargo. I was awestruck. Such a *little* thing. Yet, at that moment, he was a genius.

As I bit into my burger, I reflected on all the places customer care had taken me, literally, and figuratively, all the way back to *Love's*.

I wish you the best on your own customer care journey.

INDEX